BASEBALL AS MEDIATED LATINIDAD

GLOBAL LATIN/O AMERICAS
Frederick Luis Aldama and Lourdes Torres, Series Editors

BASEBALL AS MEDIATED LATINIDAD

RACE, MASCULINITY, NATIONALISM, AND PERFORMANCES OF IDENTITY

JENNIFER DOMINO RUDOLPH

THE OHIO STATE UNIVERSITY PRESS
COLUMBUS

Library of Congress Cataloging-in-Publication Data

Names: Rudolph, Jennifer Domino, 1973– author.

Title: Baseball as mediated Latinidad : race, masculinity, nationalism, and performances of identity / Jennifer Domino Rudolph.

Other titles: Global Latin/o Americas.

Description: Columbus : The Ohio State University Press, [2020] | Series: Global Latin/o Americas | Includes bibliographical references and index. | Summary: "Builds on historical and critical race perspectives to analyze the recruitment and use of (im) migrant Latin/o American bodies in major league baseball, and locates baseball as a site of Latino masculinity and identity negotiation for understanding nationalist anxieties and tensions over race, nation, and language"—Provided by publisher.

Identifiers: LCCN 2019048600 | ISBN 9780814214312 (cloth) | ISBN 0814214312 (cloth) | ISBN 9780814277898 (ebook) | ISBN 0814277896 (ebook)

Subjects: LCSH: Hispanic American baseball players—Social conditions. | Baseball—Social aspects—United States. | Masculinity in sports—Social aspects. | Nationalism and sports—United States. | Hispanic American baseball players—Race identity.

Classification: LCC GV867.64 .R84 2020 | DDC 796.3570973—dc23

LC record available at https://lccn.loc.gov/2019048600

Cover design by Susan Zucker
Text design by Juliet Williams
Type set in Adobe Minion Pro

CONTENTS

ILLUSTRATIONS

ACKNOWLEDGMENTS

THIS PROJECT has been a long time coming, and the generosity of spirit, time, and energy of many friends, family, and colleagues has nurtured it along the way. This is truly a collaborative work, and I would not have been able to complete it without the help of my community. I apologize in advance for anyone I forgot to mention here, but know that I thank you from the bottom of my heart.

First, I am grateful for an incredibly supportive group of friends who listened to my concerns and ideas and encouraged me as I worked on this project; many thanks to Barb Weber, Cherise Harris, Jim Perkins, Amanda Durante, and Jennifer Hunt. I would also like to especially recognize my unofficial research assistants/friends/family: Mary Watts for making sure I didn't miss anything in *Sports Illustrated*, Dulmarie Irizarry for keeping me connected to all things Boricua baseball via Facebook, and Mark Rudolph for sending me press materials after the Cubs finally won the World Series in 2016 after a 108-year draught, despite being a hard-core White Sox fan! Finally, endless brainstorming sessions with Ron Flores over the last several years have grown the seeds of this project.

I thank Connecticut College for the financial and technical support for helping me to bring this project to completion. A very special shout-out to fellow baseball enthusiast Mike Dreimiller for hunting down high-resolution images that have immeasurably enhanced this book!

At The OSU Press, I have had the privilege of working with a great team that believed in this project early on. Elizabeth García, thanks so much for putting me in contact with Fred Aldama. Fred has been a tireless supporter of my work prior to this book. Many thanks to Fred Aldama, Lourdes Torres, Kristen Elias Rowley, Rebecca Bostock, and Rebecca Bender for your work and care in bringing the manuscript to publication. I also thank my reviewers, whose time and engagement have strengthened my work in myriad ways.

In closing, I dedicate this work to my mother, Carol Domino Rudolph, for introducing me to baseball. I wish you were here to read this. The Domino and Madia families are my baseball heritage, having lived in the shadow of "Sox Park," as we always called it, on Chicago's South Side.

Mediated Latinidad

Race, Masculinities, Spectacle, and
Globalization in Major League Baseball

IN 2016, the Chicago Cubs won the World Series after a 108-year drought. In 2016, Donald J. Trump became the forty-fifth president of the United States, having won the electoral but not the popular vote. Baseball intersected with politics as these two events unfolded in that Mexican American Los Angeles Dodgers first baseman Adrián González refused to stay at a Trump Hotel in Chicago, after candidate Trump made a series of inflammatory remarks against Mexicans as part of his divisive campaign strategy (Samuel 2016). Following the November election, then Chicago Cubs pitcher Jake Arrieta, himself of partial Puerto Rican descent, tweeted, "Time for Hollywood to pony up and head for the border #illhelpyoupack #beatit!" (Sullivan 2016). Though Major League Baseball (MLB) and its teams try not to publicly take sides in political debates, this created tensions within the Cubs organization as president Theo Epstein quietly donated and fund raised for Democratic candidate Hillary Clinton while the Ricketts family, who own the team, are Republicans.[1] Neither González nor Arrieta would acknowledge their tweets as political acts. After the win, the Cubs visited the White House on January 16, 2017, just days

---

1. MLB players have engaged in far less racial and political activism than have NBA and NFL players. As an example, unlike the several NFL players who have knelt during the national anthem as a part of the Black Lives Matter movement, only one MLB player, Bruce Maxwell, has knelt, prompting a mixed and noncommittal reaction from MLB personnel. I will return to this topic throughout my argument in this book.

before Barack Obama's presidency ended. Amid speculations that the team preferred to visit the Obama White House over the Trump White House, politics was not mentioned during the visit, with remarks directed instead to the Cubs / White Sox rivalry, Obama's notorious status as a White Sox fan, and the "audacity of hope" that had propelled both Obama to the White House and the Cubs to a World Series win (Sullivan 2017). The tensions described here involving González's and Arrieta's engagement with the presidential campaign amid Trump's anti-Mexican and implied anti-Latina/o rhetoric, and the audacity of hope parallel with Obama, show how baseball mirrors social, racial, and political tensions in the US. González's and Arrieta's divergent viewpoints also highlight the varied political views among Latina/os, as part of the fraught nature of Latinidad, or Latina/o identity.

These players and media and fan receptions of them underscore the ways in which popular culture and audience participation reflect current political debates, in this case immigration, what it means to be "American," tensions around Spanish language use in the US, and economic and labor tensions. These famous or "spectacular bodies" of players stand in for the "ordinary bodies" of Latin/o American men in the US. The introduction maps concepts such as Latinidad (Latina/o identity), the Latino threat narrative, race, masculinities, globalization, spectacle, and new media use to lay the foundation for the analysis of the above mentioned political topics via media and fan consumption of MLB's Latin/o American players, defining baseball as mediated Latinidad.

Though the largest fan base for Major League Baseball in the US remains middle-aged white men, Latina/os, particularly those of Caribbean descent, also consume baseball and associate it with their cultural identities as Latina/os. This is due to both the popularity of the sport in the Caribbean as well as the established system of recruitment of young talent by MLB in the Caribbean region such that young men in the Dominican Republic have come to view the prospect of a career in US professional baseball as perhaps their best option for economic mobility given the high poverty rate and economic woes of the island. Its aging fan base and loss in popularity to the National Football League (NFL) and National Basketball Association (NBA) on the domestic front are not lost on MLB, leading the league to expand efforts to globalize its presence (Bjarkman 2016; Klein 2006). According to Klein (2006), in addition to the aging fan base and decline in popularity compared to other sports and sources of entertainment, MLB expansion makes it increasingly difficult to staff players domestically given the decline in youth playing baseball as compared to football and basketball. Also, economists have pointed to a lack of "competitive balance" where large-market teams often dominate the recruitment of talent and thus the MLB post-season as a downfall of the sport in the US. In an attempt to grow its brand and internationalize in Europe, Africa, and Asia, the league launched Major League Baseball International (MLBI) as a corollary to MLB. The most significant public act of MLBI has been the establishment of the World Baseball Classic (WBC).

In the twenty-first century, baseball is again at the forefront of social and political developments in the US as MLB's labor structure employs roughly 27 percent Latin/o American players, most from the Spanish-speaking Caribbean, particularly the Dominican Republic, where it has established a sophisticated recruitment and training infrastructure for young talent (Klein 1991, 2006). This is significant because we are currently living in a heightened nativist moment as a result of anti-immigration sentiment and the struggle for immigration reform. What does it mean that a large supply of the labor populating "America's pastime" is not considered "American" by dominant mainstream US nationalist standards? What do media constructions of and fan reactions to iconic Latin/o American players tell us about current sociopolitical tensions over economies of labor and belonging? Conversely, how do Latin/o American players and fans evince a sense of their own Latinidad[2] via participation in and consumption of baseball?[3] In what ways does baseball mirror and depart from other labor markets in terms of its treatment and management of Latino men as both an invisible labor force and a threat to dominant narratives of US nationalism? These are some of the core questions of this project.

The Americas' Game: (Re)claiming
Baseball's Latin/o American History

In 2005, KNBR radio host Larry Krueger described San Francisco Giants players as "brain-dead Caribbean hitters" and likened the mind of Dominican team manager Felipe Alou to "Cream of Wheat" during a time when the team was struggling to win games. Alou took particular offense to this state-

2. Molina-Guzmán and Valdivia (2004, 207) define *Latinidad* as an imagined community of recent, established, and multigenerational immigrants from diverse cultural, linguistic, racial, and economic backgrounds.

3. A note on terminology: Throughout this book, I use *Latin/o American* to refer to MLB players born and raised in Latin America and the Caribbean, players who came to the US as children, and players of Latin American or Caribbean descent born in the US in order to capture the layered history and nature of those identified as Latino in MLB and the US more widely. I use *Latina/o* as a gender-inclusive term, whereas *Latino* refers exclusively to those considered male. I use the term *Latina/o,* as opposed to *Latin@* or *Latinx,* to honor the advocacy and scholarship of feminists who seek to both destabilize the a/o gender binary of the Spanish language and highlight the forward slash (/) as evoking a productive tension, instead of a limiting gender binary (Vargas, Mirabal, and La Fountain-Stokes 2017, 1).

ment, citing his experiences of racism in US baseball since the 1950s. Alou responded, "I'm going to make sure that it is known worldwide. I had zero means when I was a 20-year-old kid in Louisiana, but I'm 70 now. I have the means now to identify people like that. They're going to know in my country tonight. (Even) the president of my country" (J. L. Ortiz 2005). This exchange between Krueger and Alou captures the racial and sociopolitical tensions surrounding Latin/o Americans in baseball within a historical context. Krueger's assertion that the poor performance of the San Francisco Giants was the fault of Caribbean players echoes the hostility toward (undocumented) immigrants in the US labor force. Alou's response mirrors that of the Latina/os activist community, which reminds us of the long history of racism against Latina/os and the need to speak out against it. The fact that this took place in the media attests to the significance of the media in representing, fomenting, and disseminating debates around race and nationalism embedded in MLB's history. This story joins a history of intersection between MLB and media in representing baseball history, a history steeped in institutional racism in the US.

Indeed, throughout his career, Alou has spoken out and advocated for the rights of Latin/o American players. The November 1963 issue of *Sport* magazine featured an interview with Felipe Alou that outlined the ways that MLB controlled Dominican players and reproduced racism, turning its back on the transnational economic reality of Dominican players. Dominicans would struggle economically and racially compared to most US players, particularly in the off-season, when there was ample opportunity for employment in the US, but little to none in the Dominican Republic, and they would also endure racism and segregation during the season in the US. The article, reproduced in its entirety in Alou's biography, outlines five rules for players that continue to ring true: (1) "Do not expect a bonus," (2) "In the minor leagues he must outhustle everybody else," (3) "The Latin player must learn English," (4) "If the Latin is a Negro, he should understand the racial situation in America, and not expect perfection," and (5) "Do not expect to become rich" (Alou and Kerasotis 2018, 138–39). While some of this has changed—that is, players now earn much more than they did in the 1960s—many do not make it far enough in MLB to earn the big salaries and must pay high taxes if they are not citizens. Questions of race and language remain prescient for current players, as institutional racism tied to the devaluing of Spanish and brown and black bodies persists. Alou's observations and warnings about the conditions for Latin/o American players in the US parallel what Samuel Regalado (2008) has termed the "special hunger" of Latin/o American players, born of the desire to present themselves as ambassadors of their culture, articulating pride within a hemispheric economic system that has subordinated and racialized Latin/o Americans for centuries.

Thus Alou's critique of racism in MLB and Regalado's construct of "special hunger" attest to the evolution of baseball as a part of US history and a way to understand and process race and masculinity in the US as integral to national identity. Indeed, such is the importance of baseball as a cultural institution that National Public Radio dedicated an entire show to it as part of their *Latino USA* series. "Béisbol," hosted by María Hinojosa and Michael Simon Johnson, premiered on July 10, 2015, presenting an expansive look at the history of baseball in the US and Latin America, particularly Cuba and the Dominican Republic, since the nineteenth century. Hosts and guests argue that to fully understand the history of race relations and the visibility of Latina/os in the US, we must understand baseball and desegregation of the sport, along with its fraught labor history, from players in the Negro Leagues to the present *academia* (baseball academy) system that provides a significant amount of MLB labor. "Béisbol" concludes with the statement, "As baseball goes, so goes the nation" (Johnson 2015). Producer Michael Simon Johnson further argues that baseball is the most visible site of Latino men in the US; he remembers that as a child growing up in Pittsburgh, Pennsylvania, the only Latino man visible in his life and community was Roberto Clemente. In this way, baseball, and media coverage of it serve as sites to interrogate US history as it intersects with race, nationalism, and Latino masculinities. This project builds on the work of baseball historians such as Jorge Iber, Samuel Regalado, José Alamillo, and Adrián Burgos Jr., focusing on recent events and players within a cultural studies framework. As such, I will begin with a historical contextualization of baseball's development as a marker of (inter)national and racial identity, before presenting two cases, the limited inclusion of Latin/o American players in Ken Burns's *Baseball* documentary and the Facebook page "La Vida Baseball," to connect historical and national ideologies to media treatment of baseball in the present.

Baseball has long been woven into the fabric of nationalism in the US. In the nineteenth century, baseball played a pivotal role in the urbanization process and the integration of various ethnic groups within developing US cities (Iber, Regalado, Alamillo, and De León 2011). In *Latinos in U. S. Sport: A History of Isolation, Cultural Identity, and Acceptance,* the authors trace the history of Latin/o American participation in US baseball from the 1880s to 2010, illustrating that the influx of major waves of players from Latin America starting in the 1930s has fueled racial tensions resulting in the need to prove whiteness in the early twentieth century and a continued lack of representation of Latin/o Americans at the managerial and front office levels despite the large player presence at the major and minor league levels. DiAngelo (2018) notes that any consideration of the historical formation of the US must include the premise that US American nationalism is linked to and defined by the development of whiteness as a racial category to organize social institutions and afford privilege to some while withholding it from others. One of the ways that MLB has participated in this is via its celebratory narrative around the act of signing Jackie Robinson in 1947 to desegregate baseball as an initiation of the desegregation of other social institutions. DiAngelo (2018) signals the crafting of what MLB has identified as one of its most significant historical moments as an example of how racism and white supremacy operate in the US in noting that it is not Robinson's great talent, nor the good works of white advocates that brought him to the major leagues, but rather that whites who controlled MLB decided that desegregation would benefit them economically and allowed Robinson to desegregate baseball in 1947, an act that did nothing to change the racism behind whites' exclusive control of the sport (26). I would add that the narrative surrounding the life and death of Puerto Rican Roberto Clemente does similar work in lauding an exceptional individual as worthy of MLB inclusion, but it does not move the needle on institutional racism, as MLB would like us to think. Indeed, both Robinson and Clemente were aware of this and critical of how race, be it skin color (Robinson/Clemente) or language use (Clemente), shaped their MLB careers. In his recent autobiography, *Alou: My Baseball Journey* (Alou & Kerasotis 2018), Felipe Alou, one of the first black Dominicans to play and manage in MLB starting in 1956, chronicles lived experiences of segregation and access to a professional career, including not being allowed to play in the Evangeline League in Louisiana (36), to illustrate intersections of language and complexion in the careers of Latin/o American players.

In addition to the domestic context, MLB's internationalization, especially in the Dominican Republic and Spanish Caribbean, generally has marked its history. As a result of the waning interest among youth baseball players in the US, and to abate labor costs, teams have long established *academias* (baseball academies) in the Dominican Republic, and to a lesser extent, Venezuela due to low operating costs and a generous economic relationship between the US and the Dominican Republic. Despite documented abuses of young labor in the *academias* (Marcano Guevara and Fidler 2002), the MLB presence thrives in the Dominican Republic. In 2009 MLB formed the Dominican Development Alliance, a program to grow MLB's stated commitment to "social responsibility" and aid the Dominican economy (MLB n.d.-e). This initiative illustrates the additional internationalization of MLB and perhaps also answers criticisms of imperialism and abuses on the part of MLB.

If, as Iber et al. (2011) argue, the history and development of baseball are linked to national identity formation and the industrialization of US cities, desegregation, and the contours of masculinities in the Caribbean, particularly the Dominican Republic, Puerto Rico, and Cuba, the sugar refining industry most contributed to the growth and development of the game (Klein 1991, 6). Baseball continues to promise one of the best chances for men to escape poverty in the region and has thus contributed to the association between the *pelotero* (baseball player / baller) and masculine power linked to economic privilege. As Klein (1991) argues, "Americans may love the game of baseball as much as Dominicans do, but they do not need it as much. For Dominicans, baseball is a wide-ranging set of symbols, every turn at bat is a candle of hope, every swing is a wave of a banner, the sweeping arc of a sword" (1). Klein's description captures the images of nationalism and national pride (the wave of a banner) and masculine power (the sweeping arc of a sword) that drive young Dominican men to dedicate their lives to securing tryouts and minor league contracts with MLB. Though the history of baseball has ebbed and flowed since the late nineteenth century as a result of economic, political, and foreign interventions, currently the Dominican baseball system and its leagues largely cater to the cultivation of talent in the MLB system (Klein 1991, 2006; Ruck 2011).

The Dominican Republic remains the center of MLB recruitment and operations due to the aforementioned development through sugar refinery leagues to the sustained US economic intervention via MLB. Other Spanish Caribbean nations—Cuba, due to its sustained political tensions with the US since the 1959 revolution, and Puerto Rico, where, due to the island's status as a US territory, young players are obligated to participate in the MLB amateur draft and thus are not the attractive source of cheap labor to MLB that are Dominicans—constitute a diminished presence at the major league level today. In the case of Mexico, the Mexican Leagues have historically fought to retain sovereignty and not allow their national system to cater to US and MLB interests. Tensions between the US and Mexico also escalated in the 1940s as MLB and the Mexican League fought for players in the Caribbean (Ruck 2011, 118–42). However, this is not to say that other Latin American and Caribbean countries are absent entirely. Indeed, Latin/o American players also come from Cuba, Venezuela, Curaçao, Costa Rica, Mexico, and Panama. Latin American and Caribbean countries have made baseball their own, creating rivalries and in-game traditions such as cheerleaders and musical performances that contour and claim the game as a Latin/o American cultural and nationalist tradition. According to former Chicago Cubs director of Latin American operations Oneri Fleita, "There is a tendency for us to say, 'This is how we are going to do things.' What makes baseball great is the different styles of play. . . . It's their culture" (Orozco 2008b, 35).

To further globalize baseball and grow its brand, MLB debuted the World Baseball Classic in 2006. The WBC illustrates the tensions and lessons in nationalism inherent in the globalization of the MLB brand. Heralding the WBC as a "baseball World Cup," the commissioner's office obfuscated the existence of a baseball World Cup under the auspices of the International Baseball Federation (Klein 2006, 243). Perhaps this competition is viewed as less important in the US because the US participants are amateur players, as opposed to the MLB players who participate in the WBC as household names representing their country. Conflicts arose both internationally and among MLB teams as to the scheduling of the event so that all interested parties could participate. Team managers were concerned that their players would have a shortened spring training and be susceptible to injuries before the MLB season started if the tournament took place in March as proposed. The Japanese League was additionally concerned that it would disrupt the start of their season in early March. Much debate over venue and control over the rules and economics of the series and what countries would occupy the sixteen slots in the round robin series led Japanese representatives to declare the WBC as "smacking of imperialism on the part of MLB" (Klein 2006, 246). A further political conflict resulted from the US government initially banning Cuba from participation as a result of the political embargo. Klein (2006) sees this as a teachable moment for MLB as it fought for Cuban participation:

> As Paul Archey and other officials were busily trying to get the government to rescind its decision, they should have had an epiphany: MLB was, for the moment, standing in opposition to the parochial nationalist impulses—the very ones it often acts upon. In resisting the dictates of its own government, MLB had a mirror held to its face—a valuable transnational lesson. (248)

Though the US government did in fact allow Cuba to participate in the event, MLB has yet to reach equity in its policies related to internationalization and global markets.

Within this historical context, two media interventions highlight the concurrent invisibility of and efforts to (re)claim Latin/o Americans in baseball history: Ken Burns's *Baseball,* a multi-episode documentary on the history of baseball that initially excluded the place of Latin/o Americans, until criticism drove the later addition of 'The Tenth Inning," and the creation of Facebook page "La Vida Baseball" to document the historical and contemporary significance of Latin/o Americans in baseball. In 1994, PBS aired Ken Burns's nine-part documentary *Baseball,* a documentary spanning baseball history with special attention to topics like African American players, player-owner relations, and the resilience of the game. Critics of the series—which is similar to Burns's work on World War II and jazz—noted the relative absence of Latin/o American history in the game, despite their already significant numbers in the game, prompting Burns to add a tenth inning in 2010 focusing on developments in baseball since 1994. Burns felt it was necessary to cover more "recent" topics like the steroid era and international players, particularly Dominican and Japanese players. He says he hopes to continue to update the documentary as baseball evolves. Prior to the 2010 release of "The Tenth Inning," Latin/o American players appeared in a total of six minutes of the eighteen hours of film, four minutes of which focus on Roberto Clemente. Baseball historian Milton Jamail notes that Burns erased prominent players, some now Hall of Famers, like Juan Marichal, Luis Aparicio, and Fernando Valenzuela, from baseball history (González 2007). When asked why he felt he needed to update his account with a tenth inning, Burns still did not acknowledge Latin/o Americans as significant to baseball history:

> The last two decades have been the most consequential in baseball history, and when you see the circumstances that have happened in that time, it almost demands that we examine it again, like a siren call. Baseball is the prism through which we see America, and it will continue to reveal what we know about ourselves. Yes, it has dealt with the steroid issue, but we all see great catches every week and some of the greatest pitchers who ever lived. We need the perspective away from steroids to reflect the great things in the game. The key word in baseball is "resiliency." (DelawareToday 2010)

Ironically, Burns's statement that baseball is "a prism through which we see America," a prism he describes as celebrating merit and erasing race, is a reminder of the whiteness of dominant US historical narratives.

Though "The Tenth Inning" does feature more onscreen time devoted to Latin/o American players, especially via treatment of the *academia* system in the Dominican Republic, it uses these players and their history to reify the messages of meritocracy and resilience at the expense of nuanced coverage of race. Similar to the cases of Jackie Robinson and Roberto Clemente, an iconic Latin/o American player, Sammy Sosa, represents the literal and metaphorical hunger of Latin/o American players as the "fatherless shoeshine boy" turned major leaguer. Burns frames much of MLB's steroid era through the 1998 McGwire/Sosa home-run chase to break Roger Maris's record. The narrative identifies this competition between a white US-born and a Dominican-born man as a rare historical moment that disrupts the black/white racial binary, as Sosa is identified as Latin American, erasing his blackness. As we will see throughout this book, *Baseball,* as with much media coverage, casts Afro-Caribbean players via narratives of immigration, and less often via blackness. The Latin/o American presence and MLB's recruitment in the Caribbean Basin bolster positive aspects of capitalism and globalization as examples of how both systems foster (re)invention and healthy competition that favors those who "deserve" to win on the field, and economically. Ultimately, *Baseball* gestures toward intersections of race, class, and gender in MLB's past and present but demonstrates an uneasiness to undertake a deeper analysis, lest it shatter celebratory racial myths of "America's pastime" that undergird white privilege.

If Ken Burns's initial slight of Latin/o Americans illustrates how the establishment white gatekeepers neglect, if not erase, the histories of people of color, "La Vida Baseball" uses a website and Facebook to document the historical and contemporary Latin/o American presence in baseball and provide fans a space to speak as well. It is administered and produced by Teamworks Media in collaboration with the National Baseball Hall of Fame and Museum, with Adrián Burgos Jr., baseball historian and professor of history at the University of Illinois Urbana–Champaign, as editor-in-chief, and features other prominent experts in the field. The site's content spans a broad swath of the history of Latin/o American baseball, from profiles of legendary players to current players' impact on the game, and how race and language shape baseball. Narrative content includes articles, as well as images and videos. Topics include Hall of Fame induction weekend; profiles of young and legendary players, with a special eye to pioneering players from countries such as Curaçao and Brazil; and how non-Latino players respond to and interact with the cultural impact of Latin/o American players on the game. Through a bilingual format, "La Vida Baseball" (n.d.) defines baseball from a continental American perspective: "For Latinos, our shared pastime wasn't America's game, but the Americas' game." Parting from this perspective, the "About" section contextualizes the historical development of baseball in the countries of the Caribbean Basin starting in the nineteenth century. The stated mission of "La Vida Baseball" reads in part, "We'll be experimental more than encyclopedic. The four pillars on the banner across the home page sum up what you can expect from us: Who's Now, Who's Next, Legends and Our Life. Throughout, we'll talk about the players' heroes, their journeys, their favorite food, music and entertainment and, always, about their history." Ken Burns's *Baseball* and "La Vida Baseball" historicize the larger cultural contributions of Latin/o Americans in MLB and exemplify the still contested media terrain through which we learn to understand and document mediated Latin/o American and Latina/o lives.

Theorizing Mediated Latinidad

The historical examples above demonstrate that economics, politics, race, and gender significantly contour the entrance, history, and present moment of Latin/o American players in MLB (Burgos 2007; Klein 1991, 2006; Ruck 2011). Furthermore, Latina/o identity and media use and representations contribute to perceptions of Latino/as and their identity formation via the bodies and images of MLB players. Beginning with race, Latin/o American players challenge the binary white/black racial construction of US society where the hypodescent "one drop rule" rigidly defines any African ancestry as a black racial identity. Race relations in the US have historically revolved around the construction of whiteness linked to power and privilege (Feagin 2013; Omi and Winant 1994) and presently have evolved into "color-blind racism." Bonilla-Silva (2014) defines color-blind racism as the belief among those considered white in the US that race relations have equalized such that it is no longer necessary to consider race as a factor in the allocation of resources and power (2–4). Bonilla-Silva argues that whites in the current climate of color-blind racism have parted from the biological explanation of racism where black biological inferiority dominated racial ideologies of the Jim Crow era. Presently, instead of relying on biologically defined concepts of race, whites now attribute the sustained inequality of people of color to factors such as "market dynamics, naturally occurring phenomena, and imputed cultural limitations" (Bonilla-Silva 2014, 2).

These historical and contemporary racial frames have shaped the participation and perception of Latin/o Americans in MLB. Burgos (2007), Klein (1991), and Ruck (2011) explain that before the desegregation of MLB in 1947, Latin/o American players, especially Caribbean players, would play for either MLB or the Negro League depending on how their skin color and other phenotypical features were read within the US social context. In *Playing America's Game: Baseball, Latinos, and the Color Line,* Burgos (2007) documents the strategies of players attempting to assert a Spanish-speaking Latin American cultural identity on the one hand while trying to negotiate the racial climate of the US on the other. Burgos further argues that this fraught history echoes in the present via debates over Spanish language use and media portrayals of Latin/o American players.

For players born in Latin America and for some US Latina/o fans, racial identity is more complex than the dominant binary US system. Race in Latin American and the Caribbean differs from the historical race construction in the US in that racial identities run along more of a continuum, combining issues of class and national identity as well as phenotype. In *Race Migrations:*

Latinos and the Cultural Transformation of Race, Roth (2012) argues that the sustained (im)migration of Latina/os in the US is transforming US racial construction to more closely parallel that of Latin America and the Caribbean. Roth further posits that in the US, Latina/os, particularly those that retain strong transnational ties and divide their time between the US and their country of origin, negotiate the two racial systems and fuse them in their own racial identity construction. This is significant for Latin/o American players and Latina/o fans as both groups may not define race in the same ways that media workers and non-Latino fans do. For players, understanding the position of their bodies and identities as wealthy men of color in the US may challenge their concepts of self and social positions before coming to the US to play.

Racial construction frames not only readings of Latin/o American bodies in MLB but also issues of masculinities that intersect with race, class, and what is considered normative male behavior.[4] A recent example illustrates how baseball reproduces normative gendered behavior and the limits on black and Latin/o American masculinities. In August 2018, a video circulated widely on social media depicting Afro-Latino Atlanta Braves players Ozzie Albies and Ronald Acuña Jr. embracing in the dugout during a game. Announcers and fans began to joke and speculate about the "scalp massage" and the two men's homosexuality, with fans speculating that Acuña's mother had just died and Albies was comforting him. Social media exploded with homophobic fan reactions, as well as calling for fans to reexamine taboos on emotions and masculinities, arguing that this taboo greatly harms black and Latin/o American men who are discouraged from expressing emotion publicly. As Hurtado and Sinha (2016) and Connell (2005) argue, we must understand manhood as a multilayered identity influenced by history, economic power, and cultural myths related to expectations of those considered men. Latinos and other men of color in the US, from youth to adulthood, continue to be denied equal access to institutions such as higher education that would provide them with the economic status associated primarily with white masculinity (Noguera, Hurtado, and Fergus 2011; Ríos 2011). As such, sociostructural forces funnel them into professions that rely more on physical than mental performance. Social constructions of men of color as having strong bodies and quick tempers grow out of this performance as men of color are most often seen publicly as criminals, sports stars, or entertainers, especially rappers (Kelley 1998; Rose

---

4. I use the plural *masculinities* as opposed to the singular *masculinity* to emphasize the multiple ways of being a man consistent with current usage in gender studies.

2008). This context shapes the ways that Latino men experience daily life in the US and how non-Latinos come to understand their social position.

For Latin/o American MLB players, this context is even more complex, given that many of them negotiate their identities as men within a transnational context, via both their upbringing in Latin America or the Caribbean as well as the context of the United States, a new country for some, who must learn to navigate not only a new language but also new social understandings of themselves as men. They must navigate the US American understanding of the Latino macho associated with unwanted sexual and physical aggression, crime, and violence (Gutmann 2006; Limón 1999). MLB teams assess the character of prospects via US norms of behavior and work ethic in tandem with bodies and talent. According to Hector Ortega, who has directed the Chicago Cubs' Venezuelan *academia,* "You [want to] have players with everything but not the attitude. We are very strict about behavioral problems. In the long run, it brings problems. How he behaves with peers forms part of his makeup" (Orozco 2008a, 33). For this reason, Ortega explains, the organization looks at prospects' family lives for signs of stability or lack thereof. While character and behavior are indeed important, Ortega's explanation hints at issues of masculinities of color as potentially wild and uncontrollable outside an Anglo heteronormative family structure and thus buttresses a white, middle-class heteronormative construction of masculinity. Despite MLB Latin/o American players' high level of wealth and talent, media portrayals often locate them within a context of criminality, violence, and irrationality and as an unwanted foreign population.

In this way, representations, readings, and receptions of Latin/o Americans in MLB today fall under what Chávez (2013) terms the "Latino threat" narrative that circulates through media. Parting from Rosaldo's (1997) assertion that those of Latin American origin in the US have been branded with the stigma of "alien" and "illegal," which shapes their daily experiences and questions the legitimacy of their presence in the US, Chávez (2013) defines the Latino threat narrative as media and political representations of Latina/os that paint them as a threat to US nationalism as they refuse to assimilate to the US, lay claim to the US Southwest as their homeland, reproduce at a higher rate than other groups, and refuse to learn English (23–47). Though many aspects of this narrative, such as the claim to Southwest territory, refer specifically to Mexicans, media workers and politicians have generalized them to Latin Americans more broadly. According to Chávez, these representations and meanings are not tied to any one particular historical event or moment, but rather media coverage ties historical and current events to this narrative. The Latino threat narrative flourishes, and shows no signs of shifting because it upholds commonsense beliefs of Latina/o inferiority and perpetual foreign-ness that privilege white economic, political, and social power and renders Latina/os as virtual beings seen in the media, as opposed to real people living alongside non-Latina/os (Chávez 2013, 44–47). The Latino threat narrative saturates media in an increasingly anti-immigrant political moment such that Latina/os themselves have marshaled coalitions around a shared identity, or Latinidad, to construct a counter-narrative.

Given their hyperexposure in the media, these players function as texts on which to construct and negotiate Latinidad(es). This term, often used in the plural to recognize the multiplicity of Latina/os' lived experiences and associated with both Latina/o pride and homogenization, has been deployed by scholars working in the field of Latina/o studies to understand and analyze the varied social positions of Latina/os related to cultural identity, privilege, and power. While Aparicio and Chávez-Silverman (1997) elaborate the term to understand the ways by which Latina/os use cultural production and lived experiences to build sometimes problematic coalitions, Rúa (2005) cautions that while Latinidad can unite and empower those considered Latina/o, it can also homogenize a wide range of experiences and identities related to race, class, and gender/sexuality, leading to harmful outcomes. Molina-Guzmán and Valdivia (2004) and Beltrán (2009) define Latinidad via nationalism and image marketing, respectively. Molina-Guzmán and Valdivia describe Latina/os as an "imagined community," referencing Benedict Anderson's work on nationalism to show that the term is a construct that assumes a set of com-mon cultural and linguistic practices in the name of unity. As highly visible professional athletes, these men function as building blocks of Latinidad as unity and pride on the one hand, and homogenization and stereotyping on the other. Thus, the concept of mascuLatinidad or the ways in which specifically gendered masculine traits and performances bolster and limit constructions of Latinidad (Domino Rudolph 2012) helps to unpack players', media, and fans' constructions of the men of this study.

In the current moment, Latin/o American players constitute a ready case study on the social position of Latina/os in the US, given their media coverage and the media's and public's preoccupation with their actions as sports heroes, as men, and as a not quite legitimate population that is often both lionized and vilified for being overly passionate and "fiery" on and off the field of play. As media scholars (Aparicio and Chávez-Silverman 1997; Fregoso 1993; Lopez 1991; Molina Guzmán and Valdivia 2004; Perez-Firmat 1994; Ramirez-Berg 2002; C. E. Rodríguez 1997; Shohat and Stam 1994; Valdivia 2010) have long argued, US media constructs Latina/os in relation to white gender norms, feminizing Latino men with respect to hierarchies of privilege and power.

In fact, their level of fame comes with the burden of representation as these men's bodies stand in for the invisibility associated with Latina/o immigrant and low-wage labor, and become texts upon which mainstream Americans may read, construct, and contest individual and collective notions of what it means to be Latina/o.[5] Báez (2009) and Valdivia (2010) have termed this phenomenon "spectacular bodies" that stand in for ordinary bodies in national media and social discourses.[6] Similarly Markovitz (2011) defines "racial spectacles" as events that circulate via multiple media platforms and function as "instruments of socialization" as they impart messages about race as tools of control and/or resistance for audiences (2). As such, consumption of baseball by Latina/o fans contributes to "Latino cultural citizenship," defined by Flores and Benmayor (1997) as "a range of social practices which, taken together, claim and establish a distinct social space for Latinos in this country" (1).

Furthermore, Latina/os' media use contributes to their cultural citizenship in that they gauge their belonging, or lack thereof, in the US via the frequency and types of representations of them in media (Báez 2014; Couldry 2001). According to Couldry, people tend to naturalize media power through the belief that the media legitimates who and what is important. Thus, the media is thought to imagine, legitimate, and secure Latina/os' place in the nation. Audience engagements with Latin/o American "spectacular bodies" and "racial spectacles" reveal the tensions around fear and exclusion from some non-Latina/o fans, and baseball as a place to mark Latina/o cultural citizenship for Latina/o fans. My online comment analysis follows previous Latino studies scholarship (Molina-Guzmán 2010; Valdivia 2010) that advocates for such analysis as a way of understanding how audiences make sense of Latinidad or Latina/o identities through media consumption and use.

Celebrity and star studies scholarship dovetails with this idea of spectacular bodies as Latin/o American MLB players become cultural texts upon which to read lived experiences and social relations between ethnic and racial groups and identities tied to economies and capital. Celebrities symbolically embody contradicting ideologies, open to multiple interpretations

---

5. I use the term *burden of representation* here in accordance with Mercer's (1990) work on black art, where there is an expectation that an individual can represent and speak for an entire group, despite intersections of difference within that group such as class, ability, and gender.

6. In their feminist Latina media research, Báez (2009) and Valdivia (2010) contrast famous bodies, such as those of Jennifer Lopez, Salma Hayek, and others, as hypervisible iconic figures deployed to represent a certain corpulent and sexualized Latina femininity with the ordinary, invisible bodies and labor of Latina domestic and factory workers. One could make a similar contrast between the hypervisible bodies of MLB players of this study and the invisible labor of Latino men in factories, construction, and agriculture.

from audience members in what Dyer (1979) terms "star texts." Dyer (1979), Gledhill (1991), Boorstin (1992), and Shingler (2012) advocate for studies of stars and their representations that take into account the images produced by stars themselves as well as a network of publicity, promotion, agents, and industry forces driven by economic considerations. Audiences then interpret these images in a multitude of ways contingent upon the individual's social positionality. Finally, these images then become "embodiments of ideological contradictions, through which social conflicts and crises are negotiated and resolved at a symbolic level" (Dyer 1979, 17). Similarly, sports studies scholars Andrews and Jackson (2001) and Birrell and McDonald (2000) define celebrity as a construction of being well-known that ties achievement, economies, branding, and media coverage. Marshall (1997) explains the relationship between celebrities and the public where the public uses celebrities to define and understand cultural and social spheres:

> While the celebrity is equally a complete stranger, and someone we are never likely to meet, nor ever truly know, the virtual intimacy created between celebrity and audience often has very real effects on the manner in which individuals negotiate the experiences of their everyday lives. So, as well as being a consequential force within late capitalist Western liberal economies, celebrities are significant public entities responsible for constructing meaning, crystalizing ideologies, and offering contextually grounded maps for private individuals as they navigate contemporary conditions of existence. (3)

This definition guides the current analysis of MLB players because they serve individuals in a variety of contexts, either as a means of (re)enforcing a sense of Latinidad or as proof of difference and "cultural limitations." The media, including old media such as newspaper and television as well as new media such as blogs, websites, YouTube, Twitter, and posted comments, serves as the most important conduit of communication between celebrities and audiences. The increase in audience creation of media content complicates and blurs lines between celebrities, their handlers, and media professionals in the creation of sports celebrities.

Indeed, the media has become a proving ground for Latin/o American players in terms of their self-images and public perceptions related to assimilation, capital, and gender. Burgos (2007) connects media to players' chances for success in the US:

> Media rank among the most daunting off-field tasks that foreign-born Latinos encounter as professionals, and the financial stakes involved can be sig-

nificant. The player who adroitly handles the media and his public image positions himself well for endorsement deals. Those who do not are often ridiculed by the sporting press for their inability to communicate and, over time, are often portrayed as unwilling to assimilate to the mainstream in the United States. (246)

Burgos (2007) further ties gender, language, and media in his assessment of "voice" for Latin/o American players: "The ability to speak for himself in his interactions in public, especially with the press, boosts a player's sense of masculinity. This sense of voice and masculinity is crucial to the agency Latino players can exercise in crafting a public image and manipulating perceptions through their linguistic abilities" (249). Despite some instruction in English and US laws and culture in the *academias,* many players struggle initially with media interviews (Gigley 39). In fact, language learning and practice becomes a crucial context for intercultural relationships and a sometimes fraught Latinidad. Players often employ two strategies to improve their English: (1) They seek to spend time with US-born, non-Latin/o American teammates to force themselves to communicate in English, and (2) players from other Spanish-speaking countries seek help from Puerto Rican teammates due to the greater presence of English in the US territory. According to former Chicago Cub Ronny Cedeño, "In Venezuela, it's not like in Puerto Rico. Guys learn a lot of English in school [in Puerto Rico]. I learned from English-speaking friends I had on the [Mesa Cubs] and from hanging out with the American guys. I would always ask them a lot of questions" (Gigley 38). This context of assimilation, Latinidad, language, and gender provides a context for the current study.[7] Expanding on this context, I seek to further understand how the media, fans, and players themselves articulate current racial, political, economic, and gendered tensions around Latina/os in the US.

The above examples capture the stakes involved in sports participation and consumption as part of a larger identity formation rooted in a pseudo-nationalism of sorts. Andrews and Jackson (2001) describe sports as contests where an individual or group of people competes and the audience is expected to form an "affective attachment" to the participants, akin to the affective formation of nationalism. In fact, many fans refer to themselves as part of a "nation," such as "Yankee nation" or "Red Sox nation." Duany's (2002) articu-

---

7. In evoking Latinidad in the context of this study, and particularly in the quote by Cedeño, I do not mean to argue that there exists a seamless unity among all players of Latin/o American origin in MLB. Following the definition of Rúa (2005), I argue that we must examine the multiple Latinidades or ways that Latino identity functions and shifts within MLB player relations and media content.

lation of the nation as applied to Puerto Ricans on both the island and the mainland helps us to understand the formation of sports nationalism. Duany argues that other defining traits related to belief systems and cultural pride, more than physical space, signify nationalism for Puerto Ricans economically displaced from the island. Similarly, a sports team's nation can inhabit a range of physical spaces but still remain connected to that team through technology, pride, and nostalgia. As Singer (1998) argues, technology allows sports to uniquely function as a transnational commodity as audiences across a nation or around the world can view the same game at the same time. This pride and nostalgia may lead to identity practices that unite fans and allow them to connect sports to pride in a region or in a specific image of national identity. Sport nationalism may also defy or contradict dominant forms of nationalism and should thus be understood as more of a negotiation than a reflection of the surrounding society. In response to the dominant idea that sports simply reflects social practices and mores, Klein (1991) states:

> I take a different view, one now shared by most sports sociologists: that the function of sport is complex, that sport simultaneously reflects and obscures social and cultural phenomena. This view is consistent with what is known in the social sciences as the conflict perspective, and in the field of sport sociology it is supplanting the notion that the conflicts inherent in the relations between sport and society can be ignored or explained away. (2)

The present study of Latinidad and the social positioning of Latina/os through baseball follows the complex model of negotiation proposed by Klein.

For the players and fans of this study, the conflict perspective and the negotiation through sport is rendered even more complicated due to the transnational identities of players and some Latina/o fans, as well as the continued growth of globalization as an economic model, including MLB. As we saw with the tensions over the control and implementation of the World Baseball Classic, many believe US American sports to be an imperialist mechanism, but even more than that, many name sports as a prime contributor to globalization as the influx of American culture—through the viewing of sports games and the consumption of related products such as hats and jerseys—exists in tension with or even supplants local sports. The field of global sports studies now takes up this debate. For example, Maguire (1999) provides a collection of case studies that "explore the tensions between pressures exerted by such powerful global sporting interests as American football or British cricket and local (national) responses" (qtd. in Klein 2006, 222–23). Thus, the above discussion outlines the threads of race, gender, Latinidad, transnationalism, and globalization that drive the sport of baseball, and the positioning of people of Latin American descent in global and local economic and political contexts.

Mapping MLB's Latin/o American Stars onto This Project

Three recent events surrounding Major League Baseball that engage central issues—(1) Who may be considered "American"? (2) What is the place of the Spanish language in the US? (3) What is considered proper conduct for players as men?—serve as a framework to understand baseball as a site of negotiation and articulation of the social positions of Latina/os in the US, particularly Latino men. On July 16, 2013, Marc Anthony performed "God Bless America" at the MLB All-Star game. Anthony is a salsa musician of Puerto Rican descent, and his selection drew sharp criticism among some fans who objected to a "foreigner" singing the national anthem, questioning the nationality of New York–born Anthony. A second controversy arose on March 10, 2013, when ESPN broadcast a World Baseball Classic game between Puerto Rico and the Dominican Republic in Spanish to avoid a licensing conflict with the MLB Network. Fans reacted with vitriol over a Spanish language broadcast "in America." Finally, Robinson Canó's decision to reject a contract extension with the New York Yankees and his subsequent move to the Seattle Mariners drew criticism from the New York press and fans, who accused him of disloyalty; the press coincidentally published accounts of a child support court case pending for several months in the Dominican Republic, where Canó's son lives with his mother. These cases demonstrate the perception of Latina/os as a perpetual foreign Other and threat to the national and social fabric of the US in terms of perceived refusal to assimilate, perceived excessive use of Spanish (Chávez 2013), and lack of character as men, related to "cultural limitations" (Bonilla-Silva 2014, 2).

Thus, I situate the case studies of this project within the fields of critical race studies, Latina/o studies, media studies, and global sports studies as theoretical frameworks to understand the social construction of Latinidad in the US via a cohort of MLB players. In line with previous research on sports and MLB (Andrews and Jackson 2001; Birrell and McDonald 2000; Burgos 2007), my project examines MLB players and the negotiation of power for Latina/os via the intersection of gender, class, nationality, and stardom. The material for this analysis will draw from coverage in old media, such as newspapers, magazines, and autobiographies; new media, such as websites; and new new media via fan reactions posted as comments after internet news items, Facebook, YouTube, and Twitter. The idea of "new new media," as coined by Levinson (2012, 5), is particularly important because, as Levinson explains, in new new media, the line between producer and consumer is entirely erased as users may instantaneously produce and alter content on platforms such as YouTube, Facebook, and Twitter. This provides a crucial context to understand fan consumption. Parting from the concept of spectacular and ordinary bodies already mentioned, where famous bodies stand in for everyday bodies, the guiding questions of this project are these: (1) How do media and fans process Latin/o American baseball players as symbols of productive or unproductive Latinidad and citizenship? and (2) How are Latin/o American baseball players' masculinities deployed in terms of danger or productivity? These questions emerge from the current political climate where debates over the productivity and citizenship of Latina/os, perpetually imagined as undocumented immigrants, contour perceptions and everyday experiences of Latina/os in the US, from the hardworking and docile immigrant who still believes in the hard work of the American dream to the pseudo-terrorist and dangerous drug smuggler also often attributed to Latino men.

I situate my case studies within the Latina/o media studies work of Valdivia (2010), which unpacks the various media representation of Latina/os linked to political and social ideologies from the hardworking, family-oriented, and traditional rural dwellers to the fun-loving, single, and urban residents, including the ubiquitous male *bandido* figure, a criminal invader on US soil. In an attempt to unpack and negotiate these questions and perspectives, my analysis consists of five content chapters and concluding remarks. Chapter 1, "'La crema de Sammy Sosa': MLB and Transnational Constructions of Race, Class, and Gender," opens the discussion with a focus on masculinity, racial formation, and African diasporic identity among Latin/o Americans in the US and Dominican Republic via the very public coverage of retired slugger Sammy Sosa's skin bleaching. Chapter 2, "Who May Sing the National Anthem?: MLB, the WBC, and Representations of Latin/o American Nationalisms," uses the case of Puerto Rico and the controversy over the selection of Marc Anthony to sing the national anthem at the 2013 All-Star game as well as the successful run of Puerto Rico to the final game of the 2017 World Baseball Classic as counterpoints to tease out how we define "America" within Puerto Rico's political status as a US colony. Chapter 3, "'¡Aquí no se habla español!': MLB, Media, and the Racialization of Spanish Language Use," extends the conversation on race, masculinity, and nationalism to MLB's complicated relationship with Spanish via player experiences, MLB policy, and MLB's use of media and advertising embracing Spanish within a fraught linguistic climate.

Within this racial, national(ist), and linguistic climate, chapter 4, "'You Can't Walk Off the Island': MLB's Racialized Labor Structure and the Pressure to Produce from the *Academia* to the Major Leagues," examines MLB's Caribbean *academia* system, where teams train young prospects, primarily in the Dominican Republic, alongside documentary and filmic productions depicting *academias* to reveal the ways that MLB's labor practices in the Caribbean reflect globalized, neoliberal corporate exploitation, also seen among (undocumented) Latin American immigrants in the US. Chapter 5, "'The Blizzard of Oz,' 'A-Fraud,' 'Manny Being Manny,' and 'Deadbeat Dad': MLB and the Limits of Latino Character," shifts the focus to the ways that media coverage questions Latin/o American players' character via historically documented tropes and stereotypes aimed to reproduce Latin American inferiority and dangerous Latin/o American masculinities. The concluding chapter, "'Yo quiero jugar como David Ortiz': Final Thoughts on Race and the Viability of MLB's Latin/o American Dream in the US Context," reappraises the book's argument about mediated baseball masculinities and Latinidad and offers final observations about what the cohort of players studied tells us about the intersection of race, class, masculinities, immigration, nationalism, and fame, finally offering a direction for future research. My analysis pushes us to question how far we have come in terms of uses and receptions of Latin/o American male bodies, and at what costs.

Taken together, these chapters aim to complicate our understandings of Latin/o American players as constructed via media content and Latina/o and non-Latina/o fans' consumption of media coverage of these players as a means of better understanding current social and political climates around (1) who counts and does not count as US American, (2) the racialization of Spanish in the US and the consequences for speaking Spanish, (3) questions of Latin/o American labor and presence in the US and global economies, and (4) the loyalty and character of those accepted as laborers in the US economy as representatives of "America's pastime."

CHAPTER 1

"La crema de Sammy Sosa"

MLB and Transnational Constructions of Race, Class, and Gender

ONE AFTERNOON in Chicago toward the end of Sammy Sosa's prolific career with the Chicago Cubs, I remember watching a game with my sister, when she asked me, "Is Sammy Sosa black or Hispanic?" She assumed I had more knowledge, having studied Spanish and Latina/o cultures. I responded that if you asked Sosa himself, he would say he is Dominican. She looked at me quizzically, as that option wasn't even on her radar. The framing of her question, and her confusion at my answer, illustrate the rigid ways that white US Americans understand and define race and ethnicity informed by racialized markers such as skin color and language, as opposed to more fluid definitions of race in Latin/o America, more informed by a host of physical characteristics and histories that privilege narratives of nation formation, especially when Latin Americans migrate to the US. Questions around Sammy Sosa's body and racial identity have shaped and continue to shape his public persona, questions evoking integrity, performances of masculinities, and pain wrought on still-contested black identities in Latin America and the Caribbean in general and the Dominican Republic in particular.

In July 2018, *Sports Illustrated* featured a visibly whitened Sammy Sosa on its cover as part of its "where are they now" series. The article centers the still contentious relationship between Sosa and the Chicago Cubs since his implication in the Mitchell Report and investigations on steroid use in MLB. Sosa's message to the world is that he has nothing to apologize for and is now living his best international life in the Dominican Republic and Dubai. Amid the masculinist imagery of extreme wealth and capital power, Sosa's lightened complexion only briefly surfaces in the conversation, and provides him with an additional opportunity to flex his capital muscles and say that he doesn't care what others think, motioning to the material excess of the luxury hotel where the interview is taking place and stating, "I don't take garbage from nobody. I do whatever I want" (Buckland and Reiter 2018, 44). Indeed, spaces, and particularly leisure spaces like hotels, become markers of racial and class identities for the bodies that inhabit them. Mexican American author Richard Rodríguez uses hotels and their entrances as a way to get at his raced and class identities: When he enters through the front door, others comment on his beautiful tan, assumed to be the result of a vacation, whereas if he enters through the back, his brown complexion is attributed to a working-class Mexican service profession. Rodríguez (1982/2004) states, "My complexion assumes its significance from the context of my life. My skin itself means nothing" (148). Furthermore, given the history of race and trauma, Sosa's skin bleaching belies an internalized deference to whiteness, of which he may not be consciously aware. In his 1967 memoir *Down These Mean Streets*, Afro-Cuban and Puerto Rican Piri Thomas grapples with the position of his black body, similar to that of his father, in his mixed-complexion family and racially segregated New York City. The narrative is one of pain, as Piri realizes the social and economic limitations of his black body, and the tense relationship with his black father, who blames himself for the racism Piri experiences. Read together, Rodríguez's and Thomas's observations about bodies and skin color shed light on the historically, socially constructed and malleable nature of race mapped onto human bodies and phenotypical characteristics such as skin and hair.[1] Responses to retired Major League Baseball star Sammy Sosa's very public facial whitening in 2009 provide a fruitful example of the context described by Rodríguez and the tensions over African heritage articulated by Thomas, tensions embedded in the fraught construction of racial identity in Latin America and the Caribbean in general and the Dominican Republic in particular. The Sosa case is important because as a once poor, now elite Afro-Dominican transnational athlete, his body and performance of racial identity push us to attend to intersections of race, class, and gender/sexuality. Also, stars, as Richard Dyer argues in *Heavenly Bodies: Film Stars and Society* (1986), become sites for a wider audience of fans to negotiate social issues, in this case racial construction. Furthermore, April Mayes (2014) explains the

---

1. As Synnott (1987) has noted, hair is a malleable signifier that is both public and private and thus functions as an important indicator of hierarchy and power within society. Though not typically as malleable, I would argue that skin color does share some of the symbolic social value attributed to hair.

Sammy Sosa skin-bleaching case as a continuation of the historical presence of elite, European interests, rooted in the sugar industry in Sosa's native city, San Pedro de Macorís (1). Analysis of two cultural texts referencing the Sosa skin-bleaching case—a merengue song, "La crema de Sammy Sosa," and a comedy skit featured on *A reir con Miguel y Raymond,* and comments on these texts posted by viewers on YouTube—uncover the multilayered, gendered, class-inflected, and contested nature of blackness, whiteness, and racial mixture in the Dominican Republic and beyond.

On November 5, 2009, pictures of Sammy Sosa and his wife Sonia at the Latin Grammys in Las Vegas revealed a remarkably lighter-skinned Sosa, prompting rampant speculation as to what Sosa had done to alter his complexion. Quotes in several media outlets from publicists and Sosa himself answered with the explanation that Sosa had used a rejuvenation treatment to soften his skin, which lightened his skin as an unanticipated side effect.[2] Famous bodies such as that of Sosa acquire significance beyond the individual because star images help to define power and identity for a society. This is particularly true for star images of those who occupy positions of lower status in a given society such that "spectacular bodies" take on or obscure the meanings of "ordinary bodies," sometimes hidden or subordinated by media discourses (Beltrán 2002; Dyer 1986; Molina-Guzmán 2010; Valdivia 2010).

Responses to Sosa's lightened skin in general include claims that his choice was purely aesthetic, speculation that this was a side effect of his steroid use, and accusations of racial self-hatred via explanations that Sosa is just mapping racial tensions around Dominicans' African heritage onto his own body via a cultural imperative of whiteness. Many commented that this was the next step after Sosa had started wearing green contacts. In a post on the *Chicago Tribune*'s *Exploring Race* blog, Dawn Turner Trice muses, "The reason Sosa is in the spotlight is because he appears to be yet another brown person unhappy in his skin. He says that's not true. But in the photos, Sosa's eyes appear lighter and his hair straighter. It does make you wonder. . . ." (qtd. in O'Callaghan 2009). For most Dominican and Latin/o American observers, this was just another example of internalized conflict over the histories of colonization and enslavement that have forged modern Latin/o America. Many white Americans were confused as to why Sosa would chose to alter his skin this way, while some compared his skin lightening and the likely reasons behind it to the intense body dysmorphia associated with Michael Jackson's skin lightening

---

2. An article in *Time* magazine on November 10, 2009, quoted a spokeswoman from the Chicago Cubs organization, where Sosa played from 1992 to 2004, citing the rejuvenation treatment. A dermatologist quoted in the same article stated that this explanation is unlikely as such treatments would typically darken skin tone. She instead speculated that it is possible that an ointment used to treat acne scars could lighten Sosa's complexion.

and multiple plastic surgeries. The Sosa camp emphatically insisted that Sosa was using a cream to soften and even out his complexion, with the unintended side effect of skin lightening. In an interview, Sosa explained, "It's a cream that I have, that I use to soften [my skin], but has bleached me some. I'm not a racist, I live my life happily" (Rojas 2009). This led to rampant speculation as to whether this explanation was feasible from a medical perspective, with some media coverage including dermatologists providing medical explanations as to why a simple facial cream would not likely alter Sosa's skin color in that way. Still others used humor to unpack and ultimately challenge the official Sosa narrative, also engaging racism in their criticism of Sosa. These many and varied reactions illustrate how racial spectacle functions in daily life.

The construct of racial spectacle informs the relationship between spectacular and ordinary bodies; Debord (1967) observes that racial spectacles are social relations among people mediated by images that distract ordinary people from their material realities and encourage accumulation and consumption. I would add that this consumption tied to spectacle and media representations via images imbues spectacular bodies like that of Sammy Sosa with a symbolic value as representations of Latin/o American men more broadly. The Sosa case prompted not only gossip and speculation but also expressive cultural productions depicting his whitened body and situating it within the political economies of blackness, racial mixture, and masculinity in the Dominican Republic. Such depictions connect blackness, economies, and masculinities in complex and sometimes contradictory ways as they push us to complicate historical embodiments of black and white and hint at sustained conflicts related to Dominican racial narratives.

Reactions from Latina/o fans are particularly useful and relevant to our understanding of MLB as a transnational and global actor because these fans themselves not only embody the mixed racial formation prevalent in many MLB players' physical bodies and life experiences but also possess the cultural and embodied knowledge to engage in dialogue over contested racial terrain via consumption of Sammy Sosa and other Latin/o American players. This chapter argues that MLB players serve as useful sites to understand intersections of race, class, and gender from a transnational perspective and advocates for readings of race and racialization that take into account transnational migrations and cultural paradigms. The chapter further pushes us to consider the role of class in racial formation, as much work on Latino masculinities has focused on men living at or near poverty level. Indeed, to what extent and in what ways does "money whiten," as the common saying goes in Latin America and the Caribbean? This reading of the Sosa case focused through a lens of Latin American and transnational racial optics sets the stage for receptions of Latin/o American players in the US social, political, and media contexts.

Though my argument focuses specifically on Dominicans, and one player in particular at that, the arguments advanced about racialization and MLB here apply more widely to Latin/o American players for various reasons. First, Dominicans remain the largest Latin American subgroup on major and minor league rosters, and as such have become the most visible Latin/o American group among baseball fans and players. Though some individual players from other countries have become household names, no country outside the US is more associated with MLB players than the Dominican Republic. According to data provided by MLB, at the start of the 2018 season, 27 percent of MLB players on forty-man rosters or the disabled and restricted lists were born outside of the US, including Puerto Rico and the Virgin Islands. Latin American countries, particularly the Dominican Republic, are home to most of these players. Of 254 players born outside the US, 84 are from the Dominican Republic, 74 from Venezuela, 19 from Puerto Rico, 17 from Cuba, 11 from Mexico, 5 each from Colombia and Curacao, and 3 each from Brazil, Nicaragua, and Panama (Anderson 2018). Additionally, the Dominican Republic currently houses the most sophisticated and expansive academy system to train young players outside the US. Given these historical and recruitment dynamics, Dominican players do serve to illustrate wider issues around race, economies, and masculinities, as a very hybrid population racially but very strongly associated with Afro-Latina/o identities. The Dominican Republic is also a most prolific producer of baseball talent. Sammy Sosa, in particular, because he embodies blackness and has emerged as one of the elite, if most controversial players of recent MLB history, provides a widely accessible case study to understand Latino masculinities and MLB via race, power, and economies.

The Sosa case and perceptions of racial mixture in the Dominican Republic underscore the ways that racialized bodies represent historical processes of transnational racial formation, and how the continued negotiation of mixed race subjects placed within a transnational narrative echoes this past and pushes boundaries of class and gender in the present. The Sosa case particularly signals intersections between masculinity, blackness, and wealth rendered visible through popular culture. I situate the present analysis in previous work in mixed race studies that calls for the following considerations: Readings of hybridity that go beyond the celebratory to understand global threads of white supremacy and their effects on multiracial people (Christian 2000), readings of mixed race that destabilize the idea of racial purity through nuanced understanding of mixed race (Mahanti and Moreno 2001), and readings of mixed race from an intersectional perspective that takes into account questions not only of nationalism and diaspora but also gender and class (Mahanti and Moreno 2001). A reading of representations of blackness, whiteness, masculinity, and wealth in a merengue song, "La crema de Sammy Sosa," by Nelson de la Olla, and a comedy skit featuring Sosa on Dominican comedy sketch show *A reir con Miguel y Raymond* (*Let's Laugh with Miguel and Raymond*), in conjunction with comments for each text posted on You-Tube, will reveal the contradictions and intersections of blackness, whiteness, and masculinities among Dominicans in the US and on the island, where the Dominican racial narrative illustrates the continued struggle to attribute value to blackness amid a national historic narrative that privileges whiteness.

Sammy Sosa's Body and the Performance of Power

Critiques, analysis, and speculations surrounding Sammy Sosa's body and the power it generated, more than anything else, mark his career and legacy. Born on November 12, 1968, in San Pedro de Macorís, a Dominican city associated with sugar production and considered to be the cradle of Dominican baseball talent, Sosa enjoyed a prolific MLB career from 1985 to 2007. According to Burgos (2007), media constructions of Sosa and his own public performance underscore issues of race that have long haunted MLB (243–60). In key moments of Sosa's career, the media has presented him as affable but less than intelligent, publishing quotes with English grammar errors instead of making corrections that would preserve Sosa's dignity. Common journalistic practice is to make such corrections with players who speak English as a second language, though this policy is not consistently followed, depending on the journalist and media outlet (Burgos 2007, 254). Though the media does perpetuate stereotypes, as Bretón and Villegas (1999) argue, Sosa has also deployed the endearing but not too bright figure of Chico Escuela, a *Saturday Night Live* character famous for the tag line "Baseball has been berry, berry good to me," as a means of using racial stereotypes to endear himself with US fans and to make money. Bretón and Villegas (1999) explain, "As smart as he is talented, Sosa knew the words would make Americans laugh because, until recently, they were about all Americans knew about Latin American players—that they talked funny" (35).

This context has had grave consequences for Sosa's star text and fans' understanding of him and of Latin/o American players more broadly as unintelligent or untrustworthy, a dynamic that played out in specific media events.

Events shaping media and fan constructions of Sosa include the home-run record chase with Mark McGwire in 1998; the use of a corked bat in a game situation in 2003; his involvement in MLB's performance-enhancing-drug era, culminating in the 2005 congressional hearings; his highly publicized performance of gratitude to God, kissing his hand and pointing to the sky after successful at-bats; and aggression in the clubhouse and off the field.

There was a ready-made media spectacle in the baseball world in 1998 as Sammy Sosa and Mark McGwire vied to break Roger Maris's sixty-one home-run single-season record. Dominican-born Sosa and US-born McGwire embodied the racial tensions around baseball in the late twentieth century as Latin/o American players had grown in numbers and challenged records held by iconic white players of the past. Indeed, many scholars of the history of Latin/o Americans in MLB have noted that the late 1990s is a significant period for these players as they finally began to reach prominence and garner major media attention despite their long history with the organization. However, as Regalado (2008) points out, at the beginning of the 1998 season, McGwire received far more media attention than did Sosa, and only much later did Sosa enter the story as a rival to McGwire to break the record (208–9). In the end, McGwire's sixty-second home run received much more support by media as well as Maris's family and MLB commissioner Bud Selig in attendance. Sosa broke MLB protocol to leave his position in the outfield to congratulate McGwire, a moment relished by media and fans. When Sosa broke Maris's record five days later, no comparable fanfare awaited him. As Sosa himself would describe his position in relation to McGwire's, "In America, Mark [McGwire] is the man. In the Dominican, I am the man" (Regalado 2008, 207).

A second moment in Sosa's career sparked a great deal of controversy. On June 3, 2003, against the Tampa Devil Rays, then Chicago Cub Sammy Sosa's bat shattered, revealing it to be filled with cork, leading to controversy and suspension. Though Sosa explained the incident as a mistake—he used corked bats during practice, in part to hit the ball farther and put on a show for fans—his image would never recover. Within days of the game, one could see T-shirts in Chicago with an altered Cubs logo: The large *C* with *ubs* inside had been replaced by a large *C* with *ork* inside. A litany of jokes about the incident also circulated, questioning both Sosa's integrity and his manhood.

A further scandal would haunt Sosa's career and legacy when investigations associated him (along with a long list of other players) with the use of performance-enhancing substances, culminating in congressional hearings in 2005. A heightened scrutiny of Sosa's body followed as local sports programs in Chicago contrasted images of Sosa early in his career with later ones, noting the small size of his body in the beginning of his career compared to the large physique of later years, speculating as to what prompted the change. Sosa became part of a group of players branded as cheaters and lambasted for tarnishing the reputation of "America's" game.

Besides the three crucial events mentioned above, the trademark of Sosa's career and bodily performance was his pointing and kissing up to heaven after his home runs. Though many players follow that tradition or similar ones, Sosa is perhaps the most well-known for it, so much so that it figures in imitations of him, such as the skit on *A reir con Miguel y Raymond* analyzed here. Overall, portrayals of Sosa toward the end of his career highlighted this bodily performance as excessive, egocentric, and boasting. Additionally, much talk about Sosa's clubhouse behavior, especially blasting merengue music despite protest from other players, which culminated in an unnamed player allegedly breaking Sosa's radio, cast Sosa's star text and legacy in terms of greed and black masculine aggression, as opposed to the Dominican Horatio Alger shoeshine boy turned MLB star persona ascribed to Sosa earlier in his career. The tensions surrounding the moments and characterizations of Sosa's career mentioned above provide a context for the questions of race, narratives of racialization, and pride surrounding Sammy Sosa's Latinidad and Latina/o, particularly Dominican fans' readings of Sosa's skin bleaching and performance of race. These tensions must be understood in the narratives of racial formation in Latin America forged through the discipline and pain wrought on nonwhite bodies via colonization, enslavement, and global markets, most notably through the constructs of hybridity and mestizaje.

Contextualizing Latin/o American Racial Construction: Hybridity, Mestizaje, and Transnationalism

The Sosa case is a reminder that bodily manipulation incarnates the historical pain related to race in the Americas as it delineates the tensions around and limits of Latin/o American racial narratives. The black body of one of the Dominican Republic's wealthiest citizens remains under scrutiny and pushes culture workers and Latin/o American baseball fans to examine the racial legacy of the Americas. Indeed, the game of baseball itself is enmeshed in the historical formation of racial identities in the Caribbean since the nineteenth century as a result of the Spanish American War; political/military interventions, including two US military occupations of the Dominican Republic in the twentieth century; and economic interventions, first by the sugar industry and more recently by MLB in establishing a sophisticated player recruitment system in the Caribbean Basin, especially the Dominican Republic. As such, contemporary racial formation in Latin American and the Caribbean has developed as a result of racial mixture, articulated via the theoretical constructs of hybridity and mestizaje, as well as transnationalism, via the sustained migratory flow between Latin America, the Caribbean, and the US, of which Major League Baseball is a significant example. This analysis also roots itself in the terrain of critical mixed race studies as articulated by G. Reginald Daniel, Laura Kina, Wei Ming Dariotis, and Camilla Fojas in the inaugural issue of *Critical Mixed Race Studies*. The authors (2014) define critical mixed race studies as a field that engages the intersections between the constructions of feminism, race, class, transnationality, diaspora, passing, and authenticity as points of negotiation for those who embody and study mixed race identities (25). These scholars push us to consider critical mixed race studies not only as an academic field but also as a critical tool in the arts, community-based structures, and new media (21).

Hybridity and mestizaje function as core analytical tools in negotiations of racial formation, culture, and power inherent in relationships between colonizing and postcolonial cultures/nations. Debates around race and hybridity in Latin American racial construction date back to the era of European colonization and the import of enslaved Africans. Early Latin American thinkers such as Freyre (1900–1987), Ortiz (1881–1969), and Vasconcelos (1882–1959) engaged hybridity in their work in response to biological determinists who cast racially mixed people as degenerate and inferior.[3] Despite the need for intervention, critics argue that this work romanticizes racial mixture and favors whitening discourses. Vasconcelos's construct of "la raza cósmica/ cosmic race," which constructs Latin Americans as a new and distinct racial group due to European, indigenous, and African mixture, has been criticized for positing racial mixture as a strategy toward whiteness.[4]

More contemporary definitions of hybridity and mestizaje provide a useful lens through which to read race in Latin/o America due to their emphasis on power and globalization as structuring factors in racial formations. Rosaldo (1995) defines hybridity "as the ongoing condition of all human cultures which contains no zones of purity because they undergo continuous processes of transculturation (mutual borrowing and lending between cultures)" (xi). Bhabha (1994, 225), R. Young (1995, 5), García Canclini (1989/1995, 2), and Santiago (2001, 30) expand on Rosaldo's definition, applying it to the specific context of Latin America. These scholars argue that racial formations and identities in Latin America disrupt European norms of purity and anti-

---

3. See Freyre (1933/1956), F. Ortiz (1940/1947), and Vasconcelos (1925).

4. For a discussion of the debated nature and evolution of Vasconcelos's "cosmic race" and mestizaje, see Miller (2004) and Sue (2014).

miscegenation associated with Western civilization and understand Latin American identity formation as a negotiation of hybrid sociocultural forces resulting from colonial history and globalization. As such, hybridity and racial construction in the Americas are irresolvable and in constant negotiation, as an "in-between" cultural space.

Mestizaje, meaning *mixture* in Spanish, is a theoretical concept developed by US Latina/o and Chicana/o scholars, especially the seminal work of Anzaldúa, *Borderlands / La Frontera: The New Mestiza*; similar to hybridity, it facilitates a relational and negotiated "in-between" approach to understanding Latin American and US racial constructions, power, and privilege. Anzaldúa (1987), through her development of the "new mestiza," advocates for mixture and hybridity as means of recovering the dignity of indigenous Latin American heritage and as a coping strategy for those who live in between hegemonic articulations of identity in terms of race, gender/sexuality, and class. Building on Anzaldúa's theoretical intervention, Sandoval (2000), Pérez-Torres (2006, xii–xiii), Daniel (2012), and Sue (2014) envision mestizaje as a means to challenge hierarchies built on race in both the arts and lived experiences of racially hybrid subjects as a means to understand social inequalities and develop egalitarian critical sensibilities and practices while simultaneously allowing individual and national identity formations not to appear too white or too black. Though these critical perspectives provide a needed intervention to understand mixed race, it is important to heed Shohat and Stam (1994) as they warn that hybridity and mixed race are integrationist but not always egalitarian and do not always destabilize racial hierarchies, sometimes buttressing structures of inequality, a tension still present in Latin/o American racial formations.

In addition to hybridity and mestizaje, transnationalism enables us to understand the multiple ways that audiences and media workers understand, process, and construct Latin/o American MLB players' actions, especially Sammy Sosa's skin bleaching, as an exercise in racial identity. We must consider racial formation in the broader context of Latin America, as well as specifically in the Dominican Republic and the US together. Indeed, Dominican notions of race have been shaped by the US occupation in 1916 and the resulting development of the sugar industry, which included the import of workers from the West Indies, as well as the sustained Dominican migration between the Dominican Republic and the US of the present moment, all of which have shifted racial formation on the island and among Dominicans in the US. As Roth (2012) argues in her research on Dominicans and Puerto Ricans in New York City, Caribbean migrants construct racial identities via racial systems in the Caribbean as well as those in the US, regardless of where they physically live at a given moment in their lives. This leaves a mark and begins to lead to shifts of racial construction in the US as the black/white binary sometimes broadens (Roth 2012, 1–31). The range and intensity of reactions to Sammy Sosa's whitened body illustrate that negotiations of power differentials around racial mixture related to hybridity, mestizaje, and transnationalism continue to contour Latin/o American racial formations. These tensions came through most strongly in a reaction to Sosa's skin bleaching by a fan who tried to explain the cultural and racial significance of Sosa's actions through "the mulatto escape hatch"—a reference to ways that Latin/o Americans move toward whiteness via economic status and professional success. This particular image provides a context through which to read the many and varied reactions that engage the history and historical pain around race mentioned so far, reactions that range from black pride to visceral internalized racism and antiblack sentiment.

"The Mulatto Escape Hatch": Dominican Mixed Race Negotiation in Practice

The following response from a commenter identified as "sam spade" accompanied a story on Sammy Sosa's whitened complexion posted on January 12, 2012, on Yahoo Sports:

> Ok, here it is. It's a peculiar Latin american thing. It's called—The Mullattoe Escape Hatch. If you're successful and have money. You can be honorary white. Just put that in. that's what Sammy's doing. Completely acceptable in his culture. Sammy always got mad if you said he was black. He's not. Never has been. He's from Latin america. the Mullattoe Escape Hatch is a goal. (Duk 2012)[5]

This comment signals important connections between racialization and wealth, as well as differences between racial formation in the Caribbean and Dominican Republic versus the US.[6] Most important, consistent with the research of Degler (1986) conducted in Brazil, this comment illustrates the

---

5. This and all online posts throughout are transcribed as they appear on the YouTube site, including irregular spelling, grammar, and abbreviations. Bracketed explanations are provided when necessary.

6. I use the term *racial formation* here in accordance with Omi and Winant's definition in *Racial Formation in the United States: From the 1960s to the 1990s* (1994), where the formation of racial categories is shifting rather than static, and is contingent upon the value attributed to ethnic and racial groups in a given historical moment.

extent to which class status allows Latin Americans some ability to shift their mixed race identity, historically and discursively rooted in the fusion of European, indigenous, and African ancestries, toward whiteness. Additionally, this comment underscores the emotionally charged nature of the African presence in the Caribbean, one that may have prompted Sosa to alter his body to distance himself from the black racial label he encounters in the US as a Major League Baseball player. Several mixed race studies scholars, such as Anzaldúa (1987), Camper (1994), Gordon (1997), Williams (1997), and Ifekwunigwe (1999), have written about the ambivalence, pain, identity negotiation, and colorism visited on mixed race bodies and subjectivities as a result of European colonization in the Americas and beyond. These scholars push us to understand mixed race as a means of destabilizing notions of racial purity and the power differential of the white/nonwhite binary that operates in many societies, embedded in historical narratives of colonization.

The call to employ mixed race bodies and experiences as a way to reconfigure the white/nonwhite hierarchy of the history of European colonization of Africa and the Americas informs the work of Bhabha (1990) and Hall (1990). Bhabha and Hall develop their arguments around the constructs of "third space" and diaspora, respectively, to understand mixed race subjectivities within the socioracial hierarchies that produce them. Bhabha (1990) defines "third space" as a function of hybridity:

> The importance of hybridity is not to be able to trace two original moments from which the third emerges; rather hybridity to me is the "third space" which enables other positions to emerge. The third space displaces the histories that constitute it, and sets up new structures of authority, new political initiatives, which are inadequately understood through received wisdom. (221)

The crucial element of Bhabha's argument for understanding the transnational Dominican and US cultural productions and reactions to the Sammy Sosa case is the understanding of mixed race Dominicans as inhabiting a "third Space." While the African-descended history of the Dominican Republic remains important as a structuring principle of racial construction, the sociopolitical context of the Dominican Republic as a type of "third space" combines a history of colonization of African and Native American peoples by the Spanish as far back as the sixteenth century to the present moment of globalization, where the Dominican economy is enmeshed with more powerful economies, such as that of the US, via the ubiquitous presence of Major League Baseball there. Indeed, as Hall persuasively contends, the African historical thread must not be lost because the diaspora itself is a new space, akin to Bhabha's "third space." According to Hall, "The diasporic experience . . . is defined, not by essence or purity, but by the recognition of a necessary heterogeneity and diversity; by a conception of 'identity' which lives with and through, not despite, difference, by *hybridity*. Diaspora identities are those which are constantly producing and reproducing themselves anew, through transformation and difference" (qtd. in Bhabha 1990, 221). The struggle over the construction of a "third space" and (re)production of diasporic identities is at the core of the Sammy Sosa debate, a debate that exemplifies tensions over racial formation and negotiation.

Racial classification in the Dominican Republic differs from that of the US. While the US operates via a white/nonwhite binary of hypodescent—understood as the "one drop rule," where one drop of nonwhite blood renders bodies as nonwhite, though one drop of white blood does not render bodies as white (Gordon 1997; Root 1992; Zack 1993)—Dominicans do not define racial identity so narrowly. As Candelario (2001) points out, in the Dominican Republic, as in Latin America more widely, race is constructed more along a continuum than in the black/white binary of US social structure. As in the US, though, there is a mandate and privilege attributed to *blanqueamiento*, or whiteness, rooted in economic privilege associated with light-skinned bodies. Sagás and Mayes link *blanqueamiento* to the elite class, who have deployed European ancestry to justify discourses of superiority, manipulate politics, and exploit lower classes (Mayes 2014; Sagás 2000). Mayes (2014) further posits that historical events related to Haitian and US occupation and immigration from Cuba, Puerto Rico, and Spain also drive *blanqueamiento* (1–14). This economic hierarchy stems from the justification of the colonization of Africa and the Americas via a socially and pseudo-scientifically constructed white supremacist argument that white bodies are virtuous and black bodies are sinful, rooted in the desire to exploit African labor, as well as fears of unrestrained sexuality and ethno-racial mixture (Christian 2000; Root 1992; Zack 1993). There is, however, one crucial difference with respect to socioeconomic status. According to Candelario (2001), "nonetheless, unlike the United States, racially marginalized individuals can experience some degree of upward socio-racial mobility through economic and political ascendance" (60). The Sammy Sosa case will further illustrate this point.

Pérez Cabral (2007), Candelario (2007), Howard (2001), and Simmons (2009) argue that Dominicans have accepted their racial mixture but distance themselves from blackness and Haitians. Contemporary constructions of race in the Dominican Republic emerge from the histories of Spanish colonization, the "Haitian Invasion" from 1822 to 1844, US military occupation (1916–1922, 1965–1966), migration from other Caribbean and Latin American nations, economic occupation, and more recently, transnational and global economic flows. The relatively short duration of plantation slavery, coupled with depopulation of the white creole population from the Spanish colonial period, contributes to the formation of a large mixed African-descent population (Moya Pons 1995; Torres-Saillant 1998). This fraught historical construction of blackness now permeates many social and cultural institutions in the Dominican Republic, such as mainstream media representations of meanings of Dominican nationalism tied to social class, gender/sexualities, and race.

Candelario (2001) notes that in the most recent national census that quantified race in the Dominican Republic, in 1960, few Dominicans, only 10 percent, identified as black (61). Dominican national identity constructs dark Dominicans in terms of indigenous, as opposed to African, heritage, despite the fact that there is more African than indigenous ancestry among Dominicans due to the death of much of the indigenous Taíno population after the Spanish conquest. Dominicans with visible African ancestry tend to identify via the term *índio* (indigenous), with added qualifiers such as *oscuro* (dark) or *claro* (light), classifications institutionalized through the *cédula de idenfiticación,* a national identification system dating from the Trujillo regime from 1931 to 1961 (Candelario 2001, 2007; Duany 1994; Simmons 2009). Though Dominicans acknowledge their racial mixture, there is a tendency to favor whiteness and whiten the national identity. Recent economic trends in the Dominican Republic, especially the growth of a critical mass of Afro-descended baseball players like Sosa, are shifting these dynamics.

All of the historical and social factors above shape the self-construction as well as others' constructions of Sammy Sosa's skin bleaching in relation to Dominican identity. As Candelario (2007) notes, "The Dominican case illustrates that identities can be situational, equivocal, and ambiguous, but the fact that they are also structured by power relations as self-perceptions is perforce mediated by the perceptions of others and our structured relation to them" (7). These issues are rendered even more complex by Sosa's transnational identity. Levitt (2001) underscores the importance of transnational practices in the everyday lives of Dominicans in terms of global economies and communications, as constant communications facilitated by advances in media allow Dominicans in the US to retain constant contact with those on the island and are thus mutually aware of political, economic, and social developments as they happen. Baseball players like Sosa embody the fluidity of Dominican transnational identity as they possess the cultural and economic capital to easily travel between the Dominican Republic and the US, attaining great symbolic value as icons of Dominican identity at the global level.

Having played from 1989 to 2007 for Major League Baseball, an organization that prides itself on its efforts to globalize both its labor force and fan base, Sammy Sosa specifically and Dominican players in general embody global economic movement. As Burgos (2007) and Ruck (2011) note, because the majority of players recruited in the Dominican Republic are coded as mixed race or black in the US, Major League Baseball has historically been and continues to be an important site of negotiation of racial construction, from desegregation in 1947 to current debates over recruitment processes that favor African-descent players from the Caribbean and Latin America over black US Americans. Marcano Guevara and Fidler (2002) and Klein (2006) argue that Major League Baseball has used the Caribbean, particularly the Dominican Republic, as a source of cheap labor, sometimes exploiting the bodies of young prospects to staff its teams at the major and minor league levels. The possibility of fame and fortune has fueled the desires of many of the poorest and blackest Dominican young men to follow in Sosa's footsteps. Writing in 2000, at the height of Sosa's career, in a perhaps excessively celebratory note, Bretón observes, "Everyone wants a piece of him—he is baseball's cover boy. And he is Dominican and he is black. That's progress in my book, because I can remember a time just a few years ago when the best Latin players in the major leagues felt like third-class citizens in America's game. But it's a brave new world now" (Sosa and Bretón 2000, 5). Thus, Sosa's spectacular body contributes to representations of ordinary transnational Dominican bodies that must negotiate multiple racial constructions in Dominican and US societies. The social structures of both countries are fraught with distinct hierarchies related to skin color and phenotype linked to historical, political, cultural, and economic developments around bodies socially coded as nonwhite, mixed, or black. The Sosa case demonstrates the ways that racialized social structures contour lived experiences, bodily performance/manipulation, and perceptions of black bodies.

As poster "sam spade," cited at the start of this section, indicates, the malleability of Latin American racial construction relies heavily on wealth, a malleability then literally articulated through bodily manipulation, in this case skin lightening, to distance individuals from blackness. Dominican cultural productions around the Sosa case capture this dynamic and provide sites of pointed social critique through humor, as we shall see. Textual and audience post readings of "La crema de Sammy Sosa" and the skit on *A reir con Miguel y Raymond* provide a transnational perspective on the intersection of race, class, and masculinity in Dominican culture.

Readings of texts and posts are informed by the construct of ethno-race. Candelario (2007) defines ethno-race within the transnational Dominican context:

> By ethno-racial, I mean that Dominicans are negotiating their status as racialized minorities operating in the context of histories and structures beyond their control, but they do so with a degree of agency and self-determination. They bring to the local context, in other words, their own histories and understandings of their identities and they display them accordingly. (10)

My readings stem from a perspective of transnationalism and ethno-race in part because posters on YouTube are not required to identify nationally, unless they do so in their post, and so it is impossible to identify with certainty the nationality of individuals. In addition to such practical pragmatic considerations, Dominican identity is increasingly transnational in nature, an example of which is Sammy Sosa. Thus, my analysis seeks to answer the following questions: How does popular cultural production respond and contribute to constructions and understandings of mixed race Dominican masculinity? How do audiences use cultural texts and response postings to negotiate and define mixed race Dominican identity?

"La crema de Sammy Sosa": The Body as Site of Mixed Race Negotiation

The appearance of the Sosa photo from the Latin Grammys in 2009 prompted the release of a merengue song, "La Crema de Sammy Sosa," by Nelson de la Olla, uploaded to YouTube on November 13, 2009. The fact that the song belongs to the merengue genre is significant because merengue, a genre that combines European and African musical elements, is strongly associated with Dominican national identity and pride. It is also a music originally produced primarily by poor, African-descended Dominicans, though it has now expanded to all classes. Merengue has historically been a site for Dominicans to negotiate and sometimes obscure African identity (Brito Ureña 1987; Pacini Hernandez 1995; Austerlitz 1997). Merengue also figures prominently as entertainment at baseball games on the island. Images on one of the YouTube videos for the song evoke Dominican pride via the Dominican flag, Dominican parades, Sosa's career in Major League Baseball, and iconic Dominican foods such as fried meats, rice and beans, and plantains, foods strongly associated with Sosa's working-class background. Another video posting features pictures of the whitened Sosa photoshopped onto skin care products such as Ponds facial cream. The song situates Sosa within the complex socioeconomic racial landscape of the Dominican Republic as a wealthy black man and at the same time raises questions of Sosa's masculinity as a result of his skin whitening, identifying the source of his whitened skin with women's facial creams, even as it sarcastically captures the pain wrought on black bodies willing to endure discomfort in exchange for greater social acceptance and status.

"La crema de Sammy Sosa" represents blackness and whiteness via humor and religious metaphors, describing Sosa's cream as "la milagrosa" ("the miraculous one," a name given to the Virgin Mary). It opens and ends with references to Michael Jackson's *Black and White* album. The song's reference to Jackson is significant as Michael Jackson's body has taken on global significance as a symbol of identity and struggle over blackness. It starts with a brief instrumental sample from that album and ends with de la Olla saying, "Black and white." The song presents Sosa's cream as a miraculous solution to blackness for those who no longer wish to be black: "Pa todos los morenos. Llegó la milagrosa, un producto nuevo, la crema se Sammy Sosa" (for all black people, the miraculous one has arrived, Sammy Sosa's cream).[7]

Posters on YouTube recognize and celebrate the humorous tone of the song as they link it to Dominican national pride. Several posts reference the uniquely Dominican sense of humor around race as a point of Dominican pride via posts stating that no one does humor better than Dominicans. Humor and cultural pride around race are indeed important given the contested nature of blackness and the direct nature of the song. Within this overall discourse, however, polarized opinions did emerge. For some posters, such as rosamaria14100, "La crema de Sammy Sosa" provided an opportunity to evoke black pride and admonish those perceived not to display it, directly referencing and recuperating the persona of Michael Jackson:

> Los que merecen morir son los que odian su raza o odian otra raza dios creo una sola raza LA HUMANA estupidos los negraos que odian su raza michael jackson no uso ninguna crema el sufria de vitiligo hasta que su piel se despigmento ignorantes . . . estupidos si supieran que bonito es el color que dios nos dio.

> (Those who hate their own or others' races deserve to die. God created only one race, THE HUMAN RACE. Black people who hate their race are stupid.

---

7. All translations from Spanish to English are mine.

Michael Jackson did not use any cream. He suffered from vitiligo so that his skin turned pale. Ignorant . . . stupid people, if only they knew how beautiful the color that God gave us is.) (Mr. Inoa 2009)

This poster locates black pride in biological terms via reference to a higher power that created all humans equally, and charges that those who do not realize that are simply ignorant, sublimating, or ignoring the social and historical underpinnings of racial construction. Additionally, they reclaim Michael Jackson's black subjectivity and explain his whitening as a result of an illness and nothing more. While it is certainly plausible that Jackson did suffer from a skin condition, the fact that he chose to whiten, as opposed to darkening, his skin in an attempt to even his complexion problematizes him as a figure of black pride.

Another poster, Elenibaby27, showed a greater understanding and acknowledgment of social structures, even differentiating between blackness in the Dominican Republic and the US:

I am dominican and a dark skin one but it happens in every society thats what it's thought [taught] us to think [that African descent is inferior to those coded as white] . . . I dont care how some African Americans proclaim to being dead ass proud of being black and criticize us deep down society has made blacks feel inferior but its plain out ignorance others shouldnt define your value but your self its a hard concept to understand. (Mr. Inoa 2009)

This comment indexes three important issues related to mixed race Dominican identity. First, this post contextualizes antiblack sentiment in Dominican and more global constructs of racial hierarchies and white supremacy. Second, the differentiation between US blackness and Dominican blackness via claims of black pride by African Americans and their criticisms of Dominicans for insufficiently recognizing their blackness underscore how differences in nationalism and history shape race and in some cases create hierarchies within the African diaspora. Finally, this reaction to "La crema de Sammy Sosa" reminds us that others' perceptions partially define individuals' racial identity.

By way of contrast, other posts demonstrate denial and hatred of blackness. A post by quedificilesserNico divorces the Sosa controversy from racism: "Porquee se burlan y lo critican? alomejor no es de razismo lo hace porque le gusta su apariencia mas blanco como un blanco cuando . . . se bronceaes lo mismo" (Why are they making fun of him and criticizing him? Maybe it's not racism. Maybe he does it because he likes his whiter appearance like when white people tan. It's the same thing) (Mr. Inoa 2009). This reading fails to account for the white privilege that underpins decisions about appearance and the physical body. The discussion of the historical, social, and economic threads of mixed race theories already mentioned indicates that Sosa would likely "prefer" a whiter appearance as a result of his socialization in the Dominican Republic. Further, the comparison of whitening dark skin to the tanning of light skin insufficiently attends to the malleability of complexion of those coded as white. In other words, white bodies may tan with no risk to social status as a function of white privilege, as seen at the beginning of this chapter with the Richard Rodríguez example of how leisure spaces map race onto bodies.

All of the posts thus far engage the pain faced by mixed race people as they navigate social hierarchies; one post captures intense racism, also evoking pain. MrEdwardhot posted, "Los negros son seres inmundos y putrefactos merecen morir" (Black people are dirty and putrid and deserve to die) (Mr. Inoa 2009). This extremist sentiment represents the most internalized anti-black viewpoint, certainly born out of an internalized white supremacy, and exemplifies the dangers of constructions of racial purity.

Furthermore, a direct intersection between skin color and wealth emerges in the song's lyrics. Skin color is immediately commodified as the cream is identified as a new "product," revealed to be cheap later in the song: "sólo cuesta un peso" (costs just a dollar). This representation disjoins whiteness from wealth so that whiteness, a highly desirable commodity in the song's discourse, becomes available to all who desire it. Despite the supposed democratizing power of Sosa's cream, the song later extols its virtues, stating, "Te pone como gringo de la noche a la mañana" (It makes you like a gringo from one night to the next day). This gringo reference here indexes wealth and power. Ultimately, the song informs listeners that the accessibility and desirability of whiteness is such that skin complexion is nothing more than a matter of choice, stating that now that la crema de Sammy Sosa is available, those who remain black do so "porque les da la gana" (because they want to).

Posts on YouTube express a similarly complex ambivalence toward whiteness and wealth, in one case viewing skin lightening as a leisure activity akin to Richard Rodríguez's previously mentioned argument. Poster TheDjfilip laments that Sosa had nothing better to do with all of his money so he literally bought privilege through skin cream. This poster further asserts that Sosa looked better before and that this is just another shameful example of someone who denies his blackness because he can afford to buy himself out of it. Posters also connect the idea of buying whiteness to gendered masculinist romantic desire for power and white women (Mr. Inoa 2009).

In addition to a sarcastic rendering of the Sosa case within the racial system of Dominican society in economic terms, "La crema de Sammy Sosa" underscores complexities in terms of gender and corporeal sacrifice. Skin whitening amounts to near mutilation as the ingredients listed in Sosa's cream include toxins such as battery acid and paint remover, a reference to the pain and sacrifice of skin whitening. Those willing to apply this cream are rewarded as it will make them look good and improve their skin: "Te perfila la cara. Te hace un facial" (It evens out your face. It gives you a facial). This rendering of pain and reward recalls depictions of blackness where hair is coded as good or bad based on curl and texture, and thus becomes a site of identity and power struggle, as argued by Crenshaw, Gotanda, Peller, and Thomas (1995).

"La crema de Sammy Sosa" and its YouTube responses present a social commentary that connects the contested nature of black identity not only to contexts of social class and status but also to the complexities and boundaries of masculinity and mixed race desire. As the song describes the debut of the whitened Sosa, the lyric voice asks, "¿Será que este moreno se ha bañado con cloro?" (Could it be that this black man bathed in bleach?). This question accompanies the observation, "Parecía una rubia al lado de su esposa" (He looked like a blonde woman next to his wife). It would seem that whitening his skin calls into question his manhood. Commenters on YouTube police the whitened Sosa's heteronormative masculinity by referring to him as a "*maricón*," a word that is not only an insulting term for gay men but denotes a lack of courage and masculinity in general. Posts announcing that Sosa has come out of the closet also tied his supposed whitened homosexuality to his hometown of San Pedro de Macoris, which produces baseball players and gay men, according to one post. Another post cautioned Sosa's wife about the whitened Sosa in terms of race and white desire: "Exterminate this monkey for shaming the black skin . . . this moron will never be happy. He got more problems than b4. people will be laughing at this pale pig lover. Soon he will going for a paler blonde hoe . . . watch out wifeeeee" (Mr. Inoa 2009). This warning to Sosa's wife is interesting because some Dominicans have speculated that it was wife Sonia Sosa who encouraged the skin whitening, though Sosa has never publically stated this. Ultimately, the pursuit of whiteness via his own body, or white desire, strips Sosa of his heterosexual manhood in the opinions of many audience members, whose comments buttress a masculinist gender binary that intersects with a black and white racial binary and reproduces a gendered social hierarchy that privileges a narrowly defined masculinity where potency is linked to blackness and wealth is linked to whiteness, both sustaining and subverting white (masculine) privilege.

The song concludes with the following list of descriptors for Sosa: "Seas blanco, morenito, indiecito, trigueñito eres nuestro" (Whether you are white, black, indigenous, or wheat-colored, you're ours). These descriptors illustrate the spectrum of racial identities and strategies to emphasize mixture over blackness in Dominican racial construction, underscoring the conflicts depicted in the range of comments and viewpoints, notably eschewing the descriptor *negro/negrito,* which would most directly link Sosa to blackness, revealing the ambivalence toward blackness in Dominican (American) societies. Thus the satire ends on a conciliatory note, after raising issues of gender/ sexuality, class, and race intersectionality that are further deconstructed via a reading of a skit by Raymond Pozo and Miguel Céspedes on their skit comedy show *A reir con Miguel y Raymond.*

"Los tígueres me dicen la crema": Mixed Race Masculinity as Struggle over Potency and Power

The Sosa skit on *A reir con Miguel y Raymond* (*Let's Laugh with Miguel and Raymond*) features Raymond Pozo as Sammy and Miguel Céspedes in drag as his wife Sonia being interviewed at the time of the release of the Latin Grammys photo. The conversation centers around the reasons for Sosa's whitening and unintended domestic and economic problems as a result. In particular, issues of wealth and masculinity frame the skit. Pozo as Sosa vaguely refers to fans who "give him things" as the origin of the facial cream that has changed his complexion, attributing the origin of the creams to Europe, later confessing to using Sonia's creams to retain his softer, whiter skin. The dilemma that he faces in his love of all things white—he sits with a baseball bat covered with white tape—is the cost of skin cream to maintain his new appearance since he cannot return to playing baseball to make more money because he would have to spend too much time in the sun. Paradoxically, sustained whiteness of physical appearance threatens to rob him of the economic privilege associated with white skin. These references to money and the need to use his wife's beauty products cast gender in a complicated light. Since Sosa is no longer able to maintain his prior earning potential, he must rely on his wife to attain the cultural capital associated with whiteness.

In fact, Sosa's male body becomes the site over which racial tensions are satirically fought in the skit. Consistent with research on men of color masculinities, the darkness of Sosa's body is associated with physical strength and sexual potency throughout the skit, a phenomenon linked to physical and sexual prowess as masculine strategies for men of color denied the full material and economic benefits of hegemonic masculinity (Connell 1987; Kimmel, Hearn, and Connell 2005; R. Ramírez 1993; A. Young 2004). When asked if his entire body is white, both Sammy and Sonia respond emphatically that his body remains black from the neck down. According to Sammy and Sonia, "el barrio sigue negro" (the 'hood remains black), a reference to the potency of black masculinity and criminality as they then joke about the police still coming to the metaphoric barrio that is Sosa's lower half. Perhaps neither Sammy nor Sonia would want him to be white down there. It seems that though certain privileges come with whiteness, the real essence of virility remains black.

At another point in the skit, when asked how things have changed for the Sosa family since Sammy's new look, he admits that it has caused difficulty for their children. He jokes that in the evening, after he and his wife have both applied their creams, the kids don't know which one is mommy and which one is daddy. Pozo as Sosa states that after 6 p.m., his cream is applied so he just responds if the kids call him mommy. Throughout the skit, Sonia expresses exasperation at Sammy, explaining that she literally functions as a crutch for him since he hurt his arm from applying so much cream. Finally, she stalks off stage, accusing him of stealing all of her creams in his obsession with whiteness, thus ending the skit.

The skit captures the conflicted nature of racialized and gendered identities in Dominican society. While at times the portrayal of Sonia shows irritation with her husband, she remains grateful that he possesses some of the economic privileges attached to whiteness, but at the same time stresses that he is still black where it counts. The Sammy character demonstrates this same racial ambivalence as he too celebrates his black potency but tries to ascribe masculine power to his newfound whiteness. He states, "Los tígueres me dicen la crema" (Ballers call me the cream). Though the concept of el tíguere is difficult to translate to English, it implies male potency and urban savvy, associated with black rappers and sports stars, and sometimes wealth that American culture attributes to the baller figure. Cream here, and throughout the skit for that matter, could refer to facial cream or perhaps sperm, decidedly distinct gendered images. This metaphor does, however, capture the extent to which blackness and whiteness remain complicated and unresolved as they intersect with gender in Dominican society. The most sobering moment in the skit comes when Pozo as Sosa quips, "No quiero saber nada de negro" (I don't want anything to do with blackness).

As with "La crema de Sammy Sosa," posts about the skit on YouTube highlight the use of humor as a point of Dominican pride. Many posters specifically reference the ambiguous nature of Sosa's gender in the skit once the cream is applied, as well as the images of el barrio and el tíguere as decidedly masculine references. Several posters mark Dominican identity and blackness through the images of *el barrio* and *el tíguere* in their posts. In most posts, Dominican nationality and pride are linked with blackness, denouncing the perceived shame that caused Sosa to lighten his skin, and in some cases disavowing him as a fellow Dominican. The following quote captures this sentiment through reference to the plantain, a staple of the Dominican diet as well as a cultural symbol: "Lo unico verde que sammy tiene es que el es un platanauuuu y un platano mal agradeció" (The only green that Sammy has is that he is a plantain [Dominican person] and an ungrateful one at that) (Gil 2009).[8] One poster went so far as to suggest that Dominicans collect funds to send the Sosa family to a Nordic country so that he could feel at home with white, blond-haired people.

In addition to Dominican pride, posters define Sosa in pan-Latino terms linked to black pride. For example, smartintrepid posted, "Yo creia que los dominicanos eramos orgullosos por el color de nuestra piel; hasta que aparecio la excepcion. QUE VERGUENZA Y DE UN ORGULLO HISPANO" (I thought that we Dominicans were proud of our skin color until the exception appeared. WHAT A SHAME, AND FROM A SOURCE OF LATINO PRIDE) (Gil 2009). Similarly, one poster viewed the skit as a teachable moment for Sosa, and for Latinos in general: "Eso esta bien para que sammy vea la ridiculez que hizo . . . después de ser una gloria tan importante dentro y fuera del baseball donde el mundo entero lo quería no solo los aficcionados del juego" (This is good so that Sammy can see the foolish thing that he did . . . after being such an important and glorious figure inside and outside of baseball where he was beloved by the whole world, not just baseball fans) (Gil 2009). A third poster, flyby7a, criticizes Sosa for the shame he seems to feel about having been born black, comparing him to Michael Jackson and using a litany of expletives in Spanish to admonish Sosa (Gil 2009). It is important to note that this poster uses vocabulary strongly associated with Mexican Spanish in his critique, which would indicate at least a partial Mexican identity, thus further reinforcing the idea that the Sosa case and its ramifications extend beyond the Dominican national context, allowing Latina/os overall to process social constructions of their mixed racial heritage.

Similar to the case of "La crema de Sammy Sosa," where one poster defended Sosa's skin lightening by arguing that maybe he just liked the way he looked with lighter skin, one poster defended Sosa, presenting a deracial-

---

8. The image of the plantain as a point of Dominican pride is common in popular culture and idiomatic expressions. For example, the expression "la mancha del plátano" (the mark of the plantain) is used to evoke a sustained Dominican identity that can never fade, particularly with reference to diasporic communities such as New York.

ized reading of his skin lightening: "Señores no sean asi el solamente kiere verse mejor.dejenlo vivir k ustedes no asen ni dejan hacer . . . esa es su vida y el trabajo mucho.ahora djenlo k disfrute . . . o.k" (People, don't be like that. He only wants to look better. It's better to just live and let live. . . . It's his life and he worked hard. Just let him enjoy it now . . . OK.) (Gil 2009). Though these voices are a minority in comparison with the overall admonishing of Sosa as a sellout of the African part of his mixed race heritage, they do indicate the pervasive nature of denial of racism in everyday contexts. The idea that Sosa would lighten his skin to "look better" buttresses the long-established idea of skin privilege where the economic privilege of light skin is mapped onto bodily aesthetics.

The interplay between privilege and masculinity in posters' comments, as well as the skit itself, intersects at the level of capital and the body. Pozo and Céspedes capture the unresolvable tensions between skin color and money as Pozo as Sosa expresses concern over the sustainability of his white privilege as these creams are expensive—a reference inconsistently shared in parts of "La crema de Sammy Sosa"—and his marketable skill, playing baseball, overexposes his body to sunlight so that he cannot return to the field and thus must rely on his wife to provide him with her skin creams. In effect, the tensions over racial mixture and blackness in Dominican and US society, articulated in economic terms, prevent Sosa from fully "enjoying" privilege. Furthermore, cultural producers and posters connect the relentless pursuit of whitened identity with shame and denial, both of which are embedded in historical narratives of colonization and racialization where blackness and poverty are often cast as struggles to be overcome, and at worst inspire criminalized and hypermasculine behavior, as evidenced by a cartoon circulated via email at the time of Sosa's skin bleaching.

"Money Whitens": Connecting Capital and Whiteness through Sammy Sosa

Around the release of the pictures of Sammy and Sonia Sosa at the Latin Grammys in 2009, a cartoon circulated among Dominicans via email referencing the situation in clearly masculinist and economic terms, favoring whiteness in its depiction of the images of the *pelotero* (ball player) and the *narco* (drug trafficker), two images associated with wealthy masculinities of color in the Dominican Republic. The cartoon depicts two men in suits surrounded by bags of money representing the *narco,* with the following conversation between the two:

Narco 1: "¿Cómo vamos a blanquear este dinero?" (How are we going to whiten [launder] this money?)

Narco 2 responds, "Con la crema del pelotero" (With the baseball player's cream).

This commentary links money and whiteness in direct terms and discursively links the wealth of drug traffickers and baseball players, images that fuse wealth and black masculinities with physical, as opposed to intellectual, bodily performance and danger, particularly the illicit drug trade in Dominican society. As men, Latin/o American baseball players must both manipulate and risk their bodies in pursuit of wealth, a wealth that is sometimes corrupt and often associated with the need to escape poverty, a narrative strongly associated with Dominicans in media depictions. Their bodies also represent the transnational flow of capital, culture, and racial formation. As such, they come to embody lived transnational, class-based, and gendered racial formations for ordinary Dominicans. The fusion of male bodies of color with the acquisition of wealth through bodily performance of baseball and the informal economy of the drug trade delineates both the boundaries and the malleability of race and complexity of racial mixture as individuals negotiate wealth and racial hierarchy. In whitening his skin, for whatever reason and by whatever means, Sosa alters his body and the physical embodiment of his mixed race identity to ascend that hierarchy. In a May 2018 *Sports Illustrated* interview in Dubai, where Sosa now spends much of his time, he held steadfast in his conviction that he just likes the way that he looks now, and as a retired superstar and man, he can do whatever he wants and does not care what others think (Buckland and Reiter 2018; see figure 1). For Sosa, wealth allows him not to "care" what others think and evince a simplistic masculinist attitude when it comes to questions of his racial identity.

Conclusion

Scholars of Dominican history and society remain wary of simplistic and binarized understandings of race in the Dominican Republic as vitriolic, anti-Haitian condemnations of blackness. Pérez Cabral argues that history and migration have rendered the Dominican Republic the only true "mulatto nation," while Sagás, Candelario, and Mayes argue that social class and gender matter for Dominicans when reading race. Mayes further sustains that understanding the intricacies of Dominican history beyond conflicts with Haiti serves as an impetus to reclaim a positive notion of the Dominican "mulatto

FIGURE 1. *Sports Illustrated,* "Where are they now?" Sammy Sosa, May 2018

nation."[9] As we have seen, humor has been the strategy to present commentary on Dominican racial identity mapped onto the body of Sammy Sosa in "La crema de Sammy Sosa" as well as *A reir con Miguel y Raymond*. Fan reactions to these texts demonstrate the extent to which Dominicans continue to forge and negotiate mixed race identities in relation to narratives of national history, class, and gender. Perhaps the satire and exaggeration associated with the humor employed in these cultural texts and posts provide mechanisms for individuals and societies to cope with the sometimes painful history of blackness in the Dominican Republic and beyond.

Upon arrival to the US, MLB's Latin/o American players inherit and emerge within the fraught transnational context mentioned here and are located within a US racial context as fans consume MLB games. Despite much public media discourse on racial gains made in the US, particularly associated with the election of President Barack Obama in 2008, the overall political and social climates of the US remain racially polarized, a climate mirrored in media discourses and MLB, as shall be seen throughout this book. Returning to the conversation between my sister, a white, middle-class woman, and I at the outset of this chapter, where she asked what Sammy Sosa is, Hispanic or black, I would argue that her confusion is representative of US Americans in general, who do not understand the contours of Latin/o American racial identities and as such understand and locate the bodies of Latin/o American players within a limited US racial construction. The limited understanding of race, in this case as Hispanic (not actually a racial category but often understood as such) and black evokes, on the one hand, the "one drop rule" statute of hypodescent, while also perpetuating a present-day color-blind racism unaccustomed to the complexity of transnational and global flows related to players' identities. This context carries real material consequences for MLB's Latin/o American labor force, from media perceptions of a "Latino threat" (Chávez 2013) associated with racial, political, and linguistic panic to fans' reactions to players' bodies and behaviors, as I shall explore in the coming chapters.

---

9. See Pérez Cabral (2007), Sagás (2000), Candelario (2007), and Mayes (2014).

CHAPTER 2

Who May Sing the National Anthem?

MLB, the WBC, and Representations of
Latin/o American Nationalisms

FOR THE ALL-STAR GAME on July 16, 2013, MLB chose Puerto Rican salsa musician Marc Anthony to sing "God Bless America" as part of the game's patriotic homage. The selection of Anthony follows MLB practice of choosing well-known musicians to sing the national anthem as the All-Star Game is nationally broadcast as a means of showcasing MLB talent and deciding the home field advantage for the World Series. The fact that Anthony was chosen to sing "God Bless America" further attests to the importance of Latina/os as an MLB fan base and to MLB's strategies to cultivate a Latina/o audience. The selection of Anthony ignited a controversial reaction as some fans sounded off on social media that it was un-American for someone born in a "foreign country" to sing the national anthem. Anthony is in fact of Puerto Rican descent, born in New York. This controversy illustrates the ways that professional baseball in the US has become a symbolic, if not literal, gatekeeper of what it means to be "American" as defined by the dominant US population.

In a television appearance shortly after the social media debate over his authenticity as a representative of US national identity, Anthony cleared the

A note on nationality terms: I use America(n) throughout to call attention to the cooptation of the term by US Americans, though in Latin America and the Caribbean it refers to the entirety of the Americas and its inhabitants. I use *US* and *US American* to make a conscious effort to distinguish between those in the US and the remainder of the Americas in an effort to decolonize the terms. In direct quotes, I retain original usage of the terms *American, US,* and *US American.*

air on "Live with Kelly and Michael" on ABC on July 18, 2013. In an interview segment with Kelly Ripa, promoting his then recent album release, Anthony stated, "There were some statements made that people were upset that they would have someone from another country sing the national anthem. Let's get this straight. I was born and raised in New York. You can't get more New York than me. . . . I just want to set the record straight. I'm more Puerto Rican than ever. I'm more New York than ever" (Gamboa 2013). In positioning himself as "more Puerto Rican than ever" as well as "more New York than ever," Anthony evinces the multiplicity of identity often expressed by Latina/os who negotiate their positions as Latina/os within the framework of racial construction in the US's social, historical, political, and economic contexts. Critical race scholars Omi and Winant (1994) argue that the racial categories of white and non-white/black result from shifting historical, political, and economic contexts. Feagin (2013) asserts that the nature of race as defined in the US historically grants power to those considered white, a consequence of which is the continued oppression of those not considered white. De Genova and Ramos-Zayas (2003) further theorize the position of Latina/os within this racial context via "Latino racial formation," a theoretical position that seeks to understand the ways in which *Latino* extends beyond ethnicity and becomes a distinct third racial category. These critical race studies interventions inform not only how Latina/os like Marc Anthony construct their identities but also the ways that non-Latinos understand and react to Latina/o performances of identity such as the controversy over Anthony and "God Bless America."

In an opinion piece in the *Dallas Morning News,* Tod Robberson captured the heart of the debate over Marc Anthony's performance and "right" to represent US nationalism in calling out specific Twitter users who protested Anthony, referring to him as "spic" and "F**ing Mexican," among other intended insults. In response, Robberson reminded readers that Anthony himself is Puerto Rican, not Mexican, and admonished tweeters for hiding their racism and ignorance behind the guise of supposed patriotism. He also called attention to the national identities of the actual players on the field: "And who do those Twitter-crazy racist, ignorant fools think they're watching on the field? Do they actually think all of those baseball players are from the United States? Try Japan, Venezuela, Dominican Republic, Costa Rica and (get ready for this shocker) Mexico. This country neither owns the sport nor lays claim to its best players" (Robberson 2013). The tweets mentioned by Robberson and his assessment of racist reactions via Twitter further illustrate the ways in which racial formation, rooted in a violent colonial history that privileges whiteness as a prerequisite to be US American, homogenizes those not considered white (e.g., the references to Marc Anthony as a "f**ing Mexican"), also fleshing out the theoretical skeleton of Omi and Winant,

Feagin, and De Genova and Ramos-Zayas via everyday articulations of racial hierarchy.

Marc Anthony's performance and the contrasting Twitter debate that casts him as "foreign" and "Mexican," as well as the defense of Anthony as "American," even if he were born in Puerto Rico given its status as a US territory, signals the need to look at baseball and the construction of MLB's Latin/o American players as a means of understanding how Latina/os are racialized in the US in everyday life via popular culture. Most importantly, the construction of these players through media reveals the sustained tensions related to Latina/o population growth via immigration as well as native births. These men's bodies become cultural text over which issues of language, individual character, and who should and should not represent "America" are fought and debated. Individuals use media as both consumers and creators to negotiate the roles of Latina/os in issues of belonging, nationalism, politics, and socioeconomic conditions.[1] Thus, the Marc Anthony controversy serves to introduce and contextualize nationalist and nativist tensions articulated via MLB.

Building on the Sammy Sosa case and notions of transnational racial construction in the previous chapter, an analysis of the 2017 World Baseball Classic helps to tease out the tension between MLB as "America's pastime" and its roughly one-third foreign-born labor force, most of which comes from the Caribbean and Latin America. Similar to the case of Marc Anthony, a heated debate emerged over New York–born Dellin Betances's decision to play for the Dominican Republic instead of the US in the 2017 WBC. Nationalism in the tournament climaxed in the final week as Puerto Rico entered the final game against the US undefeated. Departing from Leo Chavez's Latino threat narrative, which argues that Latina/os are often excluded from the full benefits of US citizenship as they are perceived to be disloyal and not sufficiently "American," I engage both the ways that US nationalism is articulated and contested over the bodies of MLB's Latin/o American players and also the ways that Latina/o fans, particularly Puerto Ricans, use these same bodies to perform nationalism. While for some, these players represent a "threat" to baseball's "American" character, for others, particularly Latina/os, these players represent the attainment of the American dream or a source of Latina/o pride. I argue that baseball is at the forefront of the creation and negotiation of national identities, and I investigate the ways in which narratives of threat, immigrant hard work, and loyalty function in the creation of these national narratives, ultimately questioning how viable baseball is as a site of US nationalism given the global economic forces that drive and constrain its expansion.

---

1. Indeed, Rosen (2012) signals an important shift in media production where new platforms such as blogs destabilize the power differential between media producers and consumers.

World Baseball Classic as
Culture War and MLB's Future

The World Baseball Classic is about far more than just playing baseball. Indeed, MLB itself launched the round robin–style competition in an attempt to awaken more international interest in the game and answer critiques that despite naming its final championship the World Series, only the US and Canada represent "the world," with just one team being from Canada. Its history belies the identity crisis of MLB, and I would also argue the US, with regard to globalization and nationalism. By the 1990s, MLB finally realized that it had already lost much ground in the global marketplace to other US American sports as the NFL and NBA had already established a solid presence in the international arena. Enter Major League Baseball International. MLBI is a division of MLB whose stated goal is to organize events and promote MLB internationally. In 1993, MLBI's Tim Brosnan and Paul Archey began to develop a World Cup–like concept where teams would play a round robin–style tournament to showcase the international growth and popularity of baseball and MLB (Klein 2006, 243). The commissioner's office, under the leadership of then commissioner Bud Selig, began to seriously consider the idea in 2000 and finally announced the inauguration of the World Baseball Classic on July 11, 2005 (Klein 2006, 244). The tournament would consist of four groups who would play elimination rounds until just two teams emerged for the final game. During the years leading up to the inaugural 2006 tournament, tensions surfaced around control over the event. In particular, Japan and South Korea felt that the US via MLB exercised an unfair amount of decision-making power, with one Japanese official accusing MLB of imperialism (Klein 2006, 246). Ultimately MLBI gained control over the majority of the logistics, organization, and financial matters related to the WBC. Ironically, MLB got a taste of its own imperialist medicine as the Bush administration, prompted by some members of the Cuban American community, initially denied Cubans entry to play, although it eventually reversed course. For a short while, the integrity of the WBC was in jeopardy as not only was there a danger of losing a great competitor in Cuba, but in an interesting moment of Latinidad and anti-imperialist solidarity, Puerto Rico threatened to withdraw as a site for games, with Venezuela volunteering to take its place (Klein 2006, 248). Similar articulations of nationalism and anti-imperialism also shape individual fans' perceptions of and investments in the game.

For individuals, particularly Latino/as, the WBC carries a heavy weight; it signifies national pride and allows individuals to publicly celebrate their ethnic and national identities through their teams' successes. For Dominicans in the Dominican Republic and the US, their countrymen's power and success answer back to the economic struggles of Dominicans and the Caribbean and US hierarchies that subordinate them. Indeed, Dominicans have joined nationalism and the WBC via the use of the *plátano* (plantain), a Dominican food staple that has now become a term of nationalist self-definition, as a symbol to fire up teammates. In the first game of the 2017 WBC, Diamondbacks pitcher Fernando Rodney, and later Yankee pitcher Dellin Betances, continued a tradition started in 2013 where the Dominican team uses a *plátano* as a symbol of national pride and inspiration. Players say that this is something they have been doing since they were kids and that it is also a way to relieve stress and make the game fun. As we shall see in the analysis of WBC 2017, especially for Puerto Ricans, nationalism and fun go hand in hand.

The 2017 World Baseball Classic continued to grow the international reach of baseball and indeed set new attendance records, surpassing the one million mark. Significantly, the news story featuring this statistic on the WBC official website, "World Baseball Classic Sets Attendance Record," features a crowd photo of fans in the stands waving US and Dominican flags (Kruth 2017). The games took place in Seoul, Korea; Tokyo, Japan; Jalisco, Mexico; and Miami and Los Angeles in the US. Notably, to this point, Japan and the Dominican Republic have emerged as the powerhouses of the WBC's short history, Japan having won in 2006 and 2009, and the Dominican Republic in 2013. The US won the championship for the first time in 2017. In an interview during the final game between the US and Puerto Rico on March 22, 2017, on ESPN Deportes, MLB commissioner Rob Manfred emphasized his commitment to the international aspect of MLB in pledging that as long as he is commissioner, the World Baseball Classic will continue as he sees it as the key to growth in international interest and to embracing international styles of play.

The events surrounding the 2017 World Baseball Classic highlight many of the aspects of nationalism and globalization discussed throughout this book. The final game, between the US and Puerto Rico, exemplifies how sports intersects with politics, empire, and nationalism, as well as global inequalities. While for the US, the game meant national pride tied to baseball itself as a symbol of "America" and the desire to win of professional athletes, for Puerto Ricans, both the players involved in the game and Puerto Ricans watching, a sense of pride related to the island's continued colonial status and current economic downturn made this much more than a game. Playing against the country that both largely controls its destiny and recently established a fiscal control board to regulate spending and economic development in Puerto Rico provided Puerto Ricans with the opportunity to assert a sense of agency on the ballfield.[2] Unfortunately, that would not come to pass as Puerto Rico lost the final game by a score of 8 to 0. Despite the outcome, the duration of the World Baseball Classic and the cultural production and reactions that circulated in all forms of media, especially social media, illustrate how baseball serves as a site of negotiation of national pride and negotiation of "American" identity. Tensions over individual players' decisions about which teams to play for and with what national identity or identities to associate themselves tell us much about nationalism and identity. However, Puerto Rico is particularly important given that though Puerto Ricans are legal citizens of the US, it is an uneven citizenship in terms of rights and many individuals' perceptions as Puerto Ricans first and only secondarily as US citizens.

For Puerto Ricans, the Puerto Rico versus US matchup and the possibility of a tournament win was cause for celebration leading up to the final game, given the complicated colonial relationship between the island and the mainland and the island's current economic struggles resulting from that colonial relationship. For mainland Puerto Ricans, a Puerto Rican win would also empower and embolden a group that is economically and geographically subordinated in major US cities. For example, on Saturday, March 18, 2017, when Puerto Rico beat the US, a Puerto Rican lifetime resident and activist in Chicago's Humboldt Park neighborhood, a neighborhood that continues to fight to preserve its Puerto Rican community, posted on Facebook that Division Street (a street associated with Puerto Rican identity, featuring two large steel Puerto Rican flags) was "quiet as hell," citing that silence as a sign of gentrification as, in the past, Humboldt Park's Puerto Rican community would have been out to celebrate the victory en masse. The previous day, this same individual had posted that the power of Puerto Rican nationalism has him watching baseball, despite having little interest in the sport itself.[3] Additionally, Puerto Rican infielder Carlos Correa is now featured as a narrator on a Puerto Rican tourism website, having emerged as one of the most outspoken members of Team Puerto Rico in 2017. This reception of the WBC demonstrates its significance for Latin/o Americans inside and outside of the US.

---

2. On April 12, 2016, the House of Representatives introduced H.R. 4900, the Puerto Rico Oversight, Management, and Economic Stability Act (PROMESA). This resolution established a fiscal control board that tightly regulates budgetary spending in Puerto Rico in an attempt to repay a large debt incurred by the government of Puerto Rico. Critiques of the resolution argue that this act is yet another act of colonization by the US as the decisions made by the fiscal control board, composed largely of outside regulators, have resulted in dire consequences for Puerto Ricans, including the closure of needed schools and hospitals, among other austerity measures.

3. I gained access to this post as part of the feed on my Facebook account.

An article posted on Facebook page "Latino Rebels" on March 20, 2017, asserts that Latinos are the future of baseball. In "Make No Mistake, This Year's REAL March Madness Is the World Baseball Classic," Michael Collazo (2017) argues:

> It's 2017, *mi gente,* and that baseball-is-the-national-pastime stuff is dead. Football is America's passion and has been for decades. Basketball whoops baseball in so many ways. Soccer is trying to come up, too. MLB still makes lots of money so that isn't an issue . . . yet. The average baseball TV viewer is in their 50s so unless Big Pharma develops a Fountain of Youth pill, that's a problem. America's youngest demographic, according to the US Census resides in the Latino community (median age: 29). So this tournament could serve a crucial role in growing the sport in the United States and even in other parts of Latin America.
>
> Latinos are the future of MLB because: 1) they are the youngest census demographic (median age 29), 2) the match fuels national groups' interest in the game and as such fuels revenues, 3) promotes innovative play and showcases exciting young players beyond the cities they play for, especially important for small market teams, 4) circulates on various social media platforms popular with millennials who may also consume the game through various media and at various levels of intensity.
>
> Baseball is struggling with a so-called "culture war." One faction wants the game to be "played the right way" (don't show up a pitcher by flipping a bat, for instance). Another faction (which has a large Latino contingency) embraces the bat flips and the showmanship. The bat flippers need to win. The Dominicans, Venezuelans (heck, the Koreans!) play with more of that flair. The old school fans are resistant but know your history: college basketball once outlawed the slam dunk. . . . The WBC provides more room for the players and fans to let their hair down. (And in Team Puerto Rico's case, let their bottle-blonde hair down).

Collazo gestures to a tension for survival of baseball in a modern global sports market. He underlines the aging, and I would add predominantly white male, consumer of MLB through television. MLB, like other sports, is now active in new social media platforms such as Facebook, Twitter, Instagram, and others, but this is not enough to grow the game among millennials. Scholars such as Todd Boyd (1997) have long argued that the very pace and length of baseball games work against its popularity, as more fast-paced games like basketball capture the increasingly shortened attention span of media consumers. For many, baseball is considered an old white man's game. This is due in large part to the ways that MLB regulates performances of masculinity within the game, noted by Collazo as an "American" phenomenon, one that directly contrasts to Latinidad.

Collazo (2017) uses the term "culture war" to describe the tension between presumably older and white players and fans who insist that the game be played "the right way"—defined by a restrained bodily performance with little to no on-field celebration of success—and younger players and fans, including those of color, who crave more emotion and bodily expression from players. Players have also weighed in on the subject. For example, the US WBC team expressed anger when the Puerto Rican team planned a celebration on the island before the final game of the tournament, citing that arrogance as a motivating factor in their eventual win. On the other side of the debate, in an interview for *Esquire* magazine, Carlos Correa has strongly stated that MLB needs to get with the times and allow players to perform in more expressive ways on the field, or, as Collazo insists, risk losing its Latina/o fan base (Holmes 2016). This tension/culture war engages conflicts between a perceived white masculinity associated with bodily restraint and control and a more expressive masculinity associated with men of color.[4] For some of baseball's old guard, the concern over on-field masculine performance belies a preoccupation with race, coded as not playing "the right way." In reality, this concern is one of the presence of too many men of color in the game.

MLB, for its part, is aware that changes are necessary and that its fan base continues to evolve. Known for being a politically and socially conservative institution, its governing personnel have changed some game rules to both modernize the game and shorten its length. These include the introduction of limited use of instant replay and limiting the amount and time of managerial visits to the pitcher's mound during games. The primary way that MLB has engaged with the globalization of baseball and opening it to a more expansive and diverse fan base has been through support of the WBC. The organization is also aware of the nationalist tensions that fuel competition and interest and can also help smaller-market teams, as Collazo contends, but only to a point. The primary concern remains that MLB is a revenue-driven business and players' bodies are commodities to be guarded with care during the WBC season, which coincides with spring training and ends shortly before the regular MLB season begins. This has resulted in concerns from teams over whether their best players should play in the WBC, lest they tire too quickly during the long regular season, or worse, injure themselves and risk missing part or all of the season, echoing the historically economic protectionist stance of MLB in

---

4. See Connel (2005); Boyd (1997).

limiting winter league participation for its players (Alou and Kerasotis 2018). In the end, national pride is often second to the bottom line.

MLB straddles a thin line between nationalism and economics. A conversation between members of the 2016 World Series champion Chicago Cubs' managerial and front office staff bears this out. Chicago Cubs manager Joe Maddon has suggested that the World Series champs should play the WBC champs in a best of three tournament at the end of the WBC. Maddon felt that it would put the "world" back in the game and fire up players for spring training and the regular season. One telling logistical problem emerged as a result of the idea: Who would players on both teams play for, such as the case of Javier Báez from the 2016 World Series champions? Cubs general manager Jed Hoyer disagreed with Maddon: "You want your own guys back, playing for you," he said. "We should be as a group by now. [The Classic] ends about the right time where guys need to get back and start playing for their own team. If it goes too long, it kind of hurts them" (Castrovince 2017). This sentiment echoes the politics around team spirit and dynamics, as well as the fear of injury to key players in competitive play before the season, which concerns many upper-level executives in MLB. How, then, do WBC rules and players' decisions around participation negotiate nationalist and market tensions?

"They Are Playing for the Name in the Front, Not the One in the Back": The World Baseball Classic and (Contested) Nationalism

The above quote from Puerto Rican outfielder Carlos Beltrán captures the passion and nationalism surrounding the WBC, both by design in the construction of the tournament around national teams, as well as resulting from the pride that fans feel when their teams win, especially via contentious matchups between the teams with the most talent or countries with specific histories, such as that of the US and Puerto Rico. Since the first WBC, there has been public debate over the ways that players use the rules governing how nationality is defined as they decide which teams to play for. Some players fill out the rosters of their ancestral countries despite not having lived or spent significant time in those countries, while others exercise their choices in line with transnational lives, or as citizens of a territory or protectorate (e.g., much of the Netherlands team is from Curacao, a Dutch island in the Caribbean). This is particularly salient for players born in or living in the US who retain strong ties with another country. Two countries that demonstrate this are Italy and the Dominican Republic. For example, some Italian

American players have played for Italy instead of the US under the rationale that Italy is their ancestral homeland and continues to contribute to their ethnic identities. In addition to this identity-based rationale, a more practical concern involves the difficulty of staffing teams. Since interest in baseball in Italy is low, interest in teams such as Italy would be minimal without a cadre of household names of Italian American players, such as Frank Catalanotto, Mike Piazza, Anthony Rizzo, and Chris Denorfia, since US-based fans, a large market share of WBC viewers and attendees, would not recognize player names and thus not invest time and money in some of the games. This has resulted in a somewhat curated nationalism, one that is multilayered and sometimes contested.

The curated nationalism tied to Italian Americans playing for Italy, which has a comparatively weaker professional baseball infrastructure and international presence, contrasts somewhat with the nationalism of counties with more developed baseball infrastructures and a continued history of transnational practices and circular migration connected to baseball, such as Dominican Republic. Players' decisions on what country to represent and baseball personnels' and fans' reactions to these decisions are fraught with complexities. Indeed, for transnational players and fans, the choice of what nation to represent engages complicated issues of identity and fandom, as we shall see in the case of Dominican and US American pitcher Dellin Betances.

In order to contextualize our discussion of Betances, it is first important to establish how organizers define the World Baseball Classic and its eligibility requirements. According to the official website:

> The World Baseball Classic is the premier international baseball tournament, sanctioned by the World Baseball Softball Confederation (WBSC), and operated as a joint venture between Major League Baseball and its Players Association. The Tournament features the best players in the world competing for their home countries and territories. More than 2.4 million fans from all over the world have attended the tournament games, held in March 2006, March 2009 and March 2013. Team Dominican Republic is the reigning World Baseball Classic Champion after going undefeated during its 2013 championship run. [This was published before the outcome of the 2017 tournament.] This year's tournament will again feature the greatest baseball-playing nations in the world. The tournament will be held every four years thereafter. Following a qualifying round held in Feb., March and Sept. of 2016, the 16-team field is now set for the main event from March 6–22, 2017. The games will span the globe, taking place across six venues, beginning with Seoul, Tokyo, Miami and Jalisco in the First Round. During

the Second Round, teams will head to Tokyo and San Diego on the way to
the Championship Round in Los Angeles. (MLB 2017)

The language here evokes and connects talent and home, as the idea of the
"best players in the world competing for their home countries and territories"
is tied to nationalist competition, and later in the description, the tournament
"will again feature the greatest baseball-playing nations in the world." This
juxtaposition of "home" to describe the relationship of players to the tournament and "nation" as a more general description of the tournament itself
illustrates both the fraught nature of nationalism and home in general, and
MLB's attempt to engage both in a depoliticized way via the WBC. This is
in line with Rob Manfred's pledge during the ESPN Deportes broadcast of
the final game of the 2017 tournament, where he stated that as long as he is
commissioner, he will support and retain the WBC. Manfred's promise, along
with the assertion that games "will span the globe" in the above description,
also plays to MLB's continued push to grow the game in countries around
the world. Latin/o American players and fans will play a pivotal role in this
growth via the consistent stream of young players recruited in Latin America
and the Spanish Caribbean Basin as well as migration patterns that sustain the
globalization of professional baseball. The eligibility rules for the WBC further
illustrate MLB's awareness of the complexities of nationalism and efforts to
continue to globalize the game.

If the language around "home" and "nation" as organizing principles of the
WBC allows for much fluidity and interpretation, the eligibility rules similarly
cast the tournament as inclusive of a fluid nationality. The official eligibility
rules are as follows:

> Each player on a Federation Team's approved Provisional Roster must be
> eligible to participate for that Federation Team. A player will be so eli-
> gible only if:
> The Player previously appeared on a Federation team's final roster at the start
> of either a WBC Qualifier or Tournament Round; or
> The player is a citizen of the Federation Team's country or territory, as evi-
> denced by a valid passport the player holds as of three months prior to
> the start of the Tournament; or
> The player is currently a permanent legal resident of the Federation Team's
> country or territory, as evidenced by documentation satisfactory to
> WBCI [World Baseball Classic, Inc.] and the WBSC, or
> The player was born in the Federation Team's country or territory, as evi-
> denced by a birth certificate or its equivalent; or

> The player has at least one parent who is, or if deceased was, a citizen of the Federation Team's country or territory, as evidenced by a passport or other documentation satisfactory to WBCI and the WBSC; or
>
> The player has at least one parent who was born in the Federation Team's country or territory, as evidenced by a birth certificate or its equivalent; or
>
> The player presents documentary evidence satisfactory to WBCI that he would be granted citizenship or a passport in due course under the laws of the Federation Team's country or territory (excluding any requirement of the Federation Team's country that the player would need to renounce his current citizenship), if he were to apply for such citizenship or passport. (MLB 2017)

Eligibility criteria focus on citizenship and ancestry, though players do not necessarily need to pursue legal citizenship of the countries they play for, as long as they could, in theory, be citizens. Again, the contrastive cases of Italy and the Dominican Republic illustrate varying ways that players decide which teams to play for, and also how migration to the US has impacted nationalities. While for many Dominican players, they or their parents are born in the Dominican Republic and thus are citizens, for many Italian Americans, this is not the case. Though these are individual choices, and I in no way intend to judge authenticity or a heart and soul heritage connection to players' homelands, it stands to reason that a Dominican player who has spent a significant part of his life in the Dominican and retains transnational ties there embodies a more nuanced nationality than does an Italian American who has limited contact and perhaps a largely truncated relationship with Italy. This contrast is important because it raises the question of how much investment WBC has in fomenting nationalist competition to grow the game of baseball, and how much the tournament seeks to showcase its best players for marketing purposes.

A controversy surrounding Ozzie Guillén, Alex Rodríguez, and Nomar Garcíaparra brings this issue to light. In February 2006, during the inaugural World Baseball Classic, Guillén criticized Dominican Alex Rodríguez for playing for the Dominican team and Mexican American Nomar Garcíaparra for playing for Mexico as opposed to the US. According to the ESPN news service, the Venezuelan-born Guillén, who had become a US citizen in January of 2006, fired at both players, "Alex was kissing Latino people's asses. He knew he wasn't going to play for the Dominicans; he's not a Dominican! I hate hypocrites: He's full of [expletive]. The Dominican team doesn't need his ass. It's the same with [Nomar] Garciaparra playing for Mexico. Garciaparra only knows

Cancun because he went to visit" ("Guillen Calls" 2006). While the rules governing players' choices for the countries they represent allow them to play for any country of which they are a citizen or are eligible to be a citizen, Guillén questioned the motivation and authenticity of Rodríguez's and Garcíaparra's choices, raising larger questions of Latinidad, transnational identities, and belonging. Though Guillén later retracted his criticism of Rodríguez's decision, acknowledging the fact that he was born in the US but spent his childhood moving between the two countries, he held steadfast to his claim that Garcíaparra has probably only been to Mexico on vacation and thus should not play as part of the Mexican team ("Guillen Calls" 2006).

A subsequent blog post reaction to Guillén's remarks, posted on February 28, 2006, raises questions of race, identity, heritage, and the right to claim all of these:

> Of course, the element of this that is a little ugly is when the allegations about people's heritage and patriotism start flying. Enter baseball's most annoying manager, Ozzie Guillen, and his slams on Nomar and A-Rod [Alex Rodríguez]. First of all, I wonder what somebody who every time their interviewed during the World Series feels the need to stick his fist up and say "Venezuela" as if he's practicing for the rise of Hugo Chavez' worker's paradise cares about the Dominican Republic and Mexico. It would be one thing if a Dominican questioned ARod, who was after all born and raised in Miami, about his decision, but for a Venezuelan to take it another step up from a patriotism issue by saying "He was kissing Latino people's asses" is absurd. My dictionary defines Latino as "A person of Hispanic, especially Latin-American, descent, often one living in the United States." I think that describes Alex Rodriguez to a tee, Ozzie. I guess if I ever have a hard time choosing between Cleveland and Cincinnati, which both have large white populations, Ozzie will accuse me of kissing white people's asses. ("World Baseball Classic" 2006)

There is a lot to unpack here. First of all, this blogger actually raises questions that frequently surface in discussions of Latinidad in claiming that a Venezuelan should not care about a Dominican issue. However, a contradiction appears later in the post via the "dictionary definition" of *Latino* presented. It is not clear here if Guillén should be considered Venezuelan, Latino, or some combination of the two. This post further complicates understandings of race and power in comparing Guillén's critique of Latin American authenticity to the choice between Cleveland and Cincinnati, cities with large white populations. This is problematic on two fronts, first because choosing between two large white populations does not carry the same racialized power differentials that choosing between two Latina/o identities does. Second, as these are two US cities in Ohio, questions of nationalism are not at stake here, though this does gesture to the extent to which sports fandom approximates nationalism. Read within this context, the case of Dellin Betances allows us to further tease out the issues raised here.

All of these questions and debates around national pride coalesced via press coverage of New York Yankee pitcher Dellin Betances during and just after the 2017 WBC tournament. Betances played for the Dominican Republic, as opposed to the US team, despite growing up in the US and the Dominican Republic. As often happens, the story of Betances's choice originally emerged as part of broader press coverage on his contested contract negotiations. This is important because, similar to the case of Robinson Canó and his very public child support litigation, these stories serve to further damage reputations of players as they engage stereotypes of greed and womanizing tied to Latino men, as well as broader market considerations of teams. In the cases of both Canó and Betances, New York Yankees nation, from front office to fans, used the child support and WBC stories as a means to question the loyalty, and in the case of Canó ethics, of these players. Read within this context, as well as within the above discussion of the WBC as both nationalist performance and MLB-driven market force, the Betances coverage deepens our understandings of identity and market negotiations.

In an April 17, 2017, interview with ESPN writer Marly Rivera, published in English and Spanish, Betances spoke at length about what it means to him to be both US American and Dominican. The title of the article, "For Betances, Repping the Yankees Is an American Dream," belies his commitment to his team and his belief in the possibility of success in the US, a founding nationalist principle (Rivera 2017a). Born and raised by Dominican parents in Washington Heights, Manhattan, and spending summers in the Dominican Republic, Betances feels attached and obligated to both cultures. He defines himself as Dominican first and foremost, explaining that his first language is Spanish, he was raised eating Dominican food such as *plátanos* and *mangú*, and that many consider his neighborhood to be "like the Dominican Republic" (Rivera 2017a). In *Quisqueya on the Hudson*, Jorge Duany has documented the formation and articulation of Dominican Washington Heights as Dominicans migrated to the neighborhood in great numbers from at least the 1980s. For this reason, playing for the Bronx-based Yankees allows Betances to locate his "American dream" in his Dominican heritage as the physical space of the Yankees is adjacent to Washington Heights, where friends, family, and the

Dominican community at large can witness and perform pride in his accomplishments representing both of his countries.

Betances locates the rationale for playing for the Dominican Republic in his physical space, body, and loyalty to his parents and his heritage. According to Betances:

> I think it was four years ago. I told my parents that if I had the chance to play I would play for the Dominican Republic. It is something that I owe to them. For me, growing up in that environment, growing up in Washington Heights, getting to visit the Dominican Republic, it is something that I always, I felt my blood is Dominican. As I told them I would always choose them, and I was happy with the choice I made. (Rivera 2017a)

Thus, for Betances, as for many transnational subjects, country and nation are not bounded geographic territories, but rather places (Washington Heights) and bodies (blood) on which heritage and loyalty are mapped. Amid unrelenting questions as to why he chose to play for the Dominican Republic despite having been born in the US, he responded, "Nosotros los dominicanos nacemos donde nos da la gana / We Dominicans are born wherever we want" (Rivera 2017a). Though he originally made this statement in a humorous tone, in an attempt to lighten the mood and to defuse the frequent questions, it became a rallying cry and point of pride for many Dominican fans.

In addition to the discussion of Betances's *dominicanidad* connected to language, food, ancestry, and visits to the Dominican Republic, Rivera also sought Betances's perspective on why more Latin/o American players do not get involved in politics to the extent that African American NFL and NBA players do, very pointedly asking him, "In the current political climate, why do you think players of Latino heritage do not get as involved in speaking up for Latino issues, the way maybe African-American players have spoken up on other sports, like the NFL and the NBA?" (Rivera 2017a). Betances admits to not having the answer to that question, needing to think more about the issue, but he does provide a partial explanation: "Some of us try to do the best we can in our communities and we do help out, it just happens to be in different ways" (Rivera 2017a). This complicated question merits further discussion because it gets at the very heart of the argument of this book, that is, the relationship between sports and identity. First, it is important to note that even the comparatively less conservative NFL and NBA do not fully embrace players' activism. The case of Colin Kaepernick is a good example. In the opinions of many NFL insiders, fans, and media workers, his outspoken participation in the Black Lives Matter movement has cost him professionally since, as of 2018, he had yet to be offered a contract, the theory being that it is due to political activism, not lack of performance ability on the field.[5] When Rivera follows up by inquiring if there is a need to strike a delicate balance between personal convictions and representing an organization and wearing the uniform, Betances concedes that that is an important consideration, but that players could still speak out more, and he is not sure why they don't. The complicated history of Latina/os in the US certainly underpins this situation as the category of Latina/os encompasses such a wide group of people and experiences, with Latina/os identifying along the black/white binary in complex ways, sometimes pushing for honorary whiteness. Indeed, cases of violence and police brutality, such as that of Trayvon Martin, illustrate the contested relationship between black Americans and Latina/os; Martin was black, and shooter George Zimmerman is of Latino descent.

The contested nature of nationalism and politics sparked a heated debate among fans posting comments on the Betances interview. Comments center issues of US nationalism, assimilation, racial tensions between Latino/as and other groups, and the nature of the relationship between sports and politics. The wide range of reactions to the article, and the specific questions that drew the most attention from commenters, exemplify the fragmented nature of understandings of race, politics, and what it means to be "American" in the US. While some posters simply did not understand the possibility of identifying with multiple nationalities or national identities, stating that anyone born in the US is American, period, others, many of whom talked about their own multiple national and cultural identities, underscore the importance of voices like that of Betances to understand the nuances of identities. As such, I begin with a brief discussion of the question of sports and politics, and the perception that ESPN is too overtly political, before entering into a nuanced discussion of debates around nationality and multiculturalism.

Fans bristled at the fact that Rivera asked Betances why more Latin/o American players do not speak out against racial injustice, as many African Americans do. The following post sums up the general feeling toward ESPN's intrusive role in politics: "Kudos to Dellin for not giving *ESPN* anything to chew on when served with that unnecessary leading question about politics. It would be easy for a young guy to blurt out something reckless just to sound

5. Colin Kaepernick received national media attention in 2016 when he began protesting racism and inequality in the US by not standing for the US national anthem at NFL games. Many believe that this is the reason that no team offered him a contract when he became a free agent after the 2016 season. For a detailed analysis of Kaepernick's activism, its implications, and the NFL's response, see the work of journalist Shaun King.

like he has an answer. Much better to go the Derek Jeter route and double down on whatever sounds blandest" (Rivera 2017a). The use of "reckless" here is striking in that it would seem that some fans would deprive an athlete of the right to express an opinion if that opinion is deemed controversial. The position that sports and sports media such as ESPN should be depoliticized raises complicated questions about social position and identity, especially this fan's construction of Derek Jeter, who comes from a middle-class biracial background, as a strategically apolitical public figure, an issue also taken up in the Spanish version of the article and one fan's reaction.

It is worth noting that the Spanish version of the article, published as "Dellin Betances: 'Mi sangre siempre ha sido dominicana y Yankee,'" emphasizes both Dominican and Yankee blood (*sangre*), as opposed to the ideas of representing and the American dream captured in the English title. These ideas of blood and birth are reflected in one of the only two comments posted to the Spanish version. This fan did address reasons why Latin/o American players are arguably less politically active:

> Me gustó mucho la entrevista. La pregunta de por qué los peloteros hispanos no se involucran en temas políticos, para mí la respuesta es que los peloteros no son nacidos en los Estados Unidos. Ya en sus países de origen tienen demasiados problemas sociales, problemas que son más graves que los de USA. Además está la situación de la barrera idiomática. La mayoría de los peloteros hispanos no tienen el nivel de inglés para discutir temas profundos en ese idioma y mejor ni menciono el nivel de educación. Esa es la realidad.

> (I really liked the interview. The question about why Latino ballplayers don't get involved in political topics, for me the answer is that [presumably Latino] ballplayers are not born in the US. And in their countries of origin they have too many social problems, problems that are more serious than those of the USA. There is also the situation of the linguistic barrier. The majority of Latino ballplayers do not have the level of English to discuss complicated topics in that language and better not to mention the [low] level of education. This is the reality.) (Rivera 2017b)

Like the US-based fans who claim Betances as US American, this fan claims Betances, and all Latino players, as born outside of the US, even though this is not in fact true. Perhaps a sense of pride impels such a blanket statement, a statement that also speaks to the intricacies of national identities and the stakes for those who claim them. Still more significant is that in addition to the mention of birth, linguistic ability, and educational level, this fan points out that Latino ballplayers are more focused on the greater social problems of their own countries, perhaps implying that such players must make difficult decisions as to where to spend their economic, social, and political capital. Such questions also dovetail with greater questions and implications of how teams and MLB respond to players' activism. While typically teams and MLB itself have lauded players' charitable efforts in times of humanitarian crisis, such as devastating hurricanes, politics around race are more difficult to navigate for players. For example, black American players such as retired outfielder Torii Hunter have come under fire for claiming that MLB imports its diversity via its sophisticated recruitment structure in place in the Caribbean, which brings many Afro-descent players from that region, but nevertheless largely neglects Afro-descent players in the US in its scouting and recruitment practices.[6]

As stated earlier, individual athletes do sometimes pay a literal price for their political convictions, as in the case of NFL player Colin Kaepernick, but one could also argue that the social and economic capital elite athletes wield affords them some opportunity for risk that more vulnerable members of their communities can ill afford. That said, MLB and the Yankees have crafted politically neutral brands. For example, the Yankees were among the first group of sponsors to retract their support of the 2017 Puerto Rican Day Parade in New York City amid controversy over the choice of contested Puerto Rican nationalist hero Oscar López as the parade's master of ceremonies, due to López's association with the Puerto Rican independence movement. As we shall see, on the ground conversations and representations of nationalism are indeed fraught, and it is difficult to navigate the thin line between culture and politics.

With regard to what it means to be "American," and the need to walk a fine line, the following quotes represent the strongest discourses of the US as either pluralistic society, welcoming of cultural difference, or a monolithic, English-only society whose members must relinquish other facets of their identity. Note the nostalgic portrayal of Washington Heights and the melting pot imagery of ethnic succession in this first quote:

> I suppose the kid [Betances] can have his point of view. My grandfather grew
> up and died in the Heights when it was Irish. I don't recall him saying any-

6. In a *USA Today* roundtable about baseball in 2010, Hunter criticized MLB for taking advantage of the perception among many baseball fans that Afro-Latinos and African Americans are the same, despite cultural differences between the two, allowing MLB to appear to be more inclusive of black Americans than it actually is. For its part, MLB champions its sponsorship of Reviving Baseball in Inner Cities, a program created in 1989 in South Central Los Angeles by major leaguer John Young, who grew up there, to bring baseball to poor communities of color.

thing but being proud to be from the Heights, and to be an American as well. He spent his last years still living in his "walk up," surrounded by Dominicans of course. Everyone I know that lived next door to him always looked out for him. Great people, and a great diverse part of the city. (Rivera 2017a)

This description of Washington Heights and its succession from a predominantly Irish to Dominican area elides tensions during that history as it gestures to a nostalgic past, often deployed by white Americans to describe neighborhoods where they lived in the past that are now inhabited by people of color.[7] This commenter does concede that Dominicans are "great people" and that Washington Heights is a "great diverse part of the city," parroting the often benign discourse of diversity in the US, a position exemplified in the earlier comment that Betances did the right thing in not making a political statement. This also echoes the silence in conversations of race in the US that has long existed but shows signs of changing after the presidential election of 2016.

A second quote enters into dialogue with the current political moment and tries to contest some of the nativist sentiments of the Trump candidacy and administration:

I'm currently traveling the world and the more I see of other countries, the more I feel proud to be from America, where having a mixed identity is possible and in many cases probable. It's what makes us special and important. He [Betances] is proud to be from New York. He is proud to be of Dominican decent. Those two elements are not mutually exclusive. I appreciated the article and now will root for him, except when he plays my Royals. I'm happy he will "think about" using his platform to become political. In today's heated political climate, we need high profile people to talk about real issues. I applaud his dual identity. We all came from somewhere at some point (besides native populations anyway) and that's what makes America great. Nativism is disgusting and debilitating. God bless America AND American diversity! (Rivera 2017a)

The writer of this post strives to leverage the multiplicity of US American identities as an asset not shared by many countries, from which the US should

---

7. In *Vanishing Eden: White Construction of Memory, Meaning, and Identity in a Racially Changing City*, Maly and Dalmage argue that white former residents use nostalgia as a form of coded language to talk about an idyllic past where their neighborhoods were white, contrasted with a more difficult present where their neighborhoods have become more dangerous as people of color have moved in, not accounting for structural racism as a driving force in these changes. Thus, as in the case of Washington Heights, the past becomes a mechanism to build a present anchored in a simplistic vision of community formation.

draw strength. Though this post does mimic a sanitized discourse of multiculturalism as a perceived benefit of immigration that often does not extend far beyond platitudes of pride in the US melting pot—for example, the ubiquitous acknowledgment that only Native Americans are truly from US territory—the writer does show some awareness of the need to engage in political dialogue. He at once reclaims Trump's "Make America Great Again" slogan to lend support to immigrants and multiculturalism, at the same time defending Marly Rivera and ESPN's inclusion of a question on politics and activism and the need for players like Betances to speak out against injustice.

By way of contrast, another group of comments does not show even the budding political perspective of the above quote, taking to task the idea of "multiculturalism." According to one comment,

> Everything that's wrong with multiculturalism. You wanna bring your food, dance, culture . . . great . . . melting pot! But when you stress Spanish over the English language of the country and stress a Dominican woman because she happened to be born in the same area! No. America. We share a language and a culture. Assimilate. [(Betances had also mentioned in the article that he wants to marry a Dominican woman and teach his children Spanish.]). (Rivera 2017a)

While it is certainly a valid criticism that much multiculturalism in the US is largely symbolic through food and cultural practices on display for a dominant white audience, the command to "assimilate" represents a problematic and simplistic understanding of US society that negates the systemic and structural barriers facing many immigrants and new residents of the US. Between this assimilationist discourse and the overtly celebratory discourse of the previous comment, there exists a range of perspectives concerning ethnicity and social positionality, both from nostalgic white ethnics and from Latino/as themselves.

The following exchange in one of the comment threads of the article elucidates the ways that white ethnics understand immigration from a somewhat dated perspective, as European immigrants of the late nineteenth and early twentieth centuries did not face the increasing sociostructural barriers faced by people of color today. The first commenter stated, "Shouldn't you put the us first like the italians, Irish and Germans did when they came here? no patriotic American would play for another country," to which a second person responded, "Mike Piazza played for Italy. So i guess that makes him unpatriotic?!?!? David Ortiz, Manny Machado, heck Hall of Famer Bert Blyleven all played for another country. Kind of arrogant of you to question one's patriotism" (Rivera 2017a). The first comment seems to imply that players like Betances seek to remain somehow apart from the US at large, as opposed to being affected by the residential segregation and institutional racism that often denies them access to dominant US institutional culture. The second comment harkens back to conventional beliefs of equality, mentioning a list of players including both white ethnics and Latin/o Americans to prove that patriotism is an individual choice and outsiders may not stand in judgment of others. Again, this defense misses the point that larger structures contour and limit access to full participation in US society and by extension, patriotic identification.

Another comment thread engages more social nuance and curtailed access, lamentably through an argument premised on stereotypes of African Americans, Latina/os, and tensions between and within these groups. Responding to the idea that athletes should engage in political activism, the first person commented:

> The reason why hispanics don't get all political is because we have structure in our lives. Hispanic homes have both parents, Hispanic homes have order, hispanics within the family have roles and responsibility. African Americans on the other hand have a 70% single motherhood. Children don't grow up in beneficial circumstances and are told everything is someone else's fault. Fathers give no instructions to the kids whom they have abandoned and mothers either work to provide for their kids like crazy and have no time for them or continue to get pregnant and live off the government. This lifestyle is not as common in latinos as it is in blacks. This is the difference as to why they are protesting and we are not. We have order, direction, and responsibility. Blacks unfortunately have a blame game and no direction or guidance from those who are supposed to direct and guide them. Of course this sounds racist and ESPN will probably take this down but whatever, at least it's a reasonable explanation. (Rivera 2017a)

This person encapsulates a view of meritocracy and bootstraps mentality that locates the racism experienced by black Americans in a dysfunctional family structure and releases institutions such as schools, local and federal governments, employers, and the prison industrial complex from their roles in black American outcomes. At the same time, this person trots out the conventional wisdom that Latina/os are family- and community-oriented, and as such compliant and productive citizens. This perspective ignores the ways that dominant institutions such as the federal government have leveraged profiling and anti-immigration threats to silence Latina/os.

This comment elicited a strong backlash within its thread and eventually turned to questions of Latinidad. One responder called out the racism of the post but responded with an equally racist rationale:

> You're entitled to your twisted views and comments but I won't mingle in the gutter with you and rip Dominicans (or hispanics) because I've lived and worked with many wonderful people with that background for many years. I've also enjoyed great relationships with many Caucasians but the question is; Just who are you pandering to? The majority population of North Dakota [the first commenter's home state] is nearly 90% white and you're no doubt looked down upon as an "illegal." Sure Andrew, you might have already been told, "Get out of my country!" (Bet you don't ride around with a hispanic flag on your car either) But I'm guessing you think you're a regular white boy who trolls the internet with your "racial expertise" whenever it suits your ignorance. Enjoy your day and be sure to carry your papers with you. Wouldn't want the Border Patrol to make any mistakes. (Rivera 2017a)

Again, many of the simplistic descriptions of Dominicans and Latina/os as "wonderful people" and seemingly as wonderful as white people, emerge here, alongside the accusation of pandering. Deeply disturbing, however, is the mention that this person probably does not overtly and publically perform "Hispanic" identity through the display of a flag and that the person should be sure to always carry proof of citizenship, lest he be deported, all of which amounts to silencing of cultural identity and threat. Both problematic and puzzling is that the responder goes on to call the original Latino commenter a "white boy," implying that this person has appropriated whiteness and should be put in his place.

The original poster calls out the accusation of pandering and the racist characterization of him as "white boy" as follows:

> I'm not even sure what you were trying to say in your post. But why is it that me as a minority's always end up getting called a white boy whenever I call out minorities for stupid things that we say or do. But whenever you can't attack an argument I guess the "adult" thing to do in today's time is start calling people a white boy as that's the cure to any crappy point being made. Also my dad is from Cuba, my mom is from Mexico, and when I was a kid I would go live with my sister in Mexico during some summers when her husband was fixing his papers. So yeah a little white boy is definitely the term that best describes me. (Rivera 2017a)

Though still fraught with erroneous assertions, this statement does draw attention to some of the interior conflicts of Latina/os and especially Latina/os of multiple ethnic identities as well as tensions between people of color. In addition to having bought into the dominant narrative of black American laziness and dysfunction, this commenter is acutely aware that any criticisms between people of color (founded or unfounded) bring accusations of whitewashing. This man also clearly struggles with his own identity as being both Mexican and Cuban, and thus, in a similar vein to the land-based argument that players need to play for the US if they were born and raised here, defends his own Latinidad via the birthplace of his parents and the time he himself has spent in Mexico. It is well documented that tensions exist between and are often exploited to weaken the social capital of black Americans and Latina/os.[8] The point here is that white supremacy underpins all of the perspectives represented in the comment stream analyzed here via simplistic renderings of the US as a melting pot; the nativist assertion that the US is a white, English-speaking nation; and the divide-and-conquer strategy used to separate people of color.

The above discussion shows that nationalism and identity are malleable constructs that intersect with heart and soul connections linked to physical or emotional ties to countries, as well as legal and market considerations. The WBC brands itself as a competition meant to both showcase the best baseball talent in the world and serve as ambassador of the game, and by extension MLB. The description and eligibility rules of the WBC reflect the nature of globalization as struggles between nations and markets via claims to citizenship. What does it mean that the eligibility for citizenship allows a player to represent a country he may have visited only on vacation, or not at all? How does this type of representation dovetail with those of players who represent countries to which they feel a deep heart and soul connection, if not as legal citizens, through their families' sustained transnational lives? Furthermore, how does the case of players who are dual citizens or born in a country outside the US complicate the WBC's globalized definition of citizenship? The above discussion of Dellin Betances and the controversy over his choice to play for the Dominican Republic, despite having been born in the US, serves as a means to begin to unpack these questions as a debate between fans who rigidly define citizenship from a US-centric, nativist perspective, and those

8. *Neither Enemies nor Friends: Latinos, Blacks, Afro-Latinos,* edited by Oboler and Dzidzienyo (2005), demonstrates how the histories of racial formation, politics, and economic structure uphold a framework that privileges whiteness and encourages a distancing from African heritage and thus foments tensions between Latina/os, black Americans, and Afro-Latina/os.

whose lived experiences or understandings of a nuanced social positionality allow for loyalty to two nations. It also proves that the WBC is much more than a game, and individual players' decisions and actions carry a representational weight far beyond the individual, instead reflecting current political and economic tensions.

In the interview analyzed here, Betances explains that in the Dominican Republic, there is a pressure for Dominican MLB players to play winter ball there as an act of nationalism. Betances goes on to say that Dominican teams hold a draft of US Dominican players so that even Dominicans playing in the US who are children of island-born Dominicans are selected by a team, in his case the Águilas of Santiago, his parents' hometown. Such is the level of nationalist sentiment attached to MLB players' participation in the winter league that Betances says he is not yet "ready" to accept the Águilas' invitation to throw out a first pitch at one of their games. The nationalist tensions explored and foregrounded here are even more acute for the WBC's Team Puerto Rico and its fans. Given the sustained colonial status of Puerto Rico, a successful run in the WBC, like that of 2017, symbolically contests Puerto Rico's lack of self-determination and power. Indeed, as aptly stated by Carlos Beltrán, the unique nature of Puerto Rico's statutes impels players to "play for the name in the front, not on the back" of their uniforms.

"A Cloud of Patriotic Pride": #LosNuestros, #TeamRubio, #Puñeta—Puerto Rican Pride and Struggle on Social Media

"We're just making sure y'all see us, since it's hard to see us on a map. We'll make sure we're bigger than ever this time. Show y'all what we've got!" This fan comment from an article titled "Puerto Rico Is Having All the Fun and the World Baseball Classic," posted to Facebook by Bleacher Report and subsequently shared by Latino Rebels on March 21, 2017, shows the high stakes of the 2017 WBC for Puerto Rico. The article highlights the power of the Puerto Rican team and heralds their loose style of play as the future of baseball in terms of talent and prowess, as well as entertainment for fans. Fans reacted to the success of Team Puerto Rico, taking their WBC victories to that point as a rallying cry to prove the strength of the Puerto Rican nation and the need for unity in times of struggle. A long comment stream emerged of fans focusing on the power of Puerto Rico and how this is an opportunity for Puerto Ricans to have something positive to focus on in a time of economic crisis for the island. Many focused on the idea that Puerto Ricans are a fun people and do not take life too seriously. "Blondes really do have more fun" (a reference to Puerto Rican players dying their hair blond) appeared in several comments, one even joking that Puerto Ricans looking like blond white guys will help them get accepted in baseball. Repeated emoticons include the Puerto Rican flag, arms making a muscle, hands making the OK sign, and various types of happy faces. Two posters also posted a video called "Alegría Boricua" ("Puerto Rican Happiness"), a video featuring a crowd dancing to Afro–Puerto Rican music. With regard to fun, the following comments tie having fun to an almost utopian national unity: "Puerto Rico is showing why baseball should be fun again! None of that new rules just let them have fun on the field, this [has] been a very fun team to watch and exciting since I'm from Puerto Rico, but MLB just let them have this fun during season!! . . . oh and GO PR! Make this little Island proud! We're rooting for you guys!" (Collazo 2017). This comment argues that having fun and playing seemingly effortlessly good baseball, uninhibited by rules and the institutional culture of MLB, is an act of defiance, perhaps also a reference to the US control and surveillance of Puerto Rico itself. A second comment combines sports and unity, also mentioning Puerto Ricans as fun: "Sports its suppose to unite people not to separate. Baseball fans enjoy good baseball no matter where you came from and by nature PRicans have fun of everything we dont give a real fuc . . . about skin color, religion or if youre poor or rich. We just enjoy life peace" (Collazo 2017). This quote extends the ideas of sports, fun, and Puerto Rican nationalism to a utopian space via the implication that Puerto Ricans as a people are inclusive of all, regardless of race, class, or religion. Finally, a fan simply said, "Like Beltran said, they are playing for the name in the front, not the one in the back" (Collazo 2017). The article and fan sentiments presented here form part of a larger conversation about Puerto Rican pride as the WBC drew to a close and Puerto Rico headed to the final game undefeated.

During the final week of March 2017, as the World Baseball Classic drew to a close, social media became a space for fans to articulate their Puerto Rican pride via conversations about the WBC. The hashtags #LosNuestros (roughly translated as "ours"), #TeamRubio (the blond team), and #Puñeta (a Puerto Rican expletive that can express intense frustration and anger as well as great joy, in this case analogous to saying "fuck yes!" in US English) circulated widely. While #LosNuestros and #Puñeta reference national pride and emotion most directly, #TeamRubio refers to a group of players, led by Javier Báez and Francisco Lindor, who decided to dye their hair blond, a trend that caught on with the rest of the team and fans in Puerto Rico, consolidating blondness as a symbol of pride such that several pharmacies on the island reported selling out of blond hair color during the WBC. These hashtags extend beyond national pride as the depth of frustration captured with #Puñeta reflects the complexities of Puerto Rican emotions vis-à-vis its complicated relationship with the US. Though #LosNuestros and #Puñeta express powerful feelings of ownership and passion associated with nationalism, the use of #TeamRubio deserves particular attention due to the performative and structural power differentials underpinning it.

Commenting on the #TeamRubio phenomenon, Carlos Correa references its nationalist power: "We have been able to unite our country with our blond hair" (Páez-Pumar 2017). The use of blondness as a national metaphor in #TeamRubio presents a layered and problematic articulation of Puerto Rican identity. Though this grew out of the actions of the WBC Puerto Rico players themselves, blondness inescapably indexes a white supremacist discourse as men of color alter their appearances in deference to European standards of beauty. Additionally, read within the presidency of often bleached-blond Donald Trump and his dismissal of Puerto Ricans in general, a disturbing colonial discourse emerges in the *rubio* imagery. A marketing campaign including merchandise with blond hair floating above an absent head flooded social media dedicated to Puerto Rico and the WBC. Many jokes about blonds having more fun circulated among fans, lending the game itself a lighter tone, referencing the assumption that Puerto Ricans are a fun-loving people. This image, and its adoption and responses, captures important complexities surrounding the ways that Puerto Rican empowerment operates within a colonial and patriarchal system.

Indeed, some have read blondness here as an emancipatory act to challenge patriarchal norms, thus queering the image, while others used the opportunity to uphold norms of gender performance. It is important to note, however, that some policing of gender performance circulated through social media commentary, proving how deeply entrenched gender performance and power are. Along with the hashtag itself, social media chatter emphasized that it was OK for Puerto Rican men to dye their hair blond as an act of baseball and national solidarity during the WBC, but that after that, "real men" needed to stop, lest their sexuality and masculinity be called into question. This is consistent with the research on homosociality (Sedgwick 2015) that establishes that men in patriarchal societies must carefully navigate their desire for closeness with other men while at the same time maintaining a public distance that reiterates their heterosexuality. This is important from an intersectional perspective as, through #TeamRubio, Puerto Ricans perform a bounded nationalism, constrained by the island's fraught history with whiteness and patriarchy. While we must recognize and honor the extent to which the image empowers Puerto Ricans via the consumption of baseball and national pride, both the

Eurocentric and patriarchal discourses underpinning #TeamRubio warrant critique. The complexities, ambivalence, and frustrations around patriarchy, colonialism, and Puerto Rico's political and financial status captured in these hashtags emerged most starkly in a song circulated on Facebook during the final week of the WBC.

On March 19, 2017, a Puerto Rican Facebook user identified as Leslie Ann circulated a song and video with the title "Los Nuestros" to showcase the accomplishments of Puerto Rico in the 2017 WBC to that point and to inspire the team and the nation in the final game.[9] The post included an inspirational expression of pride in Puerto Rico, including the phrase, "Ando en una nube de orgullo patriota" (I walk within a cloud of patriotic pride). On March 23, 2017, a day after Puerto Rico's loss, Leslie Ann reposted the song, rearticulating Puerto Rican nationalism, stating, "No ganamos el juego, ganamos una nación unida" (We did not win the game, we won a united nation). A closer look at the images and lyrical content of the "Los Nuestros" post underscores the tensions and fraught nature of current Puerto Rican nationalism and identity.

The image opening the song is that of the Puerto Rican flag within a fingerprint with the text "It's in my DNA" beneath. These discourses of the flag and identity, both individual and collective, as evoked by DNA and the fingerprint, circulate throughout the video post. Images of the Puerto Rican flag in various contexts connect Puerto Rican nationalism to pride, protest, and baseball itself as the core of Puerto Rican identity. These images include a black-and-white image of the flag tied to a brick wall; the black-and-white Puerto Rican flag itself, associated with resistance and anticolonialism; the Puerto Rican flag fused with baseball, in the form of a baseball with the flag superimposed over it; and a flag design with the stripes made of baseball bats. In addition to these collective images of flags and baseball, the video features images of the individual players on the 2017 WBC team, game footage, and scores when Puerto Rico won against Venezuela and moved on to the final game. Images also connect Puerto Rican pride to leisure practices of audience members during baseball games themselves, such as a Puerto Rico uniform hat beside a bottle of Medalla, a Puerto Rican national beer, and fans in the stands holding a three part sign reading "#PUÑETA," a reference to one of the popular hashtags. Images of players in black T-shirts featuring blond hair references another popular hashtag, #TeamRubio. This image resembles many anti-Trump memes and images of his famously dyed blond and sculpted hair.

---

9. A Facebook friend shared this post with me on March 22, 2017. The post has circulated widely since its original post date of March 19, 2017.

The video culminates with the following text, indexing the national pride captured in the three hashtags associated with Puerto Rico's appearance in the 2017 WBC: "Gracias por tanta alegría. Son nuestro orgullo, son Los nuestros, #TeamRubio, #Puñeta, #LosNuestros. [Thank you for so much happiness. You are our pride, you are ours, #TeamRubio, #Puñeta, #LosNuestros]." The pride associated with baseball, athletic power, and leisure in the face of harsh economic and political times in Puerto Rico captured in these images gives way to a complex articulation of nationalism amid the persistent status of Puerto Rico as a US territory, or *estado libre asociado*, a status that limits the island's political and economic autonomy, in the song's lyrics.

The lyrics begin with "salimos de aquí" (we came from here) as a means to situate Puerto Rico's history in geographic, institutional, and economic terms. The song represents Puerto Rican identity through the mention of place names and geographic features of the island, such as El Yunque and rivers and mountains; institutions such as religion, machismo, and conformity (presumably to the empires that have controlled it, that is, Spain and the US); and long-abandoned economic engines for the island, sugar and coffee. A sentiment of disillusion, unrest, and silence permeates lyrical content. Metaphors of insomnia, "dando vueltas en la cama" (tossing and turning in bed), and truncated birth and growth, "salimos de madrugada, de una cuna reciclada, recitando oraciones que aprendimos sin opciones" (we come from the early morning, from a recycled cradle, reciting prayers that we learned because we had no choice), underscore the colonial history of a Puerto Rico that persists. The description of Puerto Rico as "un pozo donde ya no queda agua" (a well that has run dry) starkly signals the emptiness of a silenced people, a theme referenced throughout the lyrical structure of the song, describing a Puerto Rico bankrupt by its lack of voice in its own destiny.

In addition to "salimos de" (we come from), the phrase "aprendimos a" (we learned to) is also used to introduce descriptions and critiques of Puerto Rico's current political and economic status. "Así aprendimos sin querer a comernos las 's' cuando hablamos y eso es todo lo que hay que saber" (This is how, without wanting, we learned to eat our "s" when we talk and that's all that you need to know) connects the history and perpetuation of colonization to language and silence, as the eating of "s" is a reference to the colonizers from southern Spain who silenced the language of the Taíno inhabitants of Puerto Rico via the imposition of their variety of Spanish. Thus, the tongue and the body itself become the strongest symbols of the silencing of Puerto Rico, a silencing answered through the athletic power of bodies playing baseball. The refrain "vivir pa' sobrevivir" (living to survive) bridges the national pride of the video images of baseball nationalism with the struggles of colonialism and disempowerment of much of the history and nationalism depicted in the lyrical content where baseball and the WBC function as desperately needed articulations of pride and voice for Puerto Rico.

This pride culminated in a planned celebration by Team Puerto Rico that ignited a nationalist conflict between the US and Puerto Rican teams just before the final game. Though Team Puerto Rico lost the game, they arrived to a celebration in Puerto Rico, including a parade that had been organized before knowledge of the outcome of the tournament. This sparked a backlash from Team USA as players felt that it was arrogant of Team Puerto Rico to plan a celebration before the final game even happened. In fact, Team USA's center fielder Adam Jones stated that this motivated them to fight even harder to win (Axisa 2017). He went on to say that the team heard that Team Puerto Rico had championship T-shirts made before the final game as well: "That didn't sit well with us, so we did what we had to do" (Axisa 2017). It is important to note that Team USA also had championship T-shirts made before the final game, but players felt that these shirts should have been held back pending results. Outfielder Andrew McCutchen further asserted, "It didn't sit well. We heard and we saw T-shirts were made and printed out for the Puerto Rican team. We even heard a flight was made for them for that parade because they said they were going to win. That ignited us, we were ready to go, and we showed that tonight" (Padilla 2017).

For its part, Team Puerto Rico did not deny its plans to celebrate no matter what the outcome. Carlos Correa clarified the meaning of the WBC for Puerto Rico as a nation and how that meaning differs for the US and Team USA players:

> It's funny because they have been talking about that, but it's all about the country; it's not about our team. Our country has been behind us since we have started [the tournament]. When we were in Mexico, we told the governor in Puerto Rico that if we made it to the finals, we need a plane to get back and celebrate with our people. There were no crimes, there were no assassinations back home while we were playing in this classic. Everybody was dyeing their hair blond, so we had our whole nation behind us that is going through tough times right now. It's as simple as this: If you ask Angel Pagan, if you ask Yadi Molina if it feels better than a World Series, they would say yes. If you ask one of the American guys, they will say, "No, not even close." So that just tells you the way we play when we represent our country is a lot different than when they play. A lot of their guys say no to the baseball classic. None of our main guys say no to the baseball classic. (Padilla 2017)

Correa's statement here indexes all of the threads of nationalism, pride, and need for celebration in hard times voiced by Puerto Rican fans during and just after the WBC. Correa additionally calls out the lack of interest and passion on the part of US players who value lucrative MLB contracts over nationalism such that they do not want to risk injury or fatigue by participating in the tournament, again gesturing to the power differential between the US and Puerto Rico. This statement implies that the white privilege associated with dominant US culture is so pervasive that it requires no reinforcement, as it affords Team USA players the choice to view the decision to play from an individual or collective nationalist perspective, whereas, as colonial subjects, Puerto Rican players must constantly struggle to gain privilege via performances of nationalism.

A Facebook post forwarded to me by a Puerto Rican friend on March 24, 2017, sums up the many threads of emotion and power differentials woven through WBC 2017 by Puerto Ricans:

Un país que lleva días defendiendo aquello de romper estereotipos de belleza, también superó 'estereotipos de triunfo.' ¿Ganar? Ganar es unir un pueblo, ganar es crear un movimiento donde los hombres se han atrevido a pintarse el pelo, donde la criminalidad disminuyó durante un lapso de tiempo, donde todo el mundo tiene desde una camisa o gorra hasta una banderita pequeña con la Monoestrellada; ganar es tener a los vecinos gritando con cada carrera del equipo, es tener un pueblo con ojeras después de cada partido, con las uñas a mitad por los nervios y esas tantas cosas que muchos países no saben. Cuando un equipo de fuera pierde, nadie los recibe con celebración y PUERTO RICO tiene fiesta!, saben porqué? PORQUE PUERTO RICO ES ORO, ES VICTORIA, ES UNIÓN Y ESO LE QUEDA GRANDE A MUCHOS LUGARES DEL MUNDO.

♥PR☺ YO VIVO ORGULLOSO DE SER PUERTORRIQUEÑO . . . QUE VIVA EL "TEAMRUBIO"♥PR☺ 🎧💯 pre!

(A country that has spent days defending the shattering of stereotypes of beauty, also overcame "stereotypes of triumph" Winning? To win is to unite a people, to win is to create a movement where men have dared to dye their hair, where crime diminished for a time, where everyone has a shirt or hat even a little flag with the Monostar [a reference to the lone star on Puerto Rico's flag], to win is to have all the neighbors screaming with every run the team scores, it is to have a people with ears on every game, with nails bitten halfway down from nerves and all these things that many countries don't know. When a team loses away from home, no one celebrates them, and PUERTO RICO has a party! You know why? PUERTO RICO IS GOLD, VICTORY, UNION AND THIS MAKES IT GREATER THAN MANY PLACES IN THE WORLD.

❤PR☺ I LIVE PROUD TO BE A PUERTO RICAN . . . LONG LIVE "TEAMRUBIO"❤PR☺ 👊🏽 💯 pre! [love PR baseball forever])

Simply put, the media coverage and comments of fans and players all indicate that the 2017 WBC has been able to provide Puerto Rico with a safety, stability, and unity that a dysfunctional government, economy, and global system have not.

Conclusion

"This country neither owns the sport nor lays claim to its best players." These words indicate that fans need to recognize that the US has relinquished its position as producer of premier baseball talent, if that were ever truly the case. In stating this in response to nativism leveled at Marc Anthony, Tod Robberson seemed to be either unveiling a secret that he thought most Americans did not know, or lifting the veil on the imperialist assumption that US players are the best. The case of Marc Anthony performing at the 2013 All-Star Game, and the Latino music industry itself, exemplify the growth of the market-driven integration of Latinidad in dominant cultural spheres. One need only listen to popular music, such as the 2017 remix of "Despacito" featuring Puerto Rican musicians Luis Fonsi and Daddy Yankee, as well as Justin Bieber, and the controversy surrounding Bieber's inability to speak Spanish and his perceived disrespect for Latina/o culture, to understand the contested dynamics surrounding Latina/os in the US culture market. As Deborah Pacini Hernandez, Frances Aparicio, and María Elena Cepeda note, the potential for profit drives acceptance of Latina/o cultural production, but not necessarily Latina/os themselves, in mainstream institutions.[10] Marc Anthony's All-Star performance and MLB fan reactions to it bridge MLB and the white-dominated music industry as institutions struggling to embrace inclusion while maintaining white hegemony. In the case of MLB, the stakes are even higher as it has traditionally used discourses of white US nationalism to survive and market itself as "America's game." Competition from other sports organizations such as the NFL and NBA, as well as demographic shifts within

---

10. See Pacini Hernandez (1995); Aparicio and Chávez-Silverman (1997); Cepeda (2010).

its fan base, have rendered US nationalist insularity an untenable model to sustain and grow the game of baseball.

As the events of the 2017 WBC illustrate, greater incorporation of Latina/os and Latinidad in the game are the keys for MLB to thrive and survive, but this requires the inclusion of Latin/o Americans. While MLB has long made inroads via recruitment of talent, and more recently by making MLB and individual team websites available in Spanish, tensions remain around differences in style of play and clubhouse and fan inclusion. Also, many parks remain unhospitable to nonwhite players and fans. Recall the scandal over racist fan taunts at black American Baltimore Orioles' center fielder Adam Jones at Fenway Park in Boston in May 2017.[11] The rhetoric of international competition and pride around the WBC is designed to mitigate against this, though the cases of Dellin Betances and Team Puerto Rico indicate the extent to which nationalism fuels embedded power differentials within US society and beyond.

Just as Marc Anthony's claim that he defines himself as both a Puerto Rican and a New Yorker fell on deaf, if not hostile, ears among many MLB fans, so too did Dellin Betances's embrace of his Dominican and US heritage in his decision to play for the Dominican Republic in the WBC, despite having attained his "American dream" as a US-born, Washington Heights Dominican playing for the Yankees. This stance forced a dichotomy on Betances that is inconsistent with his and many other players' transnational lives. Most Latina/o and some white fans understood that individuals can and do embody multiple nationalities and feel equally loyal to both. A litany of non-Latina/o fan reactions illustrate that for many US Americans, birthright citizenship remains as the very limited definition of what it means to be "American," though it is important to note that white supremacist undercurrents embedded in conventional wisdom still exclude people of color from the full benefits of birthright citizenship to the extent that one Latino commenter seized the opportunity to impugn the character of black American families as dysfunctional and chaotic as compared to Latina/o families. The accusation that ESPN is "too political" in asking Betances why he thinks Latin/o American MLB players do not participate in antiracist activism at the levels that black American players in other sports do further belies this point, as it would seem to indicate that fans want to consume bodies of color playing baseball, but do not want to hear about the inequalities these same bodies endure on and off the field. Sports should be about fun.

---

11. In late April 2017, racist fans taunted Orioles center fielder Adam Jones, throwing a bag of peanuts at him during an away game against the Red Sox at Fenway Park in Boston.

In the discourses of nationalism and competition displayed in the WBC 2017, even fun has its limits. Media and social media production surrounding the final game between the US and Puerto Rico depicts the narrative of Puerto Rico, an economically disenfranchised colony, asserting its nationalism by opposing the US empire that oppresses it. One of the currents of pride running through Puerto Rican nationalist social media is that this was not only a way to literally and figuratively "put Puerto Rico on the map" for the rest of the world, but, in a time of austerity, to have fun, a coping mechanism many fans attribute to the Puerto Rican spirit itself, a spirit linked to nationalism. When the team lost, Puerto Rico held a parade for the returning players. Players from Team USA stated that the perceived arrogance behind having planned a celebration win or lose inspired them to play even harder, propelling them to shut out Puerto Rico by a score of 8 to 0. Puerto Rican players defended their celebration as a means to unite the island and have fun at a time when it most needed any sign of strength and success, citing dropping crime and relative peace in Puerto Rico throughout the tournament. Infielder Carlos Correa further questioned the nationalism of US players in stating that they care more about their MLB contracts and the possibility of winning the World Series than the national pride of winning the WBC, as many star players decline to participate, whereas, in his estimation, star Puerto Rican players view participation in the WBC as a point of pride. In the end, the cases of Anthony, Betances, and Team Puerto Rico mirror larger nativist trends in the US as they push MLB and its fans to reexamine the meanings of nationalism, as no country owns the sport of baseball, nor players.

CHAPTER 3

"¡Aquí (no) se habla español!"

MLB, Media, and the Racialization of Spanish Language Use

ON SEPTEMBER 7, 2016, ESPN Deportes published an article, "Roberto Clemente fue un fiero crítico tanto del béisbol como de la sociedad estadounidense [Roberto Clemente was as much a critic of baseball as he was of US society]," written by Clemente biographer David Maraniss. The article highlights the campaign to retire Clemente's number 21 in all of MLB, akin to the retirement of number 42 for Jackie Robinson. Not only does Maraniss (2016) make the case for retiring Clemente's number, comparing the racial struggles he faced in MLB and the US more generally to those faced by Robinson, but he also outlines the ways that the legend and myth surrounding Clemente hide who he actually was, a fierce critic of racial and social injustice, as opposed to a passive and grateful immigrant, as he is often portrayed. This portrait of Clemente emphasizes his discomfort during spring training in the segregated South, his criticism of MLB for insisting on an outdated performance of masculinity that denies its players any sense of individuality on the field, and his insistence that he and other Latin/o American and African American players be treated no differently than white players. Maraniss states that Clemente, were he alive today, would take then GOP candidate Donald Trump to task and strongly advocate against Trump's racist rhetoric (Maraniss 2016). Perhaps the most powerful example of the racism faced by Clemente was with regard to language, specifically the way that he spoke English. As with Trump's assertion during the Republican National Convention that the US is a country where we speak English, not Spanish, interactions between Clemente and the press in Pittsburgh and beyond belie the monolingual mandate so often attached to US nationalism. Journalists literally changed Clemente's identity, referring to him as "Bob" in their writing, despite his never identifying by that nickname himself. Journalists changing names they deemed foreign was a common practice during Clemente's era. Furthermore, journalists reproduced Clemente's speech pattern and pronunciation in English so as to emphasize his foreignness. The sentiments behind the Clemente case and tensions around media interactions and Latin/o American players' language use continue today.

The Clemente article serves as a ready introduction to a deeper analysis of the intersection between racism, capital, language, and baseball in the US. In order to unpack this fraught relationship, I will apply the research and literature on language policy and ideology to contemporary cases related to MLB, media, and tensions around Latin/o American players and language use, including media content—MLB's #PonleAcento ad campaign, *Saturday Night Live* (*SNL*) sketches portraying fictional retired MLB star Chico Escuela and actual recently retired star David "Big Papi" Ortiz, and the use of Spanish in two ESPN broadcasts in 2013—and Ozzie Guillén's and Carlos Beltrán's criticism and advocacy around MLB's language policies and support structures. This analysis broadens the understanding of the ways that Latin/o American players come to embody one of the greatest nativist tensions, the use of language as a gatekeeping mechanism of citizenship and belonging. For Latina/os who have lived for a long time in the US, these same linguistic gatekeeping measures remind them that they still do not "belong" in the US and are not equal citizens. Grounded in the language policy context of the US, which favors monolingualism and constructs Spanish as a symbol of immigrant illegality, poverty, and invasion, this chapter investigates how language use in and around MLB and media both reiterates and sometimes parts from national anti-Spanish ideologies connected with anti-immigration political discourse. Competent English language use—defined as use associated with the white middle class—functions as a marker of loyalty to the US, while Spanish language use arouses suspicions as to players' loyalty and suitability to represent "America's game."

Policing Language and Institutionalized Racism in the US

Given baseball's role as "America's pastime" as well as the long-established relationship between sports and nationalism, language in Major League Baseball is a crucial issue for both the organization and its fans. Since the explosion of recruitment in the Caribbean Basin from the 1980s onward, announcers and fans have grappled with the fact that many of the heroes of MLB are not only born outside of the US, but do not speak English as a first language, in some cases barely speaking the language at all. As such, language has become a key issue in terms of communication within teams as well as MLB branding and fan consumption of the game. Tensions around language, and particularly the abundance of Spanish-speaking players, result from larger ideologies around race and language in the US. Simply put, since the inception of the US as a nation, nationalism has been linked to the English language as a defining factor of what it means to be "American." This dynamic plays out in both institutional culture, through schools, politics, the workforce, and media, and in everyday interactions in public spaces. Thus, it is important to ground the analysis of Spanish and MLB in a discussion of the institutional formation of language policy in the US.

There's a joke in Spanish that roughly translates as follows: "What do you call a person that speaks three languages? Trilingual. What do you call a person that speaks two languages? Bilingual. What do you call a person that speaks one language? American." This joke illustrates how commonplace the monolingual ideology of US nationalism is; even those outside of the US understand it to be a monolingual and Anglo country. This ideology manifests in myriad ways, as multilingualism is thwarted in both direct policy as well as tacit understandings that English equals "American" in daily social interactions and media productions. Some monolingual English speakers take offence to this joke because, despite the fact that roughly 80 percent of US Americans are monolingual English speakers, many US Americans want to believe that their country is accepting of all. They do not associate restrictive language policies with racism and white supremacy as pillars of US society.

There are many reasons for this, but first and foremost, the English language, specifically white middle-class English, has been inscribed into the history of the US as a core component of US nationalism, metaphorically used as the binding agent that supposedly brings US Americans together. Media, politics, the education system, and the labor market are four chief places where this ideology is indoctrinated as linked to US citizenship and nationalism. As Rosina Lippi-Green argues in *English with an Accent* (2011), in media and popular culture, some accented English is used to inscribe characteristics such as trustworthiness and diligence in certain ethnic groups, while other accented English is associated with laziness, treachery, and other traits marked as un-American. Additionally, political debates and the structure of the educational system since the formation of the United States of America have focused on the need to control language use and impart English language instruction (Escobar and Potowski 2015).

This same belief that the English language ties together US Americans as an organizing principle of national identity also racializes and marks the Spanish language and its speakers as "un-American." Two concepts, "Spanish as a racialized marker" and "mock Spanish," help us to systematically understand the relationship between race and language in the US. In the documentary *Latinos beyond Reel* (Picker and Sun 2012), Isabel Molina-Guzmán has identified Spanish as a "racialized marker." This means that white Americans use the Spanish language and accents in English associated with Spanish as a means to identify who is Latina/o and thus who should not gain full access to the rights and privileges of US citizenship. It is not enough to simply place Spanish and its speakers outside of US national belonging. White American linguistic culture also subordinates Spanish and its speakers to English and English speakers via what has been called "mock Spanish." Jane Hill (2007) defines mock Spanish as both the pronunciation of words in Spanish with a heavy US English accent and the invention of grammatically incorrect "Spanish" words by putting vowels on the end of English words, for example "no problemo" and "el cheapo." According to Hill (2007), mock Spanish functions to denigrate Spanish as an illegitimate form of communication in the US and to evoke a jovial and non-serious persona among white Americans.

The work on race, whiteness, Latina/o identity, and structural inequality of Joe Feagin (2013), Eduardo Bonilla-Silva (2014), and Leo Chávez (2013) is useful in unpacking and understanding the meanings and ideologies behind Spanish as a racialized marker and mock Spanish. In *The White Racial Frame*, Feagin (2013) documents the ways in which whiteness is embedded in the historical, political, economic, and linguistic formation of the US and has ensured the perpetuation of structural inequality in terms of poverty, residential segregation, and educational outcomes, among other things. Similarly, in *Racism without Racists*, Bonilla-Silva (2014) argues that white Americans currently articulate racism and white supremacy in ways that attempt to distance their acts from the individuals committing them and instead attribute them to perceived cultural deficiencies of people of color or structures they believe to be out of their control. Finally, Chávez identifies the "Latino threat," the widely held perception that Latino/as (1) want to reclaim the US Southwest as part of Mexico, (2) refuse to learn English so as not to assimilate to the US, and (3) intend to gain power through massive reproduction and population growth. Taken together, Feagin's, Bonilla-Silva's, and Chávez's work unpacks the histories and structures that have led to the conventional wisdom about Spanish and its speakers in the US.

The starkest manifestation of this conventional wisdom in recent history has emerged in the political sphere, specifically the campaign discourse of GOP 2016 presidential candidate Donald Trump. During the second Republican presidential debate, Trump stated, "We have a country, where, to assimilate, you have to speak English. This is a country where we speak English, not Spanish" (Marks 2016). This statement emerged within a larger discourse on Mexicans as rapists and an overall dangerous threat to the US, culminating in Trump's frequent assertion that he would build a wall on the US–Mexican border, a wall that he assures voters Mexico will pay for. The vitriolic imagery of the Mexican threat outlined by Trump in terms of language and criminality exemplifies the white supremacist ideas that Feagin, Bonilla-Silva, and Chávez put forth in their writings. As a further act against Spanish, the Trump administration, upon taking office, removed the Spanish language content on the White House website. Trump's success among a certain segment of the white US population illustrates the extent to which the history of racism, woven into US institutions, continues to thrive.

These actions and political views exemplify the ways that race and language intersect. The concept of raciolinguistics developed by Alim, Rickford, and Ball (2016) is useful to further unpack the work of critical race studies and sociolinguistics. In their introduction to *Raciolinguistics: How Language Shapes Our Ideas about Race*, these scholars present their construct of raciolinguistics via the following question: "What does it mean to speak as a racialized subject in contemporary America?" (1). They go on to map the ways that that racialization manifests through language in everyday life, and call on others to join in the movement proposed by raciolinguistics—namely, to use the study of language to examine and transform social injustice (5–6). I join the creators of the construct of raciolinguistics with this work in the hopes that better understandings of language use in MLB, considered within the politics and history of the US, contribute to the work of dismantling social inequality.

The evidence presented here amply demonstrates that linguistic discrimination is an outcome of the history and development of racialized social systems, from the formation of the US as a nation to the present moment. MLB's Latin/o American players dwell within this context. As a heralded cultural institution that enjoys a largely white, middle-class, male fan base, MLB is faced with a difficult situation in the current racial and political climate: How to balance baseball as "Americana" with a significant labor force who not only does not "look white" but speaks Spanish as a first language and is thus forever marked as "foreign."

#PonleAcento: MLB's Fraught Relationship with Spanish

Major League Baseball has a complicated relationship with Spanish. While practicality demands that the organization address the bilingual needs of its players due to recruitment practices and infrastructures created in the Caribbean to maintain a pipeline of young talent, it also does not wish to alienate segments of its fan base that reject the legitimacy of Spanish due to the ideologies, polities, and racist linguistic culture outlined above. Yet another factor enters into MLB's language balancing act. Given the popularity of baseball in the Caribbean, many US Latina/os are fans. As both a young and fast-growing demographic, Latina/o fans could save the game from extinction. In recent years, MLB has lost ground to the NBA and NFL in terms of overall popularity. MLB executives are well aware that cultivating a greater, and possibly bilingual, fan base could help the sport survive in the competitive US market. As such, collective and individual interventions engage Spanish as a part of the Latinidad that MLB hopes to support and profit from.

At the collective level, MLB and its teams have largely engaged with Latin/o American culture and identity through ceremonial interventions honoring specific players or Latin/o Americans in general. Many teams sponsor Latino Days during the season but particularly incorporate the national celebration of Hispanic Heritage Month, from September 15 to October 15, to recognize Latin/o American fans and players, where game-day promotions and entertainment activities are geared toward aspects of Latina/o culture. Team websites' simultaneous broadcasts in Spanish also present an avenue for Spanish-speaking Latina/os to consume MLB. MLB also has a Spanish language website, LasMayores.com. The organization's efforts are also supported by ESPN Deportes' simultaneous online content in English and Spanish, focusing particularly on Latin/o American players, as well as a host of blogs, Facebook groups, and player Twitter and Instagram accounts in Spanish (Sanchez 2016b).

Though some rightly criticize the model of heritage months as a superficial way of paying homage to multiculturalism through a façade of celebration that can occlude the reasons why many heritages are disparaged and in need of such recognition in the first place, it is worth noting that MLB organizations publicly recognize Latin/o Americans, a population that has strongly shaped the game of baseball and continues to constitute a significant amount of its labor force. With this perspective and caveat in mind, another MLB initiative, #PonleAcento, whose very name defines the Spanish language as the core of Latin/o American identity and presence in MLB, merits some attention.

FIGURE 2. MLB #PonleAcento logo developed by
LatinWorks for Hispanic Heritage Month 2016

MLB has worked with LatinWorks, a Texas-based branding and marketing agency, since 2015 to build an intergenerational campaign, #PonleAcento
(figure 2), to recognize the contributions of Latin/o American players on all
thirty MLB teams through marketing and merchandising throughout the season but particularly tied to Hispanic Heritage Month. It encourages players
and on-field staff to add the accents that their Spanish surnames customarily
include but that have often been lost in the immigration process or for other
reasons. Since the campaign started, more than twenty players and on-field
staff have put accents on the names on their jerseys. Additionally, the MLB
batter symbol was redesigned to include an accent or tilde over the bat. As
part of this initiative, in 2016, twenty-three teams hosted Hispanic Heritage
games (Sanchez 2016b).

The #PonleAcento campaign underscores many of the intricacies of
Latin/o American identity and language at the heart of this study. MLB
describes the campaign as follows:

Created by LatinWorks, MLB's Hispanic marketing agency of record, the
#PonleAcento initiative—which literally means "to put an accent on it"—

shows all the ways Latinos have put an accent on the game, both on and off the field. This month, logos with accent marks on the silhouetted batter will be featured in ballparks, on MLB traditional and social media, as well as on batting practice T-shirts worn by players prior to select games. (Kramer 2017)

Players such as first baseman Adrián González have noted the importance of this initiative: "It's great that players have caught on and the actual initiative has taken a more important role, and more players are doing it and wanting to do it. And it's great not just for baseball, but for Latinos everywhere. Hispanic Heritage Month is part of that whole process, and hopefully it will gain some more traction and continue to move forward" (Kramer 2017). In fact, González is credited with putting #PonleAcento on the map as he referred to it in a tweet in May of 2016. As part of the #PonleAcento campaign in 2015, MLB also debuted its first bilingual—English and Spanish—spot in general-market national media on ESPN's *Wednesday Night Baseball*; it was subsequently featured on ESPN, Fox Sports 1, MLB Network, MLB.com, and MLB's social media platforms. ESPN Deportes, Fox Deportes, and LasMayores.com aired the Spanish version.

The very name #PonleAcento casts language at the heart of the identities and contributions of Latin/o American players as it uses a linguistic feature, the accent mark or tilde, as a metaphor for the presence and contributions of Latin/o American players in MLB. The description of the campaign as highlighting the accent that Latino players put on the game on and off the field seeks to bridge potential cultural and linguistic tensions. According to LatinWorks's associate creative director Alberto Calva, MLB embraced the idea: "[MLB] owned the idea since day one. They were very brave in approving [#PonleAcento], because it not only takes a stand in America's favorite pastime; it stands for minorities and inclusion in American culture as a whole" (Natividad 2017). In a political climate where white supremacist discourses have emerged with force in mainstream media, LatinWorks executives recognize the pressures on MLB in adopting this campaign at this time. Executive creative director Gabriel García locates #PonleAcento within this context as a fraught but contestatory symbolic intervention for Latino/as, linking it to respect, inclusion, tradition, and competition:

It also gives Hispanics permission to insert their personal passions and interests into the conversation, yet always with a reference back to MLB, the game that recognized the need to not only put an accent on a name, but on a sport and on your life. Through an idea that is irrefutably Hispanic, we showed how something as simple as an accent could be embraced by Latinos as a thoughtful invitation to participate in a game that in many ways they've already helped make great. (Natividad 2017)

This allusion to making the game great is perhaps an unfortunate choice of words as it harkens to the presidential campaign slogan of Donald Trump, "Make America Great Again." In an alternative reading, this statement could also reclaim the idea of greatness, linking it to a population of color.

On May 18, 2017, LatinWorks posted a promotional video to YouTube titled "MLB's 'Ponle Acento' case study. Putting the Accent on Béisbol." The video tells the story of how the "acento" of Latinos has been lost as a result of the push to assimilate to English-only US culture. The video situates the campaign within an immigrant and intergenerational narrative as it opens with the image of a passport and explains how the accent has been lost for Latino immigrants. The camera zooms in to last names that should have accents on passports but do not, before transitioning to MLB uniforms also missing assents. From here, the uniform arrives at a sewing machine placing the accent mark on MLB jerseys. This is significant as it indexes work, especially the garment industry, an industry that employed large numbers of Latino/a immigrants in the early twentieth century. This image is important not only because it ties baseball to the garment industry as pillars of Latino/a labor history but also because it recognizes the production of the jerseys themselves and renders visible the often invisible production process. Accompanying these images, a narrator describes the officially deleted accents as a loss of a part of "Hispanics' identity" upon arriving in the US, stating, "Nowhere is this more evident than MLB," situating the importance of Latinos in MLB in the statistic that 27 percent of players are Hispanic. This statistic also appears on-screen to match the narrative. According to the narrator, MLB has sought to correct this historical erasure: "In 2016 MLB set out to do something about it by speaking to a new generation of fans and highlighting the role of Latinos in America's pastime" (LatinWorks 2017). Enter the intergenerational promotional campaign #PonleAcento.

The video engages an intergenerational audience through images of both youth and MLB stars playing baseball and the reach of the #PonleAcento campaign via social media to show the extent to which Latino/as have embraced and shaped the game of baseball and continue to shape its future. It also features other sports and entertainment stars, such as boxing champion Canelo Álvarez, Marc Anthony, and George López, who have embraced the campaign, even in some cases asking for accents on their names on stars on the Walk of Fame in Hollywood. Additionally featured are scores of headlines, news clips, and tweets attesting to the wide reach of the campaign and the pride it has awakened among Latino/as. According to LatinWorks, #PonleAcento has more than five hundred million social media impressions, as the narrator notes that the hashtag connected with players' and fans' sense of pride and became a movement. The video connects social media, the accent symbol, and MLB through images of accented words that evoke the celebratory and passionate tone that MLB seeks to connect with Latino/a fans, "béisbol, acción, celebración, pasión." Describing it as a "bold move" on the part of MLB, the video narrator defines #PonleAcento as "a culture changing 360 campaign celebrating everything Latinos contribute to the game. #PonleAcento in one of the biggest social media campaigns in MLB history." The narration closes with the accented MLB batter logo and the voiceover, "We didn't just change the sport, we left a mark in America's pastime for generations to come." The message and social media efforts attached to #PonleAcento underscore commitments made by MLB commissioner Rob Manfred during the 2017 World Baseball Classic to continue to reach out to an international audience via support and promotion of the WBC, and a commitment to enhancing MLB's social media presence to engage younger fans. The Spanish language is at the heart of both of these commitments.

In addition to these US-based efforts to attract and engage US Latina/o audiences through Latin/o American on-field personnel, language plays a crucial role in the academy system that MLB has established in the Caribbean. Teams provide educational training as part of the preparation of prospective players. The *academias* (academies), as they are known in the Dominican Republic, purport to provide residential, nutritional, cultural, and linguistic support to young players hoping to travel to the US and one day play in MLB. *Academia* personnel have stated that their role is to give these young men the tools for success, both as potential future MLB players and for whatever their professional lives might hold. This includes not only a place to live and a consistent diet but also language training in both English and Spanish. In some cases, *academia* prospects have dropped out of school young and need language support in their native Spanish as much as in English. MLB, through the formation of the Dominican Development Alliance, has attempted to formalize and standardize *academias* in the face of allegations of insufficient facilities and untrained training and medical personnel in the past.[1]

---

1. In *Stealing Lives,* Arturo Marcano Guevara and David Fidler (2002) document the injuries to Venezuelan recruit Alexis Quiroz's body to demonstrate the physical damage resulting from the lack of oversight of the Dominican *academia* system in the 1990s, when teams cut costs by hiring improperly trained trainers to treat players, among other offenses, and the abuses of MLB's aspiring young labor force in the Spanish Caribbean.

On the individual front, many players have spoken about the difficulties of navigating English on arrival as young men. Retired outfielder and manager Felipe Alou captures the tensions around players speaking Spanish in the 1950s during his time with the San Francisco Giants, when manager Alvin Dark instructed the players not to speak Spanish, claiming that some of the other players didn't like it. Alou and first baseman Orlando Cepeda protested by speaking in Spanish, saying that they would not stop speaking the language. Dark relented, but his relationship with Spanish-speaking players never fully recovered (Alou and Kerasotis 2018, 89). More recently, retired player/manager Ozzie Guillén and infielder Carlos Beltrán have denounced uneven language assistance provided by MLB and its constituent teams. In still other cases, Spanish has been used to smooth over trades and market individual players. For example, during trade negotiations moving outfielder Manny Ramírez from Boston to Los Angeles, his agent, Scott Boras, advocated for the trade, citing the large Spanish-speaking Latina/o population in Los Angeles (Rhodes and Boburg 2011, 277–84). Players such as outfielder Yoenis Céspedes appear in commercials speaking Spanish and linking their careers as baseball players to the pride in their Latina/o communities in the US.

A 2004 *USA Today* article puts the issue of language into greater context within the histories of individual players, presenting two contrastive player stories to illustrate the role language plays in player success as it connects to questions of race and acculturation. In "Spanish-Speaking Players Get Lessons in American Life," Tom Weir and Blane Bachelor (2004) use the careers of retired players Davey Concepción and Virgilio Mata to show that athletic talent is but one part of the puzzle for successful careers in MLB. According to Weir and Bachelor, while Davey Concepción adjusted well to speaking English and to US American life in general, Virgilio Mata struggled with the adjustment to life in the US, an issue that cut his career short. This is consistent with Felipe Alou's observation that not speaking English can lead to loneliness and hurt players' careers (Alou and Kerasotis 2018, 134). Sal Artiaga, who was a player development executive in Cincinnati in the 1960s, when both players were drafted, says of Mata, "Gosh damn, that kid could play. It's important to point out that he was not a bad kid. It's just that he had trouble with the adjustment, as many do. If they're overwhelmed, they're obviously going to have problems" (Weir and Bachelor 2004). As such, Artiaga has emerged as an advocate for support structures for players recruited by MLB in Latin America, preparing manuals in Spanish on issues from baseball and MLB procedure to how to rent an apartment. He couches these initiatives in corporate logic as part of doing good business: "If you work for Dow Chemical and you're assigned to a foreign country, they're going to take time and introduce you to that new language and the customs, not only to you, but to your family, too. I think we have a moral obligation to do that for our players" (Weir and Bachelor 2004). MLB teams began incorporating English language training in their Dominican operations in the 1980s, and by 2000 access to language training was part of the collective bargaining agreement with the Players' Association.

Becky Schnakenberg emerged as a liaison for Latin American players in terms of language and culture training in the early 2000s, using both her bilingual and clinical counseling skills to train players not only in English but in proper masculine behaviors in the US. She says it costs a team only about $15,000 a year to provide English and cultural classes. As a sign of the changing attitude, Schnakenberg notes that Kansas City has hired her to give Spanish lessons to its American-born staff. Schnakenberg notes that acculturating to gendered norms of behavior challenges Latin American players as much as learning English with regard to relationships between men and women and particularly flirting. She explains that US American men flirt with their eyes, whereas Latin American men flirt with their mouths, through whistling and spoken compliments to women they find attractive. Though this explanation overgeneralizes both US and Latin American men, and fails to take into account any nuance or intersectionality related to gender, sexuality, race, or class, it is a useful example of how MLB defines "American" cultural behavior through a white, middle-class lens, at the same time that it attempts to negotiate difference and protect its players from misunderstanding. It also sheds light on ways that players are racialized and cautioned against interactions that might lead to potentially risky interactions with law enforcement vis-à-vis questions of sexual harassment. As Dominican pitcher Pedro Martínez explains, "Sometimes you make a mistake just trying to be nice. Like you whistle at a girl. Girls don't like to be whistled at here. In the Dominican, that's flirting with a girl. You might scream something, 'Hey, beauty' or whatever in Spanish. In the Dominican, that's OK. Here, some of the girls will take that as sexual harassment or whatever" (Weir and Bachelor 2004). Despite these increases in attention and infrastructure for language training and intercultural communications, there remains work to be done in terms of larger racist ideologies that persist around baseball and MLB.

Indeed, the progress mentioned in the USA Today article reproduces a common narrative of the continued struggle for equality that pits the present against a presumably worse past, celebrating an era of progress, evidenced here by Sal Artiaga's stance that MLB has improved its support system for players from other countries and linguistic background since the 1960s. While it is true that MLB and most individual teams have increased resources given to language support, equity, and player development, Weir and Bachelor (2004) construct a narrative of appreciation in quoting top-performing Dominican-born left fielder Manny Ramírez and pitcher Pedro Martínez in 2004. Weir and Bachelor cast MLB personnel and practices as white saviors within a highly unbalanced power differential between Latin American players and the organizations that make up MLB. Both Ramírez and Martínez acknowledge that Latin American players need MLB more than MLB needs them as players. For example, when asked if MLB needs to do more, Martínez responded, "They are doing more. They're trying to actually educate us about how life is going to be in the United States because that's one of the most difficult adjustments we have to make" (Weir and Bachelor 2004). While it is certainly true that players must partner in their learning of English, the idea underpinning this depiction of MLB as savior to young men born in conditions of poverty in the Spanish Caribbean and Latin America is a colonial one in that it does not take into account the fact that these countries provide a robust and relatively cheap labor stream from which MLB may continually draw.

More recently, New York Yankee pitcher Dellin Betances has spoken about the experiences of Latin American–born players in the major and minor league systems in terms of the difficulties of communication in English, but also the more nuanced interactions between players who came to the US as young adults to play baseball and those that came younger with their families. In an interview about his decision to play for the Dominican Republic in the 2017 World Baseball Classic, when asked about the advantages of being bilingual in everyday interactions as a minor league player in 2017, Betances responded:

> Playing rookie ball, I would say 70 percent of the team is Spanish-speaking, Latin players, and 30 percent are American. At that point I felt I was the guy in the middle that had to order pizzas for them at night, if they wanted me to order stuff for them, and be that guy that just translates and making sure that Americans understand the Latin ballplayers and vice versa. The Latin ballplayers, most don't know any English, so I was the guy that spoke both. (Rivera 2017b)

This feeling of being "the guy in the middle" gestures to the "in-betweenness," to use Gloria Anzaldúa's term for the bicultural nature of the lived linguistic experiences of immigrants like Betances who came to the US before finishing high school, often referred to as a 1.5 generation immigrant.[2] When further asked if other Latin American players make fun of his slight American accent

---

2. In *Borderlands / La Frontera: The New Mestiza* (1987), Gloria Anzaldúa theorizes the border as a space of hybrid and deeply regulated identities. She posits the idea of in-betweenness to capture the feeling of belonging to neither US nor Mexican culture fully. According to Anzaldúa, language is a critical site where this dynamic manifests.

when speaking Spanish in the minor leagues, he continued, "Even now they make fun of me! There are certain words that I have trouble saying in Spanish, but for the most part, I think I do all right" (Rivera 2017b). Betances's comments here belie the power differentials between bilingual players, differentials around language and identity that often go unnoticed in conversations about language and power as these conversations typically focus on an English versus Spanish binary that occludes important subtleties in language and identity. Betances's story contributes to an understanding of the intricacies of communication among players and keeps the discussion of bilingualism at the forefront of MLB coverage.

Language, politics, and MLB coalesced in the 2017 Baseball Hall of Fame Induction Ceremony in Cooperstown, New York. Famed catcher Iván "Pudge" Rodríguez became the ninth Latin American and the fourth Puerto Rican player to be inducted in the Hall of Fame. The context surrounding his induction intersects with politics in two significant ways: First, the Puerto Rican government has selected Rodríguez to participate in a commission to encourage the US Congress to adopt Puerto Rico as the fifty-first US state of the union after a pro-statehood plebiscite in June 2017.[3] In a second political act, Rodríguez elected to speak at his induction ceremony roughly half in Spanish. Rodríguez's induction into the Hall of Fame amid a heated political battle in Puerto Rico—indeed, Puerto Rico's economic and political status emerges in much media coverage and social media chatter during the 2017 World Baseball Classic and MLB season—and his performance of *puertorriqueñidad* and Latinidad via an acceptance speech in Spanish capture the ways that MLB intersects with political and national identities, whether it wants to or not.

Rodríguez's speech exemplifies the connections between MLB protocol, adjustment, identity, and Spanish in MLB that contour this project on MLB and mediated Latinidad. Beginning with the transcript itself, now part of the archive of the induction, two striking linguistic themes emerge: First, the transcription is verbatim in English, in the sense that it captures the English of a second-language speaker, as Rodríguez is, instead of including native-like grammar changes.[4] This is important because historically Latin Ameri-

---

3. The results of this plebiscite do not tell the whole story when it comes to Puerto Rican politics. Though 97 percent of the vote favored statehood, as opposed to continuing the status quo for Puerto Rico, or independence for the island, only 23 percent of registered voters cast ballots. As such, Puerto Rico's status remains a contested and politically manipulated matter. It is also important to note that this plebiscite does not actually obligate the US Congress to take any action based on its outcome.

4. The transcript of the speech is provided by ASAP Sports (2017) (http://www.asapsports .com/show_interview.php?id=132649), a company that specializes in transcribing sports interviews and conferences to media professionals. MLB and several media outlets are listed among

can players such as Roberto Clemente have experienced an uneven respect in the media in terms of reproduction of their spoken English, as some media workers would "correct" their English, under the assumption that it made them sound more educated, while other times, media workers would reproduce second-language English speech in an attempt to satirize or play down the intelligence of players. While it is likely that in the case of the induction speech, the intent is to capture verbatim, and for the record, the words of Iván Rodríguez, a second linguistic aspect of the speech, removing some Spanish excerpts while including others in English with "speaking Spanish" in parentheses, buttresses the dominance of English in the US as the only "official" language of communication, also calling into question the official nature of the record. Perhaps a better, and more inclusive, option would be to include the Spanish portions with English translations. In any case, the silencing of Spanish in the transcript assumes a monolingual audience and discounts the people of Puerto Rico that Rodríguez addresses in Spanish. Even more telling, in his introductory remarks, when thanking Hall of Fame chairpersons Jane Forbes, Jeff Idelson, and commissioner Rob Manfred, Rodríguez thanks Manfred for "let[ting] me do half of this speech in Spanish and English" (ASAP Sports 2017).

Rodríguez weaves language into the beginning of his speech as he recalls the first time he caught pitcher Nolan Ryan, explaining that he did not speak much English but after the game was able to answer reporters' questions about pitch selection in English. Thus, from the beginning, Rodríguez marks language as a defining aspect of his career as a player. After that anecdote, Rodríguez explains that he will do part of his speech in Spanish so that his loved ones in Puerto Rico can understand it. That part of the speech is totally omitted from the transcript, The Spanish language speech content omitted from the transcript includes both personalized thanks to family, friends, and coaches in Puerto Rico, as well as a sentiment of pride in Puerto Rico and Rodríguez's great honor at being able to represent Puerto Rico, and Latin America more broadly, via his MLB career. Of note is both the fact that Rodríguez expressed his nationalist pride and identity in Spanish, as well as the absence of that information from the transcript, which then represents an incomplete and decidedly depoliticized record of his induction into the Hall of Fame, a significant public performative act that could provide a forum for speaking out and expressing Puerto Rican and Latina/o pride. It is interesting to note that Rodríguez said he would not, and did not, mention his advocacy work with

---

their clients. This transcript, referred to by the company as a Fastscript given its availability within minutes of the event, is the transcript of record quoted by many media sources and used in my analysis.

the Puerto Rican government on behalf of the statehood movement. In the case of Iván Rodríguez's induction to the National Baseball Hall of Fame, as I argue throughout this book, bilingual and bicultural Latina/os experience a more nuanced and politicized version of this event as it is the coverage in Spanish, particularly that of ESPN Deportes, that ties the induction to Rodríguez's political work and allows fans to listen to Rodríguez articulate his gratitude and Puerto Rican / Latino identity in Spanish. The above discussion lays the groundwork for an analysis of media content in and around Spanish, and the often tenuous relationship between the Spanish language, MLB, and media workers, to which I shall now turn.

"Baseball Been Berry, Berry Good to Me!": Race and the Spanish Language in Media and MLB Policy

On November 11, 1978, comedy sketch show *Saturday Night Live* debuted a character, Chico Escuela, portrayed by black American comedian, Garrett Morris. *Chico* was also a nickname applied to Latin/o American players, such as Chico Carrasquel. Escuela was a retired all-star, Dominican baseball player from the Chicago Cubs (in subsequent appearances, he is introduced as a retired New York Met). During this first skit, when asked to give a speech, he coined the tagline, "Thank you berry much. Baseball been berry, berry good to me. Thank you. God bless you. Gracias!" When asked if that was all he had to say, Escuela responds "Keep you eye . . . keep you eyes . . . on de ball." This became a repeated skit on *Saturday Night Live,* and "Baseball been berry, berry good to me" became a catchphrase associated with Latin/o American players ("Baseball Been" 2018). I remember my father saying it and chuckling when players such as Sammy Sosa appeared on television well into the 1990s. An analysis of the Chico Escuela performance lays the groundwork to understand the broader context of the racialization of Latin/o American players through press coverage. Though the Escuela character exaggerates phonological, syntactic, and morphological features of the English of Latin Americans, it is useful to understand how performance undergirds the racist ideologies mapped onto language in the US, ideologies that still operate in much media content and negotiation with players in the present.

According to Morris, Bill and Brian Murray created Chico Escuela as an amalgam of their experiences in the Catholic church growing up and the Latin American players they had seen as baseball fans. According to Morris, Latin American players were often invited to speak at church meetings and paid "a couple of thousand dollars," but since they did not speak English, this amounted to a few hundred dollars a word. This became the seed for the jokes around Escuela's brief utterances on the show (FoundationINTERVIEWS 2012). Morris also drew inspiration from Latin American players themselves, stating that his performance referenced no specific baseball player but he did base it largely on Brazilian soccer player Pelé (FoundationINTERVIEWS 2012). The Escuela storyline further developed around his failed attempt to make a comeback in MLB.

In his second appearance, Chico Escuela is hired on as the "Weekend Update" sports correspondent. In that role, he repeats his tagline and shows a total ignorance of any sport other than baseball. Morris would play Chico Escuela a total of ten times before leaving the show in 1980. Below is a transcript of his appearance:

> JANE CURTIN: Now, we'd like to welcome a new member to our Update team, the former All-Star second baseman for the New York Mets, Chico Escuela. Welcome, Chico. [Chico clears his throat, photo of smiling Chico Escuela in baseball uniform and holding a bat] Chico will be covering the sports scene for Weekend Update. [applause for Chico, a Dominican ballplayer who sits opposite Jane—he has a thick Dominican accent and speaks very little English]
>
> CHICO ESCUELA: Thank you. Thank you, berry, berry much. . . . Base-ball . . . been berry, berry good to me. . . . Thank you, Hane. . . . [Photo of major league ballplayer Pete Rose] Pete-ee Rose . . . Base-ball been berry, berry good to Pete Rose. . . . Three—point—two—million—dollar para Pete Rose. Charlie Hustle, you bet. . . . Thank you very, very much. [National Football League schedule is shown] In—foot-ball . . . I don't know—football. . . . In Dominican Republic, foot-ball is—how you say, Hane? Um—Oh!—soccer! Your football—[pause] I don't know. . . . [Hockey graphic] In National Hockey League . . . [shakes his head] I don't know hockey . . . [applause, photo of smiling Chico again] In base-ball—Base-ball been berry, berry good to me! . . . Thank you very much. Thank you. Thank you very much. [applause] Hane? Thank you, Hane.
>
> JANE CURTIN: [genuinely enthusiastic] Great job, Chico. I'm glad that we haven't hired just another stupid ex-jock sportscaster. . . . ("SNL Transcripts" 2018)

A reading of the content and form of this skit reveals a characterization of Latin/o American MLB players as unintelligent, opportunistic, and perpetually foreign. The implication is that Escuela is unqualified for his job, except for having played professional baseball, and knows nothing about any other sport. He says "I don't know," twice in the short skit and repeats his tagline, also applying it to Pete Rose. When discussing Pete Rose, all he mentions is that Rose has recently signed a lucrative contract and should "hustle," implying that unless extremely well compensated, players will not perform at a high level. With respect to US sports, he simply states that they do not have American football or hockey in the Dominican Republic. Despite living in the US long enough to retire from MLB, he has not learned anything about other US sports, let alone US culture or language.

His spoken English also belies this "foreignness" and buffoonery. First, with regard to syntax, or sentence structure, several of his utterances either lack verbs—"Base-ball . . . been berry, berry good to me"—or the word order is inconsistent with a native English speaker and exaggerates the features of a second-language speaker. His phonology, or pronunciation, similarly demonstrates these characteristics. Words such as "berry" (very) and "Hane" (Jane) are meant to mimic the influence of Spanish on English pronunciation. Here, the aforementioned work of Lippi-Green (2011) and Hill (2007) is useful. Consistent with Lippi-Green's argument about the use of accent to evoke characteristics related to morals, ethics, and trust, Chico Escuela comes across as lazy and unintelligent. Further, though Hill's construction of mock Spanish applies to the use of grammatically and phonologically incorrect Spanish to devalue both the language itself and its speakers, I would argue that Escuela's English serves a similar function as the way he speaks marks him as outside of what is considered to be middle-class, white English and thus not deserving of belonging in the US. These features of exaggerated pronunciation and non-native syntax remain present in current media representations and quotes from MLB players, as well as fans' attitudes toward the presence of Spanish in MLB.

More recently, since 2014, *SNL* has featured occasional appearances by retired Boston Red Sox outfielder / designated hitter David "Big Papi" Ortiz, played by Kenan Thompson, on its "Weekend Update" news skit. Like Escuela, Ortiz talks about sports in general, from topics such as his perspective on Yankee Stadium as a member of the Boston Red Sox to the Super Bowl. Thompson uses mock Spanish to present a seemingly fun-loving but not very smart retired Dominican star. He also performs exaggerated facial movements, in particular a big smile and often raised eyebrows as he speaks to "Weekend Update" news anchors Colin Jost and Michael Che. This character demonstrates the extent that mimicry, languages other than English, perceived intellectual deficiencies, and greed continue to be mapped onto male bodies of color for the amusement of a general (read white) American public. In these skits, the following themes emerge: Language, especially puns using Spanglish; Ortiz as happy-go-lucky but not too bright; Ortiz's big body, which is always hungry; and Ortiz as greedy pitchman willing to endorse anything for money. This exaggerated and money-hungry pitchman somewhat recalls the "clowning" that black players performed in the Jim Crow Negro League era, where some players would perform sleight-of-hand tricks to entertain fans as a means to attract more interest and money to the League (Burgos 2007, 251). Clowning, like the *Saturday Night Live* performances of Chico Escuela and David Ortiz, demonstrates the ways that racism positions people of color in a position to "entertain" a white audience, at the expense of their own humanity and dignity, in pursuit of capital.

With regard to language, the skits are done in Spanglish and mock Spanish, as absurd puns and Spanish words used incorrectly are used to achieve comic effect. In every appearance, Thompson as Ortiz mentions *mofongo* (a common Dominican dish made of mashed plantains and various fillings), presumably because the word itself sounds humorous to an English-dominant ear. There are also frequent puns involving rhyming in Spanish and English. When Jost asks him what he plans to do in retirement, Ortiz says "I endorsemints," which Jost interprets as meaning to endorse various products, but Ortiz quickly corrects him, saying, "No endorse mints" ("Weekend Update" 2016). Similarly, Jost asks what are some of the products he advertises. He says he endorses "little Cisers," which Jost interprets to mean the pizza chain Little Ceasars. Ortiz again corrects him, saying no, "Little scissors," pronounced with an exaggerated Spanish accent ("Weekend Update" 2014). These puns are often nonsensical as they do not actually mean anything, thus further trivializing Spanish and Ortiz as a Dominican native, in line with Jane Hill's concept of mock Spanish outlined earlier in this chapter.

An alternative reading of the use of mock Spanish in the Ortiz skits shifts the power differential among Thompson as Ortiz and Jost. An interesting power differential does emerge in one of the skits in an exchange between Colin Jost and Ortiz. Ortiz says, "¿Qué pasa contigo, Jost [pronounced Yost]?," to which Jost responds, "Más o menos. Y Ud?" Ortiz responds, "Shut up. We already got a deal with Tim Kaine" ("Weekend Update" 2014). This response is significant for three reasons. First, it references then Democratic vice presidential candidate Tim Kaine, who spoke Spanish and delivered a bilingual speech in Miami during the campaign. This resulted in media backlash from some, in particular CNN pundit and Trump supporter Scottie Nell Hughes. The argument was that by speaking Spanish, Kaine was ignoring most of the monolingual US population (Domino Rudolph 2018, 91). In contrast, some Latino/as interpreted Kaine's use of Spanish during the campaign as pandering to them as voters. In referencing this political figure, Thompson as Ortiz engages both the political importance of Spanish and its contested nature as part of the national imaginary. Second, Ortiz tells Jost to "shut up" since there is already one prominent white man speaking Spanish, perhaps gesturing to the power differential tied to differential bilingualism. Differential bilingualism refers to how the social position of an individual or ethnic or racial group imbues the languages that group speaks with meaning and social capital based on the individual or group's prestige level (Aparicio 1998). Furthermore, Ortiz might be expressing an uneasiness about too many white people appropriating Spanish for their own use or entertainment, thus further disempowering Latino/as. Third, in stating, "We already got a deal with Tim Kaine," Ortiz potentially references both a strategic attempt on the part of Spanish-speaking people to cultivate the support of a prominent white male figure, at the same time reducing Kaine's public speaking in Spanish to a mere business deal made by pitchmen like Ortiz, rendering visible the capitalist logic behind Kaine's language use.

The most egregious example of the pitchman persona came after Ortiz's 2014 selfie with President Barack Obama and the subsequent media scandal. When the World Champion Boston Red Sox visited the White House, Ortiz took advantage of the opportunity to pose with Obama and take a selfie, which immediately went viral. When Obama asked Ortiz to pose for an official photo, Ortiz replied, "Do you mind if I take my own?" Obama later coined this "the Big Papi selfie" (Stampler 2014). Shortly after the photo was taken, it appeared in what appeared to be advertising photos for Samsung. ABC News reported that it was indeed a publicity stunt, though a Samsung spokesman would not commit to that interpretation, stating, "We have a relationship with David and the Red Sox. We partner with people who have like-minded values and fit with who we are as a brand" (Newcomb 2014). Media reports speculate that the Ortiz photo with Obama was a calculated selfie, having come on the heels of a star-studded selfie taken by comedian Ellen DeGeneres as part of a Samsung campaign. Both photos are believed to be part of Samsung's 2014 quest to own the selfie market. According to the *Washington Post,* prior to the White House visit, Ortiz had reached a deal with Samsung to be its MLB social media insider. White House staff responded swiftly to criticize the Ortiz/Samsung deal's inclusion of the president's image for commercial purposes. Senior adviser Dan Pfeiffer told CBS's *Face the Nation* that the president had no knowledge of the selfie as advertising but that there would likely be no future selfies at the White House. According to White House press secretary Jay Carney, "I can tell you that as a rule the White House objects to attempts to use the president's likeness for commercial purposes. And we certainly object in this case" (Bever 2014).

In an *SNL* sketch about the incident, when asked how much Samsung paid him for his endorsement, Ortiz says 100,000 chickens, further rendering him both naïve and excessively hungry. Thompson as Ortiz claims that he did not know that the selfie might be interpreted as a publicity stunt, and that he talked to "Sam Sun" and "Sam" and that everyone said it was OK. When Jost asks Ortiz if he is concerned that Obama is angry that he was used for advertising purposes in this way, he says that he made it up to him by sending a big basket of food ("Weekend Update" 2014). The Ortiz as innocent persona shifts in this sketch as he appears to disrespect the president of the US for his own gain, indexing the narrative of the greedy and arrogant athlete of color.

In contrast to the Chico Escuela character, David Ortiz is a real person, interpreted by an actor. As such, fans consume the character in a different way because they bring to the character and sketches their opinions and knowledge of Ortiz, and his overall public persona as an optimistic, humanitarian-oriented ballplayer, often praised for his charitable interventions in Boston, and the US in general, as well as his native Dominican Republic. The Ortiz sketches also engage current events such as the Obama selfie and the presidential election of 2016, with the mention of Tim Kaine. Additionally, Ortiz himself has reacted to the impersonation and the content of the sketches, both the sketch about his possible post-baseball career in athletics and advertising, specifically the suggestion that he open a gym for iguanas, and the one about the selfie with Obama. In both cases, Ortiz approved of the portrayal and showed that he can laugh at himself. With regard to the iguana gym, he took to Twitter, posting a picture of himself with an iguana with the following text directed to Kenan Thompson, "Hey @officialkenan. . . . .found the first member of our new gym @nbcsnl" (McDonough 2015). With regard to the selfie with Obama sketch, Ortiz called it "hilarious" and joked that he was in New York City for a series with the Yankees so he could have stopped by. "They should have called me," he said (Mastrodonato 2014). This history with *Saturday Night Live* provides a rich context through which to read and understand how players position themselves within media productions and representations, as shall be seen via analysis of Ozzie Guillén's sustained criticism of MLB language support for Latin American players, culminating in a call for policy change from Carlos Beltrán and a response from MLB itself.

Indeed, players themselves are well aware of this dynamic and have navigated it in differing ways, some, such as Sammy Sosa, embracing the opportunity to engage in humor and quite possibly call out linguistic racism, while others, like Ozzie Guillén, have spoken out against the lack of Spanish support for Latin American players in MLB, especially when it comes to dealing with press. Adrián Burgos Jr. (2007) has noted that Sosa is familiar with the Chico

Escuela portrayal analyzed above and has reclaimed it as a means to ingrati-
ate himself to white US American fans (251–52). As such, Sosa exemplifies a
contestatory strategy to combat white supremacist ideology. Sosa's embattled
career, including accusations of using a corked bat and steroids, has under-
mined this effort, especially the scandal around his steroid use and testimony
before Congress. For that testimony, Sosa stated that he would need the support of an interpreter, causing criticism that he had lived in the US for a long
time and thus should be fluent in English, with many claiming it as a strategic
way to evade charges of steroid use.

For his part, Ozzie Guillén has been an outspoken critic of how MLB
treats its Latin/o American players in terms of race and language. Guillén
himself has conducted press conferences bilingually, especially when he wants
to speak specifically to Latin/o Americans, as was the case in April 2012, when
he apologized to the Latino/a community for remarks he made that were perceived to be in support of Fidel Castro and the ways that his regime oppressed
sectors of Cuban society. Guillén spoke mainly Spanish during the press conference, changing to English only at the request of media workers present.
Perhaps, similar to the case of Sammy Sosa, he felt that he needed to address
such an emotionally charged and serious issue in his first language. This could
also be an act of resistance to an English-only media that limits his ability to
fully express himself. In fact, as part of his explanation/apology, Guillén cited
a miscommunication and imperfect translation of his sentiment from Spanish to English as contributing to the misunderstanding of his true opinion of
Fidel Castro.[5] This is significant because it demonstrates that Guillén is very
aware of the intersection between language and identity, especially as a means
to speak out against racism against Latino/as in and outside of MLB, forging
for them a space of public pride for Latino/as and Spanish.

In addition to publicly speaking in Spanish when he deems it necessary
to communicate with other Latino/as for whom Spanish is either their dominant language or their affective language of choice, Guillén has criticized the
uneven treatment of nonwhite players in terms of race and language. In 2004
and 2010, he referenced the disparate treatment of Latin American and Asian
players in MLB vis-à-vis language support. In 2004, he first pointed out in
USA Today how Japanese players come with interpreters but Latin American
players don't, stating, "I always make a joke that we always bring a Japanese
guy (as an interpreter) because (the Japanese players) don't speak the language.
Why don't we bring a Latin guy to help? . . . I told Tony Bernazard (of the

---

5. In chapter 5, I provide a more thorough analysis of Guillén's remarks and the ensuing
controversy among media workers and fans.

player's union) we bring guys here who can't speak the language and we don't care. Then they tell us to learn the language" (Rhoden 2010). Subsequently, in August 2010, Guillén talked about the difference between playing in the US for Cuban and Japanese players, referencing a recently signed White Sox player, Dayán Viciedo, who had defected from Cuba and thus would probably not be able to return to his country as a Japanese player would at the end of his career. Guillén further contrasted the experiences of Latin American and Japanese players in terms of language on August 1, 2010, when he asked, "Why do we have a Japanese interpreter but not a Spanish one?" (Rhoden 2010). This remark referenced the fact that the handful of Asian-born players that come to play for MLB have translation support services, often escort interpreters that travel with them and translate for their daily needs as well as scouting reports that players may wish to consult. Guillén later visited his son's Class A minor league team and observed the linguistic dynamic where an interpreter supported the sole Korean player there but his son and bilingual coaches were the only support for the seventeen Latino players, further supporting his argument about differential language support for Asian and Latin American players. He punctuated his argument by saying, "I just want my people, these kids, to have a better life on the field, off the field. That's all we want. That's what I was saying. I was saying I want to help Latino kids" (Rhoden 2010). Guillén questions the logic where MLB provides interpretation and translation services to one relatively small population within the game, while denying such services to a significantly larger population, a population that the organization aggressively recruits in the Spanish-speaking Caribbean and Caribbean Basin in countries like the Dominican Republic and Venezuela. Guillén's point is that MLB should have a consistent policy with regard to providing translators, not one that provides translators to some but not other groups. These observations gain more importance when read within the larger monolingual ideology of the US already mentioned. It is certainly reasonable to assume that MLB might fear a backlash from its white (male) fan base, which doubtlessly includes many who are anti-immigration and resent if not outright wish to eliminate the presence of (Spanish-speaking) Latino/as as a demographically significant US population (Shaw 2010).

MLB, for its part, responded and attempted to deescalate Guillén's comments, pointing out that though his advocacy is laudable, perhaps Guillén is not fully aware of the efforts of MLB and individual teams in supporting their significant Latin/o American player population. MLB cited the response from Guillén's then team the Chicago White Sox as follows: "The White Sox, fairly accustomed to issuing rebuttals to its outspoken manager, made it clear with its statement issued Monday that Guillen's apparently missing out on a lot of what's being done to help Latin American players in the game these days" (Schlegel 2010). The phrasing of this quote is telling in that it highlights the outspoken nature of Guillén's persona while it also places his observations within a context of rebuttal, thus discrediting the value of the possible racism behind uneven MLB policy. On its own website, MLB defended and further explained its support structures for players, starting with their recruitment and training in the Dominican academies, where players are given language and culture training, as well as information on MLB's anti-drug policies. The article states that, as per the collective bargaining agreement with the Players' Association, teams must provide Spanish translations of notices, contracts, and other key documents, as well as translators if even one player requests this. As Adrián Burgos Jr. (2007) notes, this is not always the case, as teams have sometimes denied players' requests for interpreters, even if the player has offered to pay for the interpreter, under the logic that seasoned players who have lived in the US for at least a few years should be able to speak English.[6]

The article listed a number of services for international and specifically Latin American players to further cast Guillén as an out-of-date malcontent who does not fully recognize, or bother to remain aware of, MLB initiatives in this area. The defense consists of cultural and language training, including written translations and English as a second language (ESL) classes as long as at least one players requests them. The article cites continued negotiation of interpretation/translation services with the Players' Association in official contracts, as well as the presence of MLB personnel in the Dominican Republic and Venezuela to work with prospects, as well as drug education and testing programs in both countries as key supports for Spanish Caribbean players. MLB further argues that it actually practices a sort of Latin/o American exceptionalism in that it invests more financial resources in its Caribbean academies than its minor league system (Schlegel 2010).

It is worth noting the connection here between language training, assimilation, and anti-doping education for players in the Dominican Republic.

MLB's response connects language to capital and drug use in its defense of its policies and practices. The language used to describe the services provided by MLB and its teams is laden with references to imperialist practices like "assimilation" and "acculturation." The assessment of the work of MLB in its Caribbean facilities and recruitment infrastructure by then vice president for

---

6. According to Burgos (2007), when Yankee Pitcher Orlando Hernández offered to pay for his own translator, the organization denied the request, stating that a translator was a "crutch" for the Cuban player and that five years in the US was ample time to learn English (247).

labor relations and current commissioner of Major League Baseball Rob Manfred underscores the economic bottom line as a driving force for MLB actions and policies there. Manfred stated on ESPN, "Often, baseball is criticized for its efforts in Latin America. Looking at numbers on a per player basis, we spend approximately 40 percent more on our programs in the Dominican and Venezuela than we do on our Minor League programs domestically. Part of it is lack of awareness at the depth and breadth of programs available" (Schlegel 2010). It is certainly telling that Manfred's defense of MLB practice indexes money spent on players as an indication of all forms of investment in players, ignoring that systemic and institutionalized racism can and do exist apart from the amount of money spent on player development. Additionally, the explicit mention of MLB's anti-drug policy as the key document that MLB provides in Spanish references a hyper-concern over the possibility that Latin American players might use drugs to gain a competitive edge and thus endanger their presence in the game. While it is certainly true that issues of drug use must be addressed for all MLB players and recruits, the framing of this story, diffusing tensions around race by pointing out MLB's commitment to spending money on player development and making Latin American players aware of anti-drug policies in their first language, indicates a preoccupation with bodies and capital that does not do the deeper work of addressing the assumptions around race and the use value of young male bodies of color that underpin the concerns expressed by Guillén.

Guillén has become a voice and advocate for Latin/o American players, starting a conversation about language and inequality in MLB. Indeed, in the period between 2004 and 2010, MLB instituted many of the changes it cited in its response to Guillén's 2010 criticism about unequal treatment of Japanese and Latin American players. Though it is not possible to directly attribute this change to Guillén's 2004 intervention, his remarks and consistent outspoken nature have certainly brought that conversation to the attention of MLB, which likely resulted in the action taken to better support players from Spanish-speaking countries. Guillén's remarks opened a larger dialogue where other players, current and former, told their stories of discrimination. Many players admit to initially avoiding interviews or saying little, referencing insecurities in their spoken English and concern about making a mistake. Most players feel that after a couple of years, they can function in basic English in their daily lives and discuss basic baseball topics in media interviews. There is, however, an important distinction to be made between discussing basic elements of the game, using English phrases that players have likely heard often and memorized within their pragmatic context, and the demands of using English in a more sophisticated context, beyond basic baseball vocabulary and descriptions, which demands a much higher proficiency in English, as Puerto Rican outfielder Carlos Beltrán points out.

Similar to Guillén, Carlos Beltrán underlines the serious nature of language competence and the media with regard to an incident with New York Yankee Dominican pitcher Michael Pineda being asked about unauthorized use of pine tar. In April 2014, Pineda was ejected from a game for using pine tar. Pineda said that he was having trouble gripping the ball in the cold and did not want to hit a batter. MLB suspended him as a result. Then Yankee manager Joe Girardi applauded Pineda's decision not to seek the help of a bilingual teammate or bullpen personnel for his interview in English, stating, "I think Michael did a tremendous job last night, standing up in front of you and not necessarily maybe using an interpreter and hiding behind an interpreter or doing anything like that" (Castillo 2014). Girardi's comments link linguistic competence and a willingness to risk misunderstanding to a masculine sense of honor associated with not asking for help and "standing up" to media workers to address his behavior instead of "hiding behind an interpreter." Beltrán sees this as a more serious systematic issue. He realizes the gravity of the conversation involving Pineda as media coverage of an ejection for not following authorized procedure in the use of pine tar carries potentially harsh ramifications for a player's career, such that any language barrier is dangerous for the player. Like Guillén, Beltrán points out the presence of professional interpreters for Japanese players, such as Ichiro Suzuki and Masahiro Tanaka, who are never expected to speak to media without the benefit of an interpreter. Though Beltrán acknowledges that players should try to learn English and MLB does provide some support for language learning, it is simply not enough, especially in situations like that of Pineda. According to Beltrán, "In the big leagues, we aren't given an interpreter. Personally, I understand that it's also on the player to find help if he doesn't feel he can express himself in the way he wishes to. But, like I said in spring training, there should be something available for these situations because at the end of the day I know it's a difficult moment for him [Michael Pineda] as a person" (Castillo 2014). The tension between Girardi's and Beltrán's responses to Pineda's case—Girardi viewing it as honorable male behavior in not asking for help and instead standing up for himself, and Beltrán asserting that this is a systemic issue where players feel pressure to communicate without the benefit of interpretation in sensitive and complicated situations—underscores ideas of individualist masculinity and honor as cornerstones of US and MLB ideology, while at the same time upholding the notion that Latin American players who do not speak native English are less trustworthy if they "hide behind" an interpreter.

Despite this tension and the perception among some in MLB that players should learn English as soon as possible and be fully bilingual within a couple of years in the US, MLB continues developing initiatives to address Spanish language support. In January 2016, MLB published an article on its website lauding the fruition of Beltrán's vision for translators for MLB teams. In January 2016, MLB reached an agreement with the Players' Association for a jointly funded translator to be provided by each team by Opening Day 2016, expanding the efforts some organizations already had in place (Sanchez 2016a). The idea is that each team will have this person available for players throughout the year for assistance with translation and understanding of documents and policies related to players' contracts and duties in MLB, as well as assisting with cultural adaptation as needed. The description of the duties and qualifications of the translator reveal subtle ways that MLB still does not yet fully embrace Spanish language support in the way that it does Japanese language support. The qualifications mentioned in the article are that the person be "fluent in English and Spanish, with excellent written and oral communication skills in both languages" (Sanchez 2016a). Missing is any mention that the person must be trained as a professional interpreter. The arrangements for payment of this new personnel indicate a lukewarm investment on the part of organizations. According to the announcement, "The translators will be paid from the proceeds of the penalties paid by teams for exceeding the signing bonus pools for acquiring international amateur talent during the international signing periods" (Sanchez 2016a). This arrangement places interpreters as an extra expense compensated via monies accrued through a punitive system, apart from organizations' customary operating budget, a financial allocation that echoes the Othering of Latin American players. It also further demonstrates the weakly regulated, capital-driven structure of MLB's international recruitment, where teams may pursue top talent unfettered if they can pay the highest signing bonus and the penalty for doing so. It is important to note that MLB and the Players' Association have subsequently fleshed out the translation mandate to include requirements that translators be both trained and assessed, including through a mock post-game translation exercise. Despite this being now written into Players' Association contracts with teams, two teams, the Kansas City Royals and the Arizona Diamondbacks, chose to exercise the option to be grandfathered in and use a member of the current team personnel who would continue in his informal translation role, in an effort not to disrupt team chemistry in players' trust in the translator speaking for them. The fact that the commissioner's office allowed teams to opt out of hiring a trained and tested translator further echoes the conventional wisdom among many in MLB that time in the US and English training at team academies in the Spanish Caribbean via Rosetta Stone software and supplemental materials is enough. Indeed, according to Royals personnel, the organization encourages its Spanish-speaking players to conduct interviews in English on their own (Torres 2017). Not only does this buttress the incomplete labor support infrastructure inherent in global capitalism, it follows a larger US political and social imperative to racialize Spanish as a language to be silenced in deference to a monolingual assimilationist stance.

Though this 2016 initiative inspired by Beltrán's advocacy does further address questions of equity and inclusion in MLB, one interpreter for several players does not come close to the escort interpreters that work with Japanese players. Special advisor to the executive director of the Players' Association Omar Minaya captures the true motivation behind the initiative, crediting Beltrán's advocacy in stating, "We felt this was something that helps the media and helps the players and it's a win for everybody. It's a player-friendly and media-friendly initiative. As someone that has been in the game so many years, this was needed, and something we wanted for a while as a group and we pushed. But the guy who started it all was Carlos Beltran" (Sanchez 2016a). Minaya mentions the media before the players, an acknowledgment of both the importance of appearance and public discourse for MLB and the need to carefully navigate a linguistically conservative dominant media sphere that remains largely English only. This emphasis on the need for MLB to support language use that caters to media and fan consumption emerges most strongly in reactions to the use of Spanish on ESPN.

A "World" Baseball Classic in Spanish, ¡Ni Modo!, No way!: ESPN AND ESPN Deportes and the Production of Baseball Narratives

Two ESPN broadcasts further illustrate the tensions over language that surround US politics and the ubiquitous presence of Latin/o Americans in MLB. On March 10, 2013, ESPN broadcast the World Baseball Classic game between the Dominican Republic and Puerto Rico in Spanish on its flagship network. The World Baseball Classic is a round robin–style competition designed to increase interest in the game at a worldwide level. Given its popularity in the Spanish-speaking Caribbean, Caribbean countries have performed well in the WBC's short history, with the Dominican Republic having won in 2013 and Puerto Rico making it to the final game in 2017. ESPN elected to broadcast the game in Spanish on both its flagship network and ESPN Deportes because the MLB Network owned exclusive broadcast rights to the English language broadcast. A *Deadspin* post by Timothy Burke with a headline reading, "'Is It Me or Has ESPN Been Taken over by Wetbacks?' Viewers React to Tonight's WBC ESPN Deportes Simulcast," captures the vitriol and anti-Spanish-language reaction of the network's viewers (Burke 2013a). Despite the fact that the game was between two Caribbean opponents, one (Puerto Rico) a US territory, several fans angrily demanded to know why ESPN was broadcasting in "Mexican," and asking, as the headline indicates, had ESPN been taken over by "wetbacks"? (Burke 2013a).

Consistent with previous discussion of language, politics, and race throughout this chapter, this anti-Mexican sentiment extends beyond issues of baseball and broadcasting to the pervasive monolingual ideology that has operated in the US since its early days of national formation, when fears of the spread of other languages, such as German, permeated congressional debates (Perea 1998). In the current political moment, the Spanish language and Mexicans have become symbols for anti-immigration and racist propaganda. The issue of the perception of Spanish as a particularly problematic language emerges in one tweeter's reaction to the broadcast: "Effin mexican bullshit on ESPN. .spreken z English please" (Burke 2013a). This sentiment positions German ("spreken z") above Spanish in the racial and linguistic hierarchy of the US as a language associated with whiteness. The vast majority of the quoted tweets in Burke's post position "English" and "America" in opposition to "Mexican" and to a lesser extent "Spanish" in their content. Having purchased exclusive rights to the English language broadcast, MLB and its television network forced ESPN to make a calculated business decision that many interpreted as un-American, thus placing baseball and media at the center of debates around language and US identity, as a manifestation of Leo Chávez's Latino threat narrative. According to Chávez (2013), dominant images of Latino/as in mainstream English media and politics cast them as (im)migrants who refuse to learn English and assimilate to white "American" culture, constructing the core of a media, political, and social anti-Latina/o campaign.

Burke also covered a second ESPN broadcast that once again ignited the anger of fans when on July 15, 2013, Pedro Gómez conducted a bilingual interview with Cuban players Yoenis Céspedes and Aroldis Chapman (Burke 2013b). As with the broadcast of the World Baseball Classic, comments equated US nationalism with speaking English, and stated that English is the official language of the US, though no law currently denominates it as such. Thirty-one states have passed laws declaring English as their official language. A debate over the meaning of "America," namely the US-centric expulsion of the rest of the continent from the name *America* versus a more inclusive and hemispheric definition, ensued in the Twitter feed included in the article.

The Twitter debate captured in Burke's article underscores the complexities over language use and US national identity. A few tweets called into question the very construct of "America" as defined in a US-centric manner both linguistically and geographically. Much Twitter feed content tied the need for MLB players to reach a high level of English proficiency to "deserve" to be in this country, the economic privilege of MLB salaries, and the need to appear as an educated person. One tweet questioned why Chapman did not speak English, speculating that he was a child "left behind," a reference to the education reforms of George W. Bush's administration (Burke 2013b). ESPN viewers labor under the false impression that it is easy to learn a language, and thus only those who have just arrived from Spanish-speaking countries are in true need of help. One dissenter rightly pointed out that even the conversational English demanded by many tweeters is complicated for players as such English conversations appear in the media and thus expose players to high risk of scrutiny, similar to the Michael Pineda case discussed earlier. The fact that Chapman is specifically targeted for his lack of English proficiency is curious given that both he and Céspedes are Cuban-born. Perhaps some mistakenly associate Chapman with a black American identity as opposed to a Cuban ethno-racial identity, thus further exemplifying the ways that a black/white binary impedes many in the US from understanding race in nuanced and intersectional terms, in this case with respect to blackness and Spanish.

Though many signaled education, or the perception of a lack thereof, in both the players interviewed and their fellow tweeters, the core of the debate centered around the idea of privilege, both to be in the US and the economic privilege of an MLB salary—minimum salaries in MLB range in the hundreds of thousands per year—both indicators of the sustained imperialist nature of the US on a global scale. One tweeter posted the image of cartoon character Homer Simpson dressed as Uncle Sam taking a bite out of the globe, with the caption "try and stop us" under the image. Above the image was the following tweet: "That's right, foreigners—you want to come here, you'd better speak fluent English. Just like Americans do when we go to other countries" (Burke 2013b). Below the image, author Timothy Burke posted, "On another note, I'll happily join these people in calling for fluent English when *they* can prove that they're capable of speaking and writing it" (Burke 2013b). Burke's intervention captures the many shades of the debate as he calls out US cultural and linguistic imperialism, tied in this case to a strict adherence to formal grammar rules. Despite this critical intervention, many other tweeters continue to focus on economic status and a supposed respect for another country's culture in their reactions, even wondering what happens when US players play in Japan, where they are sure they at least learn some of the language (Burke 2013b). This unsubstantiated observation projects an image of multilingual acceptance that is inconsistent with current monolingual ideology in the US. It also further illustrates the extent to which the Spanish language, and Latina/o speech in general, has become what Isabel Molina-Guzmán terms "a racialized marker," as language is used to exclude Latino/as from the full privileges of US cultural, social, and institutional citizenship and belonging (Picker and Sun 2012). Thus, Spanish as a racialized marker, as evidenced by all of the examples mentioned thus far, intersects with the Latino threat narrative.

Conclusion

Returning to the case of Roberto Clemente discussed at the outset of this chapter, his experiences continue to resonate with some players' experiences and media coverage in the present, where Latin/o American players often receive the de facto message that they should learn English as quickly as possible to connect with (white) fans and media, and to belong in the US. Despite the commonly circulated narrative of MLB as a site of racial reckoning, where US society has supposedly advanced significantly toward racial equality, the lived experiences of Clemente and others illustrate the ways that narrative rings hollow. In addition to the black/white color line, MLB has had a stake in the language line in the US, where English only has been the white nationalist ideological norm, with Spanish as its racialized opposite. MLB itself has yet to fully come to terms with its position as linguistic ambassador via its robust Spanish-speaking labor force. Indeed, though MLB promotions and narratives often highlight the breaking of the color line, they present race and ethnic relations in black and white, leaving aside the extent to which a significant portion of its Latin/o American players not only challenge, but do not identify within that racial binary. MLB, along with media coverage of its players, further spreads the racial and linguistic ideologies of the US.

Both MLB and media producers and consumers live in and are aware of a changing demographic, political, and social landscape. As institutions and as individuals, all of the above struggle with their own social position as well as those of others in terms of race and language. As has been seen throughout this chapter, MLB and media production around it have functioned as terrain on which to reiterate and contest the language(s) by which we communicate in public. While for many monolingual viewers, the broadcast in Spanish of a WBC game between two Caribbean opponents flies in the face of all things "American," for others, like Ozzie Guillén and Carlos Beltrán, MLB needs to adapt to the linguistic realities of a group of players from whose talent it most strongly benefits, and as such can and should promote Latin/o American culture, including the Spanish language. For its part, MLB occupies a market-driven in-between space in that it can neither engage fully with the monolingual rhetoric undergirded by white supremacist discourse nor fully embrace the culture and bilingualism of roughly one-third of its labor force. Only under pressure from players and managers like Guillén and Beltrán did MLB institute more robust Spanish language support and the language- and identity-based #PonleAcento campaign. It is perhaps through humor that we see the most nuanced, if also problematic, undertaking of Spanish and MLB. From the 1970s Dominican caricature of Chico Escuela to the recent depiction of retired Dominican designated hitter David "Big Papi" Ortiz, played by Kenan Thompson, *Saturday Night Live* has held an exaggerated mirror to hegemonic US society with regard to Spanish. While the exaggerated pronunciation and bilingual word play in the Escuela and Ortiz sketches amount to linguistic brownface, Ortiz's refusal to allow white "Weekend Update" host Colin Jost to speak to him in Spanish, citing a deal already in place with Tim Kaine as a white voice speaking Spanish, complicates the intersection between race and the Spanish language and commodifies it, perhaps the truest representation of the motivations behind MLB's limited embrace of Spanish. In this way, MLB reproduces a linguistic angst where policies and economies often clash around conflicting imperatives, sending the message, ¡Aquí, no se habla español!

CHAPTER 4

"You Can't Walk Off the Island"

MLB's Racialized Labor Structure and the Pressure to Produce from the Academia *to the Major Leagues*

"If you hit it, they will come, even to a dirt field in Washington Heights"
—Executive Assistant District Attorney Jack McCoy,
Law & Order, "Foul Play," 2002

THE ABOVE QUOTE from long-running crime drama *Law & Order* captures the intersection between baseball, economic success, the American dream, and race. In referencing a well-known tag line from the film *Field of Dreams* (1989), *Law & Order*'s creators locate the show's narrative within the American dream imagery associated with *Field of Dreams,* an American dream that includes hard work, respect for family, and the bucolic setting of white, rural America struggling to fight the disillusionment of economic hardship. When Jack McCoy adds the ending line, "even to a dirt field in Washington Heights," he references the desperation of poor communities of color, given that until very recently, Washington Heights in Upper Manhattan has been an almost exclusively Latina/o American community, fueled by a major influx of Dominican immigrants in the 1980s. He also suggests that communities like Washington Heights are not quite part of what white Americans would consider to be their country, instead viewing these communities as a wasteland of crime, violence, and neglect to be avoided, the type of place where options for upward mobility are severely limited, such that families rely on their sons' participation in baseball to improve their economic situation.

The show's "ripped from the headlines" storyline fictionalizes the case of Dominican Bronx Little Leaguer Danny Almonte. In August 2001, the Rolando Paulino All Stars Little League team rose to success in the Little League World Series. As the team gained success, competing teams became suspicious that the Dominican-born talent on the team were older than they claimed to be, and thus ineligible to play in the league, especially their star player, Danny Almonte, leading them to hire private investigators to look into players' birth certificates as proof of age. Based on this case, the "Foul Play" episode portrays the desperation of talented young Honduran Miguel Soto and his family, who immigrated to the US after suffering economic devastation and the death of Miguel's mother in the aftermath of Hurricane Mitch in 1998. As the episode develops, it traces the transnational trajectory of the Soto/Benítez family from Honduras to New York in search of a better life, particularly for the children. The fictional Youth Baseball League (YBL) becomes a vehicle for a white, middle-class coach to cash in on the talents of young Latin/o American young men and their families, who serve as a bottomless labor pool of young talent.

The homicide under investigation results from the accidental shooting of a private investigator hired by another team to investigate Honduran Miguel Soto's age, due to suspicions of age falsification so that Miguel can play despite being too old for the YBL. When Soto's coach learns of the investigation, he threatens Miguel's father with stripping him of his job and possible deportation if he does not threaten the private investigator at gunpoint to end the investigation. The unfolding of the investigation reveals the underlying tension between individual greed, embodied by the coach and Miguel's father, versus the virtue of the American dream, symbolized by the immigrant success story of Miguel's possible rise to MLB stardom and support of his family both in the US and in Honduras. Since this episode was written and aired in 2002, recently following the September 11 terrorist attacks, it not only fictionalized the Danny Almonte story, with one of the investigating detectives even mentioning his name, but also reminded viewers of recent media coverage of falsified birth certificates of a group of Dominican MLB players, including Miguel Tejada, after recently passed anti-terrorism legislation revealed that some Dominican players had falsified their ages to be younger so that they could increase their chances of a major league career. The addition of the anti-terrorism discourse likened a young man's age falsification to the violence and destruction of the events of September 11, 2001, and reified long-held perceptions of men of color as threatening the security of the US. As Adrian Burgos and Frank Guridy (2010) argue with respect to the Almonte case, "Suspicions of Danny Almonte and the Rolando Paulino All Stars [Almonte's Little League team] were always about more than the on-field success of young boys; it reiterated suburban fears about urban (barrio) residents, as it projected the racialized suspicions and tensions about national belonging among adults onto the boys" (83). The question of national belonging becomes particularly prescient when we consider MLB scouting practices, which seek a significant portion of talent, especially among men of color, outside the US. This reality has led to criticism and accusations of racism embedded in the recruitment structure of MLB and its constituent clubs from both black Americans who feel that MLB imports its diversity under the assumption that nondomestic black men will be more docile players, as well as nativist white Americans who map anti-black, anti-immigrant, and anti-Spanish ideologies onto the bodies of black Latin American players.

The depiction of the Youth Baseball League and its international recruitment practices as a proxy for MLB in "Foul Play" encompasses much of the debate over recruitment, diversity, and labor within the structure of MLB, given the organization's ubiquitous presence in the Dominican Republic and Venezuela as leading sites for MLB to recruit young men of color for its labor force at the pre-professional and minor league levels via the presence of a complex baseball academy training infrastructure. At present, all thirty major league teams have academies, or *academias,* in the Dominican Republic, where a significant transnational labor stream continues to flow. Not only does *Law & Order* address the transnational labor flow of MLB, but it also gestures to the Othering of Latino players from urban centers in the US, such as Washington Heights, which have been marked as dangerous places by many scouts, leading to diminished scouting of black and Latino players. In fact, one scout spoke candidly about his reticence to scout retired outfielder Manny Ramírez in Washington Heights in the late 1980s due to the presence of crime in the neighborhood, despite Ramírez's exceptional hitting abilities and his being named All City Athlete for New York City: "Scouts prefer the landscape of suburbs and rural America, where they can dine at Cracker Barrels and IHOPs, to poor urban neighborhoods. In fact, they would rather go to the Dominican Republic, where it's easier to get around. It puts urban athletes at a distinct disadvantage" (Rhodes and Boburg 2011, 105). This depiction mirrors the critiques of many that MLB imports its diversity and does not dedicate sufficient resources to domestic communities of color. These strands of transnational labor flows, immigrant pursuit of the American dream, and the Othering, if not invisibility, of domestic black men and Latinos in MLB frame a wider ongoing discussion of how MLB policies and practices engage race. With this in mind, it is important to interrogate MLB labor recruitment and race from both the US perspective mentioned above, and the perspective of the Spanish Caribbean, where young men and their families see MLB as a viable option to improve their families' economic situation.

"You can't walk off the island" is a common phrase that circulates among baseball personnel to describe the aggression and style of play associated with many players of Caribbean descent. Indeed, when profiling players and analyzing their hitting and fielding styles, announcers will often note that Latin American players are "too aggressive," "impatient," and "don't take enough pitches" in the batter's box and are thus overly susceptible to striking out, having swung at pitches outside the strike zone. Similarly, the fielding of such players is also characterized as overly flashy or showy and reckless compared to the "smart" play of many players trained entirely in the US. The rationale provided by announcers is that players who come from the Caribbean *academia* system have had to develop a more aggressive and flashy playing style to get noticed and scouted by MLB personnel in their home countries. If a young player shows too much patience and takes too many pitches during an at-bat, perhaps scouts will not notice him: "You can't walk off the island." Much has been made of "playing the right way" and using "smart aggression" over the last few decades. For Latin/o American players, there is a lot at stake in the characterization of their playing style and perceived talent level. They must carefully navigate this dynamic as, should they play too aggressively, they run the risk of being considered too wild, and not smart players, while showing the more measured aggression associated with patient players might lead to the impression that they are lazy, due to racially based perceptions of Latin/o American men.[1] Additionally, readings and characterizations of Latin/o American MLB players must be understood within the context of labor dynamics related to Chávez's Latino threat narrative, which consists of the assertions that not only are Latina/os disloyal to the US and either refuse to learn English or continue to speak Spanish as an act of anti-nationalist defiance, but they are a threat to supposedly home-grown "American" labor.

Through the discussion of a group of MLB initiatives and media texts related to recruiting men of color, this chapter explores the ways that Latin/o American labor is sought after, packaged, and consumed through the MLB system, taking into account MLB's public stance of corporate social responsibility. These case studies span the journey from youth talent to arrival to MLB. Starting with the *academia* system in the Dominican Republic and the baseball-as-American-dream narrative for participants in MLB's Caribbean baseball academies, I establish the contours of race, recruitment, and immigration at the core of MLB's Latin/o American narrative. From there, I turn to the Dominican Development Alliance (DDA), a transnational initiative embedded in MLB's labor force recruitment, designed to diversify MLB and create positive impacts in economically challenged communities. I then analyze documentary and film productions depicting *academias* as texts that pub-

---

1. I discuss racially based stereotypes and perceptions for Latin/o American men in the next chapter.

licly engage the MLB labor debate with critics and audiences. Finally, the story of Cuban-born Yasiel Puig's controversial journey to the major leagues reveals the politics and costs of arrival to MLB. Though salaries are much higher and issues of immigrant documentation are less pressing in the MLB context, this chapter argues that there are striking parallels between constructions of MLB hopefuls and players and Latin/o American and Caribbean (immigrant) men at large in terms of perceptions of threat to US national identity in a nativist moment, and exploitation at the hands of global labor economies.

Pelotero Labor: Race, Exploitation, and Corporate Social Responsibility in MLB

MLB's labor practices share some common ground with the exploitive labor practices, rooted in globalization and capitalism, that are imposed on immigrants, particularly undocumented immigrants in the US. This exploitation emerges within the context of economic shifts in major cities in the 1970s and 1980s that drastically altered the labor force as blue-collar jobs left major US cities and the US in general. As a result of this, Latino men found themselves pushed toward the informal economy as casual laborers in largely unregulated sectors of the economy (H. Ramírez and Flores 2013, 33). In his "Latino threat" construct, Chávez (2013) argues that these economic conditions facilitated the mapping of foreignness and threat onto Latino men's bodies as a result of white Americans' real or perceived economic precarity. This would also lead to media and popular constructions of Latinos within a threat-based context as hardworking but invisible labor, as garden maintenance workers in wealthy private homes, "jardinero masculinity" (H. Ramírez and Flores 2013, 34), or alternatively, via images of urban violence and national threat as gangbangers or terrorists (Noguera et al. 2011). This labor and media trajectory shapes MLB recruitment practices as a multinational corporation practicing global capitalism in the Spanish Caribbean from the 1970s to the present.

With a waning recruitment pipeline in the US, MLB has followed the pattern of most multinational corporate giants, namely a search for the cheapest and steadiest stream of labor possible, which it found in the Spanish Caribbean, especially the Dominican Republic and Venezuela. Baseball scholars refer to this as the "boatload mentality," meaning that if MLB recruits a large quantity of promising young players, at least a few will pay off at the major league level (Bruns 2015; Klein 1991, 2006, 2014; Marcano Guevara and Fidler 2002; Ruck 1998, 2011). This has led to the development of a robust academy training structure in the Dominican Republic due to not only the ability to recruit players more cheaply but also the cheaper cost of operations in general. As such, similar to the exploitation of undocumented immigrants in the US, the presence of MLB in the Dominican Republic, and the Spanish Caribbean more widely, functions on the twin pillars of, first, a vulnerable and largely unprotected population, as more than half of the Dominican Republic's population lives in poverty, and second, cheap transnational facilities, since start-up costs are significantly cheaper there. In discussing the formation of the first large *academia* in Las Palmas in the early 1980s, Ralph Ávila states, "If you realize that we spent approximately $400,000 for the land, the construction of the entire camp, baseball fields, leveling the hill, equipment, the bus, you see how far money goes and what a good deal it was for the Dodgers. Imagine what that would cost in the United States!" (Ruck 2011, 169). Competition from MLB's continued quest for cheap labor has decimated Dominican baseball operations, as the money available from MLB from the recruitment and training stages all the way up to the major league level leads talented young men away from the Dominican baseball establishment. Felipe Alou's description of the rules governing winter league play since the 1950s, which limit players' participation further, illustrate MLB control over the game (Alou and Kerasotis 2018, 131). Rob Ruck (1998) cites the decline of participation in winter ball as an example, as players who make a great deal of money in the US have no incentive to participate in winter ball during the MLB off-season (190). Juan Marichal, retired Dominican MLB star and member of the Ministry of Sports in the Dominican Republic, succinctly locates the problem and the solution in capital: "They [MLB] should pay subsidies. It's the only way Dominican baseball can survive" (Ruck 1998, 190). This labor context, in conjunction with both a waning population and limited recruitment efforts among domestic players of color, especially black Americans, continues to shape MLB demographics. It is important to note that MLB's Reviving Baseball in Inner Cities (RBI) program, founded in 1989, is a direct effort to recruit in black American communities, with 41 percent black American players in the program in 2012 (Kihl and Tainsky 2013, 187). The program is now international, including teams in the Dominican Republic. The loose structure and inconsistent implementation of RBI have made it difficult to assess the program's effectiveness (Kihl and Tainsky 2013, 191–95).

From the 1970s to the present, MLB's numbers of Latin/o American and African American players have roughly flip-flopped. As MLB recruitment has expanded into the Spanish Caribbean and Asia Pacific Rim, recruitment in African American and US Latina/o communities has diminished. There are various reasons for this, including the rise in popularity of basketball and football in the US in general, as well as in black American communities, and the argument, made by scholars such as Todd Boyd, that basketball is more suited to urban environments than baseball in terms of space and pace of the game. Some players, most famously Torii Hunter, have argued that MLB imports its diversity via Afro-descent Caribbean players so as to not have to deal with African American players and communities.

Indeed, the labor recruitment and scouting of young talent in the US and abroad mirrors the history of racism in the US in general; MLB's goal to selectively reach out to communities of color engages the subtle and overt ways that race continues to operate in MLB as a social and economic institution. Additionally, recently, stories of MLB's exploitive labor practices in the Dominican Republic and Venezuela, particularly the well-documented case of Venezuelan Alexis Quiroz, who suffered a career-ending injury compounded by lack of adequate medical care as a recruit in the Cubs' organization, have compelled MLB to establish more socially responsible corporate practices. Two major interventions that demonstrate the historical and current tensions between race and social responsibility in MLB scouting and player development are the *academias* sponsored by MLB and its teams, and the Dominican Development Alliance (DDA). I explore this tension via a discussion of these programs couched within the growing literature on sport and corporate social responsibility.

The negative press brought to bear on MLB as a result of accusations of predatory scouting and labor practices raises a number of questions: To what extent does MLB simply search out and exploit the bodies and talents of Latin American men living in countries economically subordinated to the US? What is MLB's responsibility as a lucrative multinational corporation? What, if anything, is MLB doing to address criticisms of its racialized scouting and player development procedures? The answers to these questions is that MLB is, and has been, involved in practices in line with what has been termed "corporate social responsibility" (CSR) to a limited extent. Kathy Babiak and Richard Wolfe (2013) define corporate social responsibility as "an ethical ideology or theory that an entity, an organization or individual, has an obligation to act in a manner that contributes to and benefits society at large" (17). With regard to corporations, McWilliams and Siegel (2001) define CSR as a set of actions that are intended to further some social good, beyond the pecuniary interests of the firm, and that are not required by law. Of particular relevance to the current study, scholars argue that the capacity to improve reputation, brand recognition, and morale motivate corporations to act in socially responsible ways (Babiak and Wolfe 2013; Kihl and Tainsky 2013). Babiak and Wolfe (2013) have developed a specific set of pillars to reflect how CSR operates in sports. They argue that the specific context of sports, given the ways that passion, economics, transparency, and stakeholder management intersect, calls for a specific set of pillars to understand the increasing CSR interventions of sports corporations such as MLB. They identify the following six pillars: Labor relations, environmental management and sustainability, community relations, philanthropy, diversity and equity, and corporate governance (21–22). Labor relations, community relations, and diversity and equity inform our exploration of the above questions regarding MLB's presence and scouting and player development practices in Latin America. *Labor relations* refers to business practices and employee treatment that take into account the welfare of and practices that express the value of employees. *Community involvement* in turn extends the concern for individuals' welfare to the community level, where the firm seeks to work with the community to intervene in problems faced by that community and seeks the community's input in the firm's presence and activities and fosters partnerships with the community. At the macro-social level, *diversity and equity* involves creating a fair and equitable workplace, one that reflects the human diversity of the society in which it operates and establishes a climate that equally respects the views, experiences, and perspectives of all of its members (Babiak and Wolfe 2013, 22–27). The three pillars defined here serve as a needed context to understand the ways that MLB intervenes in local and global contexts in its scouting and player development initiatives with an eye to growing the game of baseball in a socially responsible way, initiatives that do not always attain the goals of corporate social responsibility.

Babiak and Wolfe (2013) contend that MLB has made significant inroads with respect to diversity and equity initiatives: "MLB has introduced a number of diversity initiatives including the Inaugural Civil Rights Game which was first played in Memphis on March 31, 2007. MLB's efforts rest on Jackie Robinson's vision to increase the percentage of African-American players as well as coaches and front office personnel" (27). Though true, this description of MLB's CSR efforts ignores MLB's transnational and Latin American–focused programming, which operates somewhat in tension with Robinson's vision as it privileges Latin American players, some of whom are of African descent. At the ground level, MLB has implemented two corporate community involvement (CCI) programs as part of its commitment to CSR, the Dominican Development Alliance and Reviving Baseball in Inner Cities. Lisa A. Kihl and Scott Tainsky (2013) define corporate community involvement programs as initiatives that address vital social problems in a given community using strategies that align with the core competencies and long-term strategies of the corporation, in the case of MLB using baseball and softball to improve educational opportunities and teach life skills that foster economic improvement in poor communities (185). As we shall see, DDA engages CSR pillars of labor relations, community relations, and diversity and equity in complicated ways that reveal tensions around race, class, and equity within MLB's inter- and transnational presence.

In its implementation of CSR and CCI programs, including *academias* and the DDA, does MLB act in a socially responsible way? This question guides the remainder of the analysis here. As we shall see in the discussion of *academias* and the DDA, the answer is yes and no. The nuanced understanding of how CSR intersects with labor recruitment and retention of men of color for MLB shows that efforts are unevenly successful, and must always be understood within MLB's desire to retain a positive corporate image and grow its brand, one linked to US American nationalism and also to its history as a major actor in the desegregation of US society with the debut of Jackie Robinson in 1947. As such, a final element to the framework to understand MLB labor interventions in communities of color is the question of CSR in sport and corporate misconduct. According to Roger Levermore (2013), professional sports organizations like MLB use CSR practices largely as a "fig leaf" that often fails to cover structural inequalities and power differentials that structure relations between the corporation and communities with which it works (52). Furthermore, some corporations engage in "greenwashing, whereby business largely uses CSR in an attempt to distract stakeholders (particularly the media and consumers) from its irresponsible actions" (Kallio 2007, 165). The following discussion will reveal how MLB interventions straddle the positive aspects of aligning competencies in terms of baseball training and economic contributions with the need for economic growth and life skills training in impoverished communities, and the negative aspects of corporate exploitation, with sometimes ethically questionable practices in Caribbean scouting and player development, embedded in the grossly unequal power relations that favor MLB economically and politically in the international context.

"It's Different Here Than Down There": *Academias* and Recruitment in the Dominican Republic and Venezuela

Though Latin American players have been a part of MLB almost since its inception, the major shift that has grown that population, especially players from the Caribbean, particularly the Dominican Republic and Venezuela, is the development of a sophisticated recruitment structure termed *academias*. Though a handful of teams had established *academias* in the Caribbean since at least the 1950s, the current system developed largely as a result of the Summer League of Baseball, started by a group of players and investors, including

Felipe Alou, with the goal of developing young players holistically (Alou and Kerasotis 2018, 197–99). The Toronto Blue Jays' and the Los Angeles Dodgers' front offices subsequently decided to enhance their recruitment in the Dominican Republic. From 1965 into the 1970s, Epy Guerrero worked with Pat Gillick, first in his role as director of scouting for the Houston Astros and later as vice president of baseball operations for the Blue Jays, to develop his ideas around scouting and recruitment in the Dominican Republic. In the late 1970s, Guerrero bought a modest plot of land, including a house in Villa Mella, and established the first *academia* (Bruns 2015, 105). By the late 1970s, the Dominican Republic had become a key site of baseball talent, along with Puerto Rico and Cuba. Dodgers president Peter O'Malley and general manager Al Campanis charged Cuban Ralph Avila, a Dodgers scout for the Caribbean and Florida regions, with developing the club's first *academia* along with Guerrero, a scout for the Toronto Blue Jays (Klein 1991, 98–105). Part of the impetus for Avila's interest in aggressively scouting in the Dominican Republic comes from the way that eugenics intersects with race among baseball recruitment personnel, following a long-held conventional wisdom that men of color are better "natural athletes" than white men. According to Alan Klein (1991), "baseball men" associate certain body types and temperaments with racial and ethnic identities that they deem most well suited for success. For example, pitchers should be tall and lanky, with long limbs. Klein notes the conventional baseball wisdom that Mexicans make the best pitchers because their Native American heritage affords them an increased level of concentration. Avila, for his part, felt that Dominicans were good baseball players because of the Spanish and African descent mixture they embody, a mixture that he felt made them stronger and more skilled athletes (Klein 1991, 98–99). In 1981, he started the Dodgers academy at Las Palmas (Klein 1991, 101). Over time, other teams have seen the benefits of a cheap and seemingly endless labor stream in the Dominican Republic, and currently all MLB teams have *academias* and a significant scouting and recruitment presence in the Dominican Republic and the Caribbean more broadly, especially Venezuela.

Due to political relations between the US and Caribbean nations, namely the embargo with Cuba, and the incorporation of Puerto Rico in the MLB draft in 1989, Venezuela has emerged as a second major source of baseball talent in the Caribbean Basin. It is important to note that Curacao is also a consistent and growing source of baseball talent but has yet to reach the saturation of the Dominican Republic and Venezuela.[2] If Ralph Avila built the *academia* infrastructure and put the Dominican Republic on MLB's labor

---

2. Curacao, a Dutch island in the Caribbean, has a well-established relationship with both Little League and MLB baseball. Many Curacoans play for the Netherlands team in the World Baseball Classic and enjoy a significant and growing presence at the major league level, most

recruitment map, Andrés Reiner did the same for Venezuela. Working under the auspices of the Houston Astros, Reiner opened the Astros academy in 1989. Andrés Riener, himself an immigrant in Venezuela, having been born in Hungary in 1935 and emigrating with his family in 1946 in an effort to flee the Communist government there, used his knowledge of the Venezuelan economy and immigration hardship to craft his vision of an *academia* in Venezuela. Reiner understood that severe fluctuations and an eventual downward spiral in the Venezuelan economy starting in the late 1970s, and the subsequent devaluation of the Venezuelan Bolívar (the country's currency), created a receptive environment where families encouraged their sons to play baseball as an economic opportunity, following in the footsteps of a handful of Venezuelan stars such as Tony Armas, Bo Díaz, Ozzie Guillén, and Andrés Galaraga (Jamail 2008, 10–11).

In August 1989, Reiner formed La academia de béisbol de los Astros de Houston. Expanding the pillar of his low-cost recruitment model and streamlining the scouting and development process, Reiner explains his view that in the Latin American context, MLB must change its business plan of obtaining quality through quantity from within a large minor league system by combining scouting with development via the *academia* system, which gives MLB staff a chance to see players over more time than scouts typically do before signing them to a contract. This is in contrast to the model proposed by Billy Beane in Oakland, which emphasizes statistical analysis of collegiate prospects as the most effective scouting tool. Reiner strongly believes that the combination of scouting and development through *academias* streamlines the development process as it achieves the goal of converting raw material efficiently and at a low cost into the final product, major league players (Jamail 2008, 52–53). According to Reiner, it is a mistake to think "that money spent on scouting and development is an expense, when in reality it is the best capital investment possible in the baseball industry" (Jamail 2008, 53). US immigration and visa policy also disfavored sending large numbers of players to the US as, prior to 2007, minor league players were classified as "temporary seasonal workers" as their visa status. A new legislative bill signed into law by President Bush adjusted their status to "internationally recognized athletes," thus allowing MLB to bring in as many foreign-born minor league players as necessary (Jamail 2008, 160).

Over time, Reiner convinced Astros front office personnel that his model works. As noted by David Rawnsley, assistant scouting director and director of international development for the Houston Astros, "The academy weeds

---

notably retired outfielder Andruw Jones. There are currently sixteen players from Curacao in the MLB system.

out players. The important part of the selection process is not so much the player you bring into the academy but the player who graduates" (Jamail 2008, 60). Indeed, often when describing the biographies and histories of individual Latin American players at the major league level, announcers state that scouting there is all projection and development since most players do not come from a college baseball system, as is usually the case in the US. They talk about the intangibles related to character in addition to athletic talent that frequently make the difference in Latin American players' success.

Macro-level politics and nationality also play a role in establishing and sustaining *academias* in Venezuela. As of the 1990s, twenty-three major league teams had established facilities in Venezuela as recruitment stepped up there, due to the efforts of Reiner and other baseball personnel. More recently, however, due to political and economic tensions between the US and Venezuela, teams are withdrawing from Venezuela. Also, the worsening economic situation in Venezuela has led to safety concerns related to the high crime rate there, and food shortages such that teams cannot access sufficient food to feed their players. MLB teams now send their promising prospects to established *academias* in the Dominican Republic, a common practice in the 1980s and 1990s, before teams had established a presence in Venezuela, a topic to which we shall now turn via the case of Alexis Quiroz and questions of corporate social responsibility.

While *academias* do present certain benefits with regard to the possibility of a Major League Baseball career and make good business sense because [they] help engender the development of athletes in fertile environments (Klein 2009) as well as cultivating the growth in national pride that comes with MLB stardom, it is important to note that there is also a predatory side of the story that flies in the face of sport and corporate social responsibility described earlier. A case in point is that of Alexis Quiroz, who began training with the Chicago Cubs organization in August of 1994. *Stealing Lives: The Globalization of Baseball and the Tragic Story of Alexis Quiroz* (Marcano Guevara and Fidler 2002) chronicles Quiroz's story as an example of the ways that corporate greed and misconduct shape the lives of some *academia* prospects who do not make it to the major leagues. The obviously imperialist philosophy of scouting for cheap labor in economically troubled countries like the Dominican Republic and Venezuela has repercussions for young men's lives and bodies, as well as for MLB's image as an international corporation.

Though the story of Alexis Quiroz is that of one individual, it does illustrate deep problems with transparency and infrastructure that extend beyond an isolated case. Quiroz's story illustrates the problematic side of CSR, especially in terms of willful lack of transparency and exploitation of power differentials related to economics and language proficiency. Quiroz's experiences with scouting and eventually signing with the Chicago Cubs illustrate exploitation and a severe lack of transparency. Infractions on the part of the Cubs include not honoring contract terms, offering substandard living and training conditions, and providing improperly trained personnel, all of which contributed to Quiroz's career-ending shoulder injury. At the time of his scouting in the 1990s, no organization or governing body closely regulated *academias* or MLB personnel working in Venezuela and the Dominican Republic, allowing individual corruption to flourish. Statements by front office personnel Scott Nelson and David Wilder and director of Latin American scouting Oneri Fleita reveal the depth of unregulated abuses and treatment of the Dominican Republic as a wild, Third World space. According to Nelson, Major League Baseball did not have any written standards for academies in the Dominican Republic in the 1990s that the commissioner's office applied or checked on: "Standards are different in the Dominican Republic. I don't know what the DR standards are. I live in Chicago; it's different here than down there" (Marcano Guevara and Fidler 2002, 165). When confronted by the Quiroz family regarding the Cubs' treatment of Alexis, Fleita responded, "That's just your story" (Marcano Guevara and Fidler 2002, 128). Finally, in speaking of the Cubs' Dominican facility, Wilder states, "It's a Third World country, and that's the way [the Cubs] treated it" (Marx 2003). These statements crystalize a broader lack of corporate social responsibility among some MLB teams in Latin America in the late twentieth and early twenty-first centuries, visited on young male bodies of color.

Though Alexis Quiroz did not receive the settlement he believed he deserved, he did help to shed more light on a largely unknown issue with respect to MLB and corporate social responsibility. The case of Alexis Quiroz also calls to mind the international dimension of corporate social responsibility, and how that might differ from the US context. CSR measures sometimes do harm in the international context. According to Utting (2004), though CSR may provide some help in dealing with the worst symptoms of underdevelopment, it may also be used to deflect criticism of corporations, reduce the demand for external regulation, and undermine the position of trade unions. The above case study of Alexis Quiroz and the Chicago Cubs illustrates an attitude that MLB is not obligated as an organization to implement the same standards and practices in the Caribbean that it does in the US when it comes to best practices in scouting and player development. It would seem that from the perspective of MLB, the young men who are lucky enough and work hard enough should accept whatever infrastructure, or lack thereof, that MLB provides in what are, according to Wilder, "Third World" countries. The weak regulation of MLB and its economic relationship with the Dominican Republic exacerbates the possibility of exploitation of labor there. All of these points support Uttings's argument about the problematic side of international CSR. Furthermore, reactions to MLB's history of labor abuses against Latin American children undergird the sustainability of MLB's practices in Latin America. In their research, Marcano Guevara and Fidler (2002) document two predominant reactions to stories like that of Alexis Quiroz: "Disbelief syndrome," meaning that people unfamiliar with the situation simply don't believe that MLB would engage in such abuses, and the "opportunity thesis," where those with more knowledge of the situation acknowledge that there have been problems but assert that MLB is working to resolve them, and that even harsh conditions provide young men in Latin America a chance at a successful future that they could not attain any other way (49). This history provides an important context to understand MLB's chief international CSR initiatives, the DDA and MLB en la Comunidad, initiatives that strive to both diversify the population of MLB players and provide supportive intervention in communities where there is economic need. The following discussion looks at these programs from within the context of the history of the *academia* system and CSR theory outlined above.

MLB and Social Responsibility: The Major League Baseball Dominican Development Alliance and MLB en la Comunidad

In May 2009, myriad reports of age and identity falsifications, kickbacks, rampant use of performance-enhancing substances, and deplorable conditions in many *academias* led then commissioner Bud Selig to commission the Alderson Report, a study conducted by former MLB executive vice president for baseball operations Sandy Alderson in the Dominican Republic. Alderson recommended addressing the above issues through education programs, increased MLB oversight, and working with the Dominican government to hold unscrupulous actors such as *buscones* (scouts) responsible for the proliferation of corruption in the Dominican system (Bruns 2015, 162). Alderson's recommendations sought to develop a more robust infrastructure and checks and balances to ensure that teams know as much as possible about players' backgrounds before they enter *academias*. Further, once players are working with an MLB team, the organization would provide players with the tools to be successful at the major league level but also beyond the baseball field through educational opportunities to ameliorate the history of young men dropping out of school, washing out of the academies, and facing uncertain futures with little hopes for steady employment within the Dominican economy (Alderson 2009). MLB implemented some of Alderson's recommendations almost immediately.

In recent years, MLB has improved its interventions and facilities in the Dominican Republic, more in line with CSR best practices, particularly in the areas of infrastructure and transparency through media. MLB has accomplished this through the development of a website (MLB.com/DR), available in English and Spanish, dedicated to the history and current presence of MLB there. This site is designed "to provide the visitors with a place to learn about Major League Baseball in the Dominican Republic, its illustrious history and to showcase the efforts of MLB to improve Dominican baseball and the overall Dominican community" (MLB n.d.-a). This site is a clearinghouse for MLB to present its projects in the Dominican Republic, with a decidedly public relations spin. The following statement captures MLB's attempt to integrate corporate social responsibility into its Dominican operations:

> Social responsibility is one of the main tenets of Major League Baseball in the Dominican Republic and this commitment has helped to spur many projects that give back to a country that has produced many great players. MLB's Santo Domingo Office has made it a mission to coordinate with MLB Clubs, executives and players to implement sustainable projects and programs that impact local communities. (MLB n.d.-e)

The site also features information about MLB en la Comunidad, the DDA, and the Dominican Republic RBI, the major CSR initiatives established by MLB there. Finally, MLB's site provides information about the *academias* sponsored by all thirty MLB teams. The site includes current photos of the academies and describes the mission and infrastructure as follows:

> The Dominican Republic has been a major source of talent, as evident from the number and caliber of Dominican players on Major League Baseball rosters. As a result, each MLB Club has founded an academy for promising prospects in the Dominican Republic.
> While the primary focus remains preparing these players for professional careers, the academies, often in partnership with the MLB's central office in the Dominican Republic, have implemented education-based programs that also help prepare prospects for life after their playing careers have ended. The academies offer courses in English language, and players also participate in programs that help them adjust to life as a professional ball-player. In

addition, the Club academies encourage players to give back through Club sponsored service projects that impact their local communities.

Currently all 30 Clubs have academies in the Dominican Republic, many with state-of-the-art facilities. The academies, which often include dormitories for players and coaches, also feature playing fields, weight room and training facilities, clubhouses, classrooms and recreational areas for participating players. While many of the Clubs have erected new academies in the last several years, almost all of the Clubs have operated academy programs that date back as early as the 1980s. (MLB n.d.-b)

Note that the description emphasizes the infrastructure of MLB's Dominican office, the high caliber of the facilities, and community outreach beyond the baseball field. The inclusion of pictures highlighting the state-of-the-art facilities and engaged players also increases transparency, though as media consumers, we need to ask ourselves what, if any, images are not captured in MLB's curated presentation of its Dominican operations. These initiatives stand in sharp contrast to the early days of the unregulated *academia* system and the experiences of players like Alexis Quiroz, raising the question, to what extent has MLB improved its practices in the Dominican Republic?

Descriptions of the aforementioned initiatives begin to answer this question. From 2007 to 2010, MLB partnered with the US Agency for International Development (USAID) to develop the Major League Baseball Dominican Development Alliance, an association designed to bring together USAID, MLB, and various partner organizations to implement MLB's social responsibility and charitable initiatives. James Watson, interim director of the USAID mission in the Dominican Republic, sums up its importance: "This Alliance with Major League Baseball is the ideal channel to raise resources through baseball in order to promote community development in the Dominican Republic. This initiative is one more example of how baseball helps the underserved in the Dominican Republic" (Major League Baseball Players Association 2010). Sandy Alderson, the major league consultant overseeing sports operations in the Dominican Republic, emphasizes the connection to players' personal experiences: "The MLB-DDA is an example of MLB's commitment to improve Dominican society. Many of our players come from poor communities, and through the MLB-DDA, players, teams, and fans have the opportunity to help these communities by supporting education, health, and economic development projects" (Major League Baseball Players Association 2010). According to USAID'S website, MLB and USAID, along with a group of nonprofit organizations, officially formed the MLB-DDA in 2008. The alliance had two principal goals: To improve the quality of life in Dominican communities and to build long-term relationships with these communities. This alliance describes its approach as seeking to share and strengthen experience, technologies, methodologies, and resources (including human, in-kind, and monetary) in order to build long-term relationships with Dominican communities via cooperations between MLB teams, players, and fans. MLB-DDA was formed to provide potential donors (teams, players, agents, and fans) ways to direct their resources into sound community development activities with strong implementing partners in the Dominican Republic (USAID n.d.). Program initiatives extended beyond the baseball field to assist Dominican communities in areas such as health and education, and provide resources and support during natural disasters. MLB-DDA provided a structure to ensure that individual actors and agencies coordinated their efforts and delivered them consistently and in a professional manner. USAID ended MLB-DDA in 2010.

A more recent intervention, MLB en la Comunidad, shares MLB-DDA's goal of connecting baseball to outreach and economic assistance. It follows a similar model to DDA in seeking to integrate corporate, community, and civic partnerships to implement programs directed at Dominican youth. MLB's website describes the program as "a vehicle to impact the Dominican Republic through community outreach programs that promote positive play, education, civic pride, environmental awareness and humanitarian values" (MLB n.d.-e). These five tenets shape a host of programs, from donations of baseball equipment and clinics to strengthen young players' skills and future eligibility to play for MLB; to clean-up projects in individual communities, such as recycling programs, beautification days, beach clean-ups, and health missions; to educational initiatives, including school remodeling and university partnerships (MLB n.d.-e). MLB en la Comunidad also features Dominican Republic RBI, under the umbrella of the broader Reviving Baseball in Inner Cities program, started in the US in 1989 to recruit young urban talent in low-income areas. Since 2003, the Dominican Republic has participated in the program and has expanded to four programs located in Santo Domingo, Santiago, San Pedro de Macoris, and Villa Altagracia. These programs and tenets combine social responsibility with national pride, two areas that MLB strives to engage through its continued branding as "America's pastime," particularly as it loses ground in popularity to the NBA and NFL, and must increasingly answer to criticisms from some players and fans for being unyielding to change, in deference to tradition and racism. Questions surrounding the extent to which MLB interventions promote social responsibility and shape the lives of young men of color also emerge in cultural production via documentary and feature film.

Screening MLB in Latin/o America: Hard Work and Threat in *Rumbo a las grandes ligas / Road to the Big Leagues, Ballplayer: Pelotero,* and *Sugar*

Two documentaries, *Rumbo a las grandes ligas / Road to the Big Leagues* (Goodman 2008) and *Ballplayer: Pelotero* (Finkel, Paley, and Martin 2011), and one independent feature film, *Sugar* (Boden and Fleck 2008), introduced a broad viewing public to the labor recruitment and corporate social responsibility issues discussed in this chapter. Screened at several independent film festivals, *Rumbo a las grandes ligas* features MLB superstars David Ortiz and Vladimir Guerrero, as well as other MLB personnel in its narrative of talent, hard work, and integrity as the necessary factors to arrive at MLB. By contrast, *Ballplayer: Pelotero,* a film not authorized by MLB, narrated by actor John Leguizamo, presents a harsher image of corruption, abuse, and scrutiny of young male bodies of color as MLB pursues cheap labor in the Dominican Republic. *Sugar,* which received broader distribution than the documentaries, narrows the narrative focus from the documentaries, which each focus on a small group of players, and delves deeply in the life of one player, the fictional Miguel "Sugar" Santos, an aspiring pitcher moving through the MLB system. The narratives, as well as critical and fan reception of these films, echo the multifaceted and ambivalent understandings of Latin/o American labor as it is integrated in systemic US corporate culture, as sometimes a manifestation of the myth of US meritocracy, at other times a parasitic threat to US workers as a result of neoliberal capitalism. Through the content of the films, as well as critical reviews, and fan reviews on Amazon.com and IMDb.com, I seek to broaden the understanding of how cultural production and receptions of the same make public the MLB labor debate.

Rumbo a las grandes ligas (figure 3) seeks to depict the process of becoming a major league baseball player in the Dominican Republic from young childhood through the final contract signing and portrays the rise of MLB stars as an accessible dream for those with extreme talent and a strong work ethic. The documentary frames this narrative via the juxtaposition of the stellar careers of David Papi Ortiz and Vladimir Guerrero with the experiences of *academia* prospects. While the narrative does address some of the corruption within MLB operations in the Dominican Republic, especially age fraud, it casts the story of MLB as one of boundless dreams and hopes for those who are honest in their character and willing to work hard. Indeed, a great deal of the footage shows players working out in *academias* and elsewhere, pushing and disciplining their bodies to their physical limits. A consistent message of hard work and merit emerges from the visual narrative construction as well as

FEATURING MLB ALL-STARS DAVID ORTIZ AND VLADIMIR GUERRERO

ROAD TO THE BIG LEAGUES

RUMBO A LAS GRANDES LIGAS

"A must have film if you are a fan of baseball!"
-Dan Roche, CBS

FIGURE 3. *Road to the Big Leagues / Rumbo a las grandes ligas* (ELEMENT Productions, 2008)

the interview clips from players and training personnel at all levels. One *aca-demia* employee captures the level of competition and need for hard work in defining the MLB industry yield per *academia*: Five out of every one hundred players make it to the major leagues.

The lives of three baseball hopefuls, Vladimir Gómez, Juan Cabrera, and Miguel Mercedes, illustrate the trajectory of hard work and possible pitfalls of the undeserving who pursue the success that David Ortiz and Vladimir Guer-rero had already attained. At key moments in the stories of Gómez, Cabrera, and Mercedes, Ortiz and Guerrero interview clips and practice footage further emphasize the rags-to-riches story of baseball as the escape from poverty in a country with limited resources. The clips of children playing in abandoned fields and later, an organized youth league, along with Ortiz's fond recollec-tion of the poverty of his youth, cast the dream of an MLB career in a jovial and hopeful light, where the big leagues are available through dedication and work. The stories of Juan Cabrera and Miguel Mercedes as they train at *aca-demias* and try out for MLB teams complicate somewhat this idealized vision of childhood.

If Juan Cabrera stands for the road to success, Miguel Mercedes stands as a warning for those who transgress MLB rules and try to cheat the system. Cabrera's story features images of him working with coaching staff and in *academia* English classes, as a studious young man in pursuit of his baseball dream, a dream that ultimately pays off with a contract with the St. Louis Car-dinals and a signing bonus of $25,000. As Cabrera's story unfolds, it reiterates the well-known narrative of baseball as a means to help his family and provide them with a viable economic future as the result of ethical behavior and work. His trajectory ends with footage of the large home he has bought for his fam-ily, along with a large black SUV with tinted windows that he drives through his neighborhood, the ultimate material signifiers of success in the Domini-can Republic. His mother crystalizes this in stating, "He wiped my debt at 18" (Goodman 2008). At his contract signing with the Cardinals, an organization representative explains to him what it means to be a Cardinal, beyond playing excellent baseball, offering the following advice: Be careful of others who will want to take advantage of your wealth and success, represent the club well in terms of your behavior, and inspire youth that want to pursue the dream you have realized. The Cabrera success story is only part of the narrative about baseball in the Dominican Republic that the documentarians choose to tell; the other part is a cautionary tale of the consequences for ethical breaches.

Miguel Mercedes represents the corruption and desperation that lead to unethical practices among some young Dominicans and *buscones*. A player of the same caliber as Juan Cabrera, Mercedes follows a similar path of hard work and training, until MLB investigates his identity and age documents. According to one official interviewed for *Rumbo,* an MLB investigation agency is necessary in the Dominican Republic because 36 to 38 percent of documents presented to verify age and identity contain "irregularities." In the case of Mercedes, despite his insistence that he was born in 1984, MLB locates two birth certificates for him, one listing his year of birth as 1984, and a second listing it as 1981. As a result, his career comes to an abrupt end and he is cast out of MLB. Given MLB's participation in the documentary, and the juxtaposition of stars David Ortiz and Vladimir Guerrero against Juan Cabrera and Miguel Mercedes, it is important to note that while both Ortiz and Guerrero refer to the profound poverty of the Dominican Republic and affirm their commitment to give back through charitable endeavors, *Rumbo* casts Cabrera as a hero and Mercedes as a villain in the narrative of baseball. Though Mercedes did present questionable identity documents, I would argue that the narrative pays insufficient attention to the desperation that would lead one to make such a choice, instead further linking MLB to the ethic of hard work inherent in the American dream myth.

Reviewers and fans highlight the hard work and realistic portrayal of Dominican baseball in the documentary. IMDb users gave it a score of 7.5/10, though no one posted an actual review (IMDb n.d.-b). Comments posted on Amazon are mostly positive, comparing it to *Hoop Dreams,* a documentary about how basketball provides a path out of poverty for black Americans. Overall, users comment on the film as an inspiring depiction, especially given the presence of Ortiz and Guerrero as success stories, as well as a good teaching tool for students studying Spanish. Two comments capture the ways that hard work and perseverance are the keys to an MLB career. Roberto comments, "Great documentary, emotional and in many ways inspirational. Will recommend to any parent, or young baseball player. A lesson not to take things for granted, and to once again remind ourselves that hard work pays!!" (Amazon n.d.-b). Likewise, GSL states, "We've all heard about how many good ballplayers come from the Dominican. Here's an inside look at what it's like to be a kid with a chance to make it. It was very real and very interesting. The stories from Vlad Guerrero and David Ortiz were good, especially Big Papi's hilarious description of what they used in place of a ball for stickball—and how they got it. I highly recommend this film" (Amazon n.d.-b).

If *Rumbo* paints a picture of MLB success for deserving young Dominicans, *Ballplayer: Pelotero* (2011; figure 4) critiques the corruption and greed of the MLB system in the Dominican Republic and its moral and ethical repercussions. Shot in 2009 over nine months in San Pedro de Macorís, an area known as a hub of baseball talent, and featuring former player and manager

FIGURE 4. *Ballplayer: Pelotero* (Cuacua Productions, 2011)

Bobby Valentine as executive producer, *Pelotero* focuses on the stories of two prospects, Jean Carlos Batista and Miguel Angel Sanó. The film follows the players as they neared their eligible MLB signing date of the July 2 after their sixteenth birthdays. *Pelotero* closely engages questions of age falsification and how the MLB system fosters it. Jean Carlos Batista's baseball journey ends with a one-year suspension for age fraud, as an MLB investigation reveals that he is one year older than he claims to be. The repercussions of this are that his *academia* trainer Astin Jacobo loses his years of investment in Batista, and the commission on the signing bonus money that would have helped him to run his *academia,* as well as having his reputation harmed. The story of Miguel Angel Sanó more deeply interrogates MLB as a predatory and corrupt corporation. Sanó's strong and muscular black body comes under scrutiny, including a lengthy MLB investigation due to allegations that he is not sixteen, as he claims to be. The Sanó case provides a pointed critique of the intricacies of MLB corruption of Dominican labor.

As the Sanó case unfolds, the Sanó family fights MLB investigators' unrelenting attempts to prove that Sanó was not born when he said he was, including the assertion that his mother used a miscarriage to falsify his birth certificate. The extreme age vetting rises to the level of MLB demanding DNA tests and a bone scan as part of its investigation. President of the Council for Responsible Genetics Jeremy Gruber critiques this MLB practice, citing concerns that this type of testing could reveal medical information that could be used to discriminate against individuals (Bruns 2015, 142). The discourse around Sanó casts the Dominican Republic as a country of liars that MLB must hold accountable via relentless interrogations of identity documents, with Dominican institutions powerless to intervene when cases reach a level of harassment, as is the case with Sanó. When the Sanó family seeks assistance from the Dominican Baseball Commission as MLB's investigation stalls due to backlogs, thus compromising his ability to sign on the July 2 date, the commission informs him that MLB is a US monopoly and can set its own rules. The numerous tests on Sanó's body reveal that he is indeed his mother's son, but cannot pinpoint his bone age to an exact year, causing MLB to close the case with a verdict that they can neither prove nor disprove his age. The delays and eventual verdict cast a shadow of doubt on Sanó and lower his signing bonus value.

Ultimately, the narrative construction and testimonials in *Pelotero* view MLB through a lens of corruption and manipulation of the labor market, with many informants calling MLB a mafia. Sanó's agent, Rob Plummer, sums up the relationship between MLB and the Dominican Republic as follows: "I basically broker Dominican 16-year-olds to Major League Baseball teams" (Finkel, Paley, and Martin 2011). Market considerations provide the most feasible explanation for the aggression of the MLB investigation of Sanó as depicted in the film. The year 2008 saw record-high signing bonuses in the Dominican Republic, and many baseball people outside of MLB suspect that in 2009, the year that Sanó was eligible to sign, MLB wanted to drive bonuses down. That is also the theory behind the role of Pittsburgh Pirates scout Rene Gayo, who befriended the Sanó family, telling them at one point that if he signed for the relatively low amount the Pirates were offering, he could make the investigation "go away." Ultimately, the Sanó family stood their ground and Miguel Angel Sanó finally signed with the Minnesota Twins for a $3.15 million bonus, with his story culminating in images of the material comforts that he is now able to provide for his family, with Sanó stating that he has finally realized his dream to "play in the US like a man" (Finkel, Paley, and Martin 2011). The story told in *Pelotero* unmasks some of the corruption behind the depiction of meritocracy in *Rumbo a las grandes ligas,* with its indictment of MLB's predatory system eliciting responses from MLB and reviewers that engage the ethics behind a market-driven labor structure involving children.

The July 2012 release of *Ballplayer: Pelotero* sent a ripple of controversy through the commissioner's office. Then commissioner Bud Selig himself exhibited Marcano Guevara and Fidler's "disbelief syndrome," mentioned earlier, in his questioning of the veracity of the documentary. The commissioner's office strenuously objected to representations of MLB and insisted that by the film's release in 2012, many of the problems it depicted had been addressed and more reforms were on the way (Bruns 2015, 141). The filmmakers insist that they attempted to present a balanced and nuanced picture of baseball operations at the time. Director Jon Paley states, "Maybe they felt we saw something they didn't want us to see." Likewise, according to director Trevor Martin, "The system is set up so it allows [MLB] to sign large numbers of players for pennies on the dollar and export them en masse to the US to be sold. It's a form of colonization" (Bruns 2015, 141).

Reception from critics and fans includes both the meritocratic baseball-as-uplift narrative associated with *Rumbo* as well as the critique that MLB is a corrupt organization that exploits children living in poverty. The strongest indictment of MLB came from Jeff Passan of *Yahoo Sports*:

> MLB made a Faustian bargain with the Dominican Republic that it can neither clean up, nor break, the fraud too deeply rooted in the system and the player pipeline too important to its daily operations. And because it happens in a place of immense poverty, where little English is spoken and less attention paid, baseball skates by with the overwhelming majority of its fan base

unaware that the foreign country producing the largest number of major league players does so with a factory-farm mentality, its waste and runoff polluting all that surrounds it. (Passan 2012)

Amazon user salmon62 similarly states:

Having worked for a Major League ballclub as one of the front-line employees, I know very well that "MLB" is "the owners," and the owners are all about the money. The little people get abused within this system, and the Dominican players, while not under the control of MLB (there is no official MLB farm system there) clearly get manipulated here by the owners (MLB), so that the owners can keep signing costs low, or relatively low. (Amazon n.d.-a)

Both of these responses to the film highlight the lack of responsibility and oversight of MLB that have allowed it to engage in irresponsible labor practices, further permitted by the uneven power differentials embedded in the poverty of the Dominican Republic and the imperial dominance of the US articulated through the observation that the lack of English spoken in the Dominican Republic enables MLB to operate under the radar and sustain systemic inequality via cheap Dominican labor. Other Amazon reviewers acknowledge the poverty and difficulties of Dominican baseball hopefuls and the need for MLB to do better (some saying they have personal knowledge of these experiences), but read the actions of MLB less as acts of abuse and corruption, and more as a means of motivation to persevere in the face of great difficulty. As with *Rumbo,* some teachers extol *Pelotero*'s usefulness for Spanish language courses. On IMDb, reviewers gave the film a score of 7.2/10, focusing their reviews more on technical aspects of *Pelotero* within the documentary genre (IMDb n.d.-a).

Sugar (2008; figure 5) differs from the documentaries, not only in that it is a fictional narrative but also in its more transnational depiction of the MLB trajectory and the personal struggles for players as they adjust to life in the US, learning English, as well as navigating the racial and gendered social context of the rural white US as Latino men. It focuses on the experiences of one player, Miguel "Sugar" Santos, in his trajectory from the Dominican Republic to the US, as he enters the minor league system with the Kansas City Royals in Bridgetown, Iowa, and finally leaves baseball and stays in New York City to pursue a life in the US outside of professional baseball when his arm begins to fail. Santos's life and struggle to find a home and employment in New York City shift the immigrant narrative from one of possible wealth as

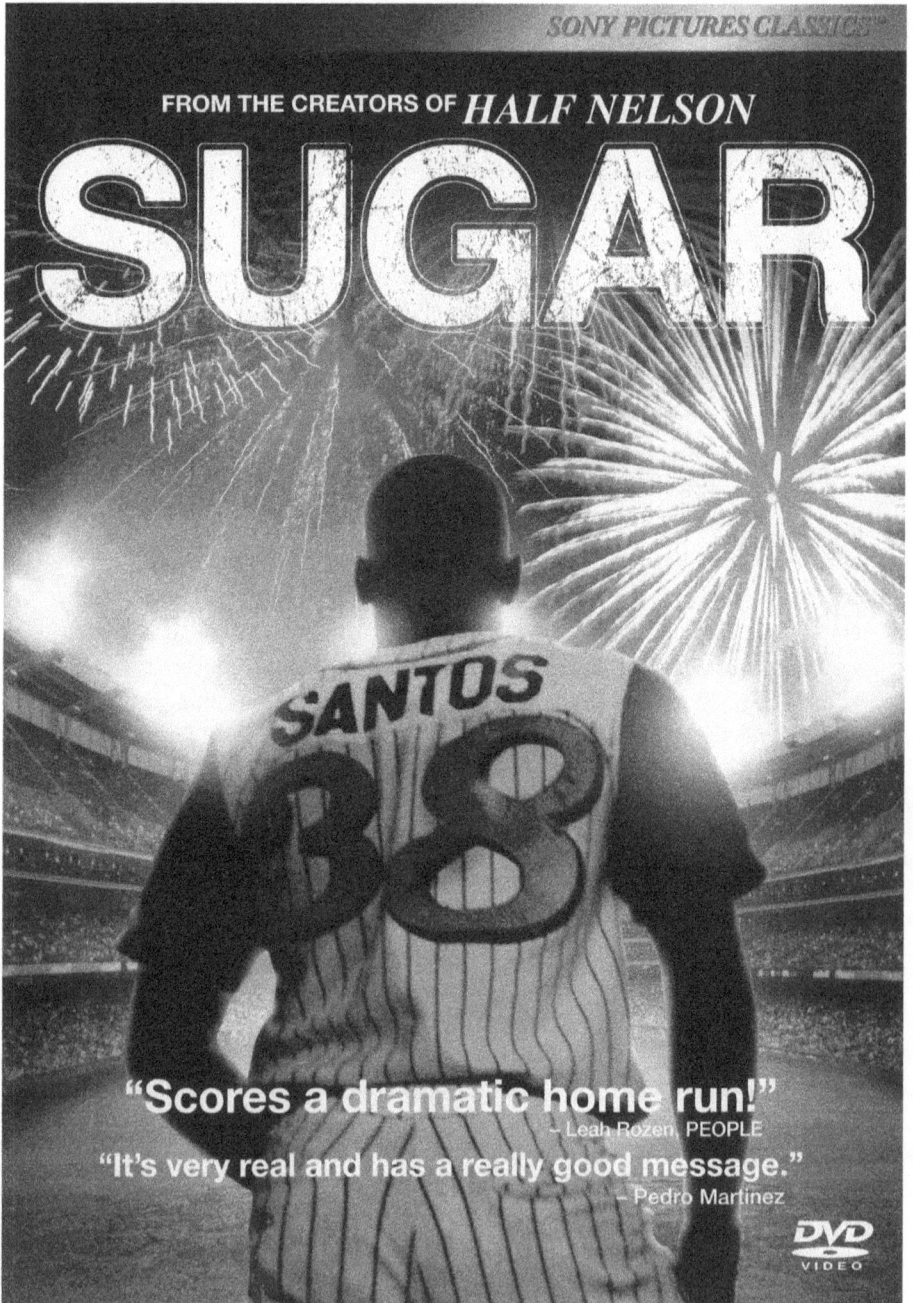

FIGURE 5. *Sugar* (Sony Pictures Classics, 2008)

an MLB hopeful to one of Latino working-class struggle as he finds work as a dishwasher in a restaurant, locates a former Iowa teammate, and integrates into the wider Latina/o working-class network of the Bronx. Indeed, the film ends with Santos and other former minor and major league players playing baseball as amateurs in New York.

As with *Rumbo*, critical and viewer receptions of *Sugar* are favorable overall, attending to the film's honest but not overtly aggressive statement on MLB's recruitment and labor practices in the Dominican Republic, and the hard work of reaching MLB. Dominican MLB stars Pedro Martínez and Robinson Canó also endorse it. User reviews on Amazon and IMDb, similar to *Rumbo* and *Pelotero*, concentrated on the hard work and challenges of pursuing an MLB career, in this case with the added dimension of the minor league experience in the rural US, with IMDb users rating it 7.2/10 (IMDb n.d.-c). Issues of race, immigration, and language emerged most strongly in viewer feedback, with one review displaying Marcano Guevara and Fidler's "disbelief syndrome" and blaming the players themselves. While most viewers acknowledge the abusive practices of MLB in the Dominican Republic, they focused more on issues of race and immigration in Santos's integration into the US. In particular, one IMDb user noted that the movie does not sufficiently address the challenges of a dark-skinned young man moving to rural Iowa (IMDb n.d.-c). Another Amazon user, Brian Maitland, connected immigration and language in his assessment of the film, which states in part:

> You watch this movie and wonder how people who have so little (the Dominicans) can have such a vibrant, interesting and fun culture yet those who live in the breadbasket of America and want for nothing live such controlled lives that seem so lost. This undercurrent of the film is not emphasised but the scenes around the billet family's table are so telling. Despite hosting numerous Latin ballplayers the billet family's Spanish is still rudimentary and, although good people, have no concept of the loneliness of the "immigrant" ballplayer or of the reality of dumping these guys in the middle of nowhere with very few English skills. (IMDb n.d.-c)

Though the first part of this review problematically casts Dominican poverty as "vibrant" and "fun," infantilizing poor Dominicans, in contrast to the economically comfortable but "lost" (read cultureless) white rural Iowans, the remainder of the review raises important points. The assertion that the billet family hosts but does not have meaningful interactions with the ballplayers living with them, especially speaking only rudimentary Spanish, exemplifies race relations in the US.

More contested responses emerge with respect to reviewers' remarks on language and its connection to identity and the film's merit. As with the two documentaries, Spanish teachers largely recommend the film for use in the classroom, with the caveat that there are a few romantic scenes that might not be appropriate. Notably, some Spanish-speaking reviewers reclaimed the use of Spanish to assert Latina/o identity. One IMDb user who identified as Dominican applauds the representation of Dominican culture in the film but critiques the fact that Santos's girlfriend does not speak Spanish as a poor Dominican would, calling into question class, language, and *dominicanidad* (IMDb n.d.-c). Likewise, one Amazon reviewer, jairo jacinto mata, posted his comments in Spanish in all caps, praising the reality of the film and its moving presentation of a Dominican minor league player adjusting to the US (Amazon n.d.-c). The fact that he posted both in Spanish and in all caps marks a strong presence, in contrast to a handful of reviewers who admonished that the film is in Spanish with subtitles and thus not worth watching.

IMDb user ldavis-2 locates the film in the "disbelief syndrome" and Latino threat narrative of Latina/os as parasitic undocumented immigrants: "Some reviewers have opined that the film is about how these poor non-white kids are exploited by rich white guys. But, as they say, it takes two to tango, and none of these kids have ever been forced to sign up for a shot at the big time. That Sugar and his fellow screw-ups decide to stay in the US after their visas expire renders the filmmakers' self-righteous screed as pointless as their little opus" (IMDb n.d.-c). Thus, the contested reception of the three filmic texts presented here further attests to the structural inequalities of MLB recruitment and ways that the public uses MLB players to form and negotiate viewpoints about race, immigration, and Latin/o American masculinity. The case of Cuban exile Yasiel Puig, and his daunting journey to play for MLB, extends this negotiation even further.

"Puigmania": Sensationalism, Excess, and the Silence of Social Responsibility in MLB

The case of Yasiel Puig further highlights the sacrifices and structural inequalities embedded in MLB recruitment in the Spanish Caribbean as they intersect with politics and international relations. As a Cuban, Puig traversed a different road to MLB since Cuban citizens must defect from the island and enter the US within a hostile political context that forces them to sever ties with family and friends in Cuba. Players who defect must either establish residency in the US, making them subject to draft rules, or establish residency in a third country and come to the US, allowing them to sign with the highest bidder, unfettered by the US draft (Bjarkman 2016; Bruns 2015, 144). Puig arrived to the US via Mexico, through a human trafficking operation organized by Miami businessman and convicted thief Raul Pacheco. Puig's journey and media coverage underscore the excesses of exploitation, corruption, bodily risk, and desperation that lead many young men to quite possibly risk their lives for the chance at an MLB career.

Despite Puig's status as a baseball prodigy, Cuban baseball officials and coaches had considered him to be a difficult player, erratic and sometimes unwilling to listen to coaches. Cuban officials suspended him from play in the 2011–2012 playing season, fueling his desire to leave the island. When intermediaries introduced Puig to Raul Pacheco, Pacheco crafted a plan to smuggle Puig to the US via Mexico, via the services of the Los Zetas drug cartel. The trip would prove harrowing and filled with details that attracted media and fan attention in their sensational detail. During the trip, the small boat carrying a group of Cubans, including Puig, ran out of gas and narrowly escaped crashing into a container ship as they awaited another boat. Once in Mexico, Los Zetas contacted Pacheco in search of the promised money for smuggling Puig, money that never came, resulting in the group holding Puig hostage in a cheap hotel for nearly a month, threatening to harm or kill him if they did not receive their money. After Pacheco sent another group to free Puig and the group traveling with him, Puig finally signed with the Dodgers after a tryout in Mexico City. Initially, Los Zetas threatened to harm Puig after he arrived in Los Angeles, causing him to pay them a cut of his signing bonus. The Dodgers hired additional security for Puig upon his arrival due to concerns over continued retaliation for Pacheco's double-cross (Bjarkman 2016, 1–30; Bruns 2015, 148–49).

An article published online on April 14, 2014, and in print in the May issue of *Los Angeles Magazine* in both English and Spanish detailed Yasiel Puig's journey to the US, sparking a heated conversation on the story's veracity as well as the political tensions, corruption, criminality, and danger captured in its content. In "Escape from Cuba: Yasiel Puig's Untold Journey to the Dodgers: The Shocking Saga of Major League Baseball's Most Controversial Player," Jesse Katz frames the story of Yasiel Puig as one of a childlike young man who exemplifies the height of exploitation of MLB labor recruitment and capitalism with a heavy dose of intrigue. The lengthy piece spans the everyday situation in Cuba for talented players like Puig to the salacious details of the smuggling of his body, to the politics surrounding the all-too-common business of trafficking Cuban players amid the diplomatic impasse between the US and Cuba. Katz raises important questions about the ethics and capitalist ideology behind the Puig story while simultaneously infantilizing him and chronicling a life of excess brought on by the sudden immersion in a capital-driven society, Puig having experienced the material limitations of life in Cuba. This tension engages common constructions of Cuba as a nation of lack, as well as well-worn perceptions of Latino men as wild and needing to be controlled.

With regard to the trafficking and selling of Puig's body, Katz draws parallels to the enslavement of Afro-descendent bodies via his worth, and the way that he arrived to the major leagues. Katz (2014) asks, "What was this gladiator-size man, with the Popeye forearms and the XXL chest, actually worth—to the people bankrolling his defection from Cuba, to the smugglers now holding him in Mexico, to the agents and scouts who would determine the US market for his talents, to the baseball team that might ultimately write the check?" References to both the large physicality of Puig's body and the market negotiations for his strength and talent recall auctions of enslaved men. The description of why Puig must defect from Cuba and endure a perilous journey further reiterates this parallel via the metaphor of the middle crossing: "Under Major League Baseball's byzantine rules and the US Treasury Department's outdated restrictions, the only way for a Cuban ballplayer to become a free agent—and score a fat contract—is to first establish residency in a third country. That detour is a fiction, winked at from all sides, and one that gives traffickers command over the middle crossing" (Katz 2014). The commodification of baseball bodies begins in Cuba and intensifies as young men get closer to the major leagues: "An elaborate underground of couriers and bagmen is forever shadowing Cuba's best ballplayers. So is a state-sponsored network of secret police and paid informants. When you are being lured and monitored at every turn, caught between ambition and duty, survival sometimes means playing both sides" (Katz 2014). The business of trafficking Cuban players via Mexico involves drug cartels as well as sports agents, resulting in the attempt to auction Puig off to a sports agent, a practice not uncommon with Latin American players. According to agent Joe Kehoskie, "Nobody's going to Cuba and bringing out a guy like Yasiel Puig, just handing him over to an agent out of the goodness of their heart" (Katz 2014). Though it is important to recognize that the trafficking of Cuban baseball players does not rise to the abuses wrought on enslaved male bodies, the buying and selling of strong, male, Afro-descent bodies for the entertainment of a largely white audience buttresses a racist labor structure, dependent on the deprivation of black men like Yasiel Puig.

Katz's characterization of Puig follows this same animalization of black male bodies, as it emphasizes his physical size and erratic personality. With regard to his character and behavior, Katz states, "He is emotional in a straight-faced game, unpredictable in a sport that glorifies routine, reticent in a town of professional image makers, and enigmatic in the eyes of the largely non-Spanish-speaking reporters who cover him—L. A.'s 'International Man of Mystery,' as the *New York Post* put it" (Katz 2014). Descriptions of Puig's interactions with other players and fans highlight a childish irrationality and the trope of the black brute: "He seemed to relish the camaraderie of his teammates, engaging pitcher Hyun-Jin Ryu in mock tae kwon do battles and feeding bananas to Juan Uribe each time the stout third baseman homered (at least until the Dodgers, sensitive to how Puig's stab at King Kong humor would be perceived, put an end to that ritual)" (Katz 2014). This portrayal of Puig culminated in the image of him in *ESPN Magazine*'s 2018 body issue featuring his dark, near-naked body, save a peanut vendor's hanging box, throwing peanuts in the air and smiling widely (figure 6).

The idea that the Dodgers needed to control Puig also surfaces in the story behind his number, 66, assigned by clubhouse manager Mitch Poole, who compares him to the Tasmanian Devil. Gatekeepers of baseball as an institution steeped in a quiet masculine respect also police Puig's behavior on and off the field, as the following assessment of his early behavior in Los Angeles indicates:

Whether it was a frivolous slide after a walk-off home run or a boys' night out at the Playboy Mansion during the all-star break, Puig had triggered something akin to a referendum on what it means to respect the national pastime. No moment symbolized the spectacle more than his Game 3 blast in the National League Championship Series against St. Louis: Having flipped his bat and trotted in triumph toward first, he suddenly realized that the ball had hit the fence and he needed to sprint—and even then he made it to third, with time for a bunny hop. "He must think that he's still playing somewhere else," an irked Carlos Beltran, the Cardinals' veteran, said after the game. (Katz 2014)

Katz mentions Puig's dedication to fans, interacting often with children and frequently autographing balls, as well as helping in the kitchen at a charitable event and Homegirls Café, a café staffed by former gang members. However, the article disproportionally highlights Puig's transgressions, be they exaggerated bodily performances on or off the field, from over-celebrating hits and home runs to driving at high speed. Katz attributes Puig's behavior to his need to adjust to life in the US, managing the excesses of the life of a professional athlete, in contrast to the deprivation of life in Cuba. While the adjustment

FIGURE 6. *ESPN* Body Issue, Yasiel Puig, 2018

to a new culture is certainly difficult, casting Cuba in antiquated traditional images, in contrast and tension with US modernity, as it intersects with the childlike and animalizing references mentioned above, reiterates problematic representations of black and Latino masculinities.

Tensions between the past and present continue to contour Yasiel Puig's life in the US. Katz describes Puig's hometown of Elipidio, a town southeast of Havana with a population of three thousand, as a small sugar-processing area whose residents have been harvesting, mashing, and extracting sugar from cane since 1873: "Slave labor helped erect the factory during colonial times; it was later nationalized, becoming an arm of the state economy" (Katz 2014). A slogan on the field where Puig played baseball as a child links baseball to Cuban nationalism: "Sports," says the hand-painted mural on the outfield fence, "has to do with the life of the country, with the future of the country, with the survival of the country!" (Katz 2014). Katz describes the 1950s-era cars and structural decay of the island that formed Yasiel Puig's upbringing and fueled his desire to leave Cuba. He creates a strong contrast between an antiquated Cuba and a modern US: "The more Puig cordoned off his past, the greater his legend grew. He had leaped overnight from the 19th century to the 21st—an experience familiar to many in L. A.'s immigrant communities— and yet he continued to insist that his only concern, his sole longing, was to help the Dodgers win" (Katz 2014). The reckoning with his past in Cuba and the precarious journey to the US and MLB most certainly contributed to the difficulties Puig experienced when he first arrived and immersed himself in the material excesses available to elite athletes. Similar to the bodily risk and physical and emotional traumas faced by many undocumented immigrants who cross the border, Puig seems to deal with his trauma by silencing his past, and focusing intentionally only on the present. When Ned Colletti spoke to him at the end of his first season, trying to orient Puig to life as an MLB star, he offered the following advice: "I want you to have a great life. You're somebody who brings a lot of joy to a lot of people. You've come to a different place in your life. I want you to think about the future. Be prepared. Be wise" (Katz 2014). Puig responded to Colletti, "Where I come from, you don't think a whole lot about tomorrow." In many ways, Puig's struggle reconciling the past, present, and future resonates with the research on undocumented immigrants who concentrate on the present moment in their physical journey, as well as during their lives in the US as noncitizens living in constant fear of deportation, unable to access the benefits of citizenship.[3] While Puig does not experience that level of hardship, similar to undocumented immigrants, he lives a life truncated from his country of birth, a place to which he may never be able to return.

Reader comments on the article highlight the truncated diplomatic relationship between the US and Cuba that requires players like Puig to risk their lives to come to the US. Within this debate among commenters, issues of masculinities of color and nativism also emerged in the discourse, some acknowledging that being a black man has probably contributed to the dangers Puig has faced along his journey. Keepingitreal5 writes, "Great article LAMAG, as a lifelong Dodger fan I'm happy to have Yasiel here in L.A, but at the same time he has brought a lot of negative attention to the team since his arrival as well as positives. I commend him and all other Cuban defectors that leave Castro's regime for a better life though and only hope he can be a good teammate and help instead of hinder the Dodger's this year and in the future" (Katz 2014).

---

3. In his research with undocumented youth, Roberto Gonzales (2015) found that precarious citizenship status leads many Latina/o immigrants in Los Angeles to focus on the present because they see the future as an uncertain and unstable, abstract concept.

This comment indexes the excesses of Puig's behavior just as it lauds the myth of meritocracy and a better life in the American dream narrative. Similarly, JP states, "Glad to see another quality player leave the tyrant's grip! Hope he makes millions, pays off the thugs that are extorting him & that he becomes an even bigger star in MLB" (Katz 2014).

Two other comments engage the journey to the US as the realization of a dream based on meritocracy, impossible to attain in Cuba, though from opposing viewpoints. Barbara voices the viewpoint of a Cuban American in tension with the government of the island:

> Excellent reporting. I am a Cuban-American who recently travelled back to Cuba. The system is totally corrupt and young people with promise and talent have no avenues to succeed. They must leave to pursue even the most basic dream. Can you imagine being 20 years old and looking at a life of struggle just to meet your basic needs, and NO personal freedoms? Can you blame Puig or any other young person for their very human desire to uplift themselves?
>
> I am sad and scared for Puig. Too much too fast, especially for such a young man. So many leeches trying to feed from his person. I hope someone with maturity, integrity and savvy takes him under their arm. He needs a good father figure. (Katz 2014)

Barbara's comments capture the desperation and loss of personal freedom that appeal to the role of the US as a place to escape tyranny and build a better life. She also casts the youth and excess of Puig's behavior in masculine terms in stating that he needs a "good father figure" to guide him and protect him from those who would leech off of his wealth. Another commenter, Doug, sees Puig himself and others who flee Cuba as leeches:

> I think we should send him back on the next raft. America needs to stop allowing anyone and everyone from anywhere to come here and leech off the system. Puig is the exception because he now has money. What if he had been a flop and couldn't go back . . . now he is in America with no education or job and on food stamps. The only people excepted should be those who go through the proper steps and legally become citizens of the USA. (Katz 2014)

Though other comments challenge Doug's stance, the assertion that immigrants abuse the system in the US as unproductive members of society who have broken the law circulates widely in political and media production, and in comments like these, locates baseball within the immigration and nativism debate around labor.

Once Puig was safely in Los Angeles as a member of the Dodgers' organization, MLB's public response to the news of Puig's journey reveals the limits of MLB's commitment to social responsibility that it highlights as a core principle on its US and Dominican websites. MLB personnel claim to have no direct knowledge of how Puig, or players like him, arrive to sign with the organization, stating that they do not want to know. According to Dan Halem, MLB executive vice president for labor relations, "We almost never hear of how players get here" (Bruns 2015, 149). Dodgers scout Mike Brito takes the point even further: "How he got from Cuba, I don't care. I don't wanna find out either. I never ask any Cuban player that. And even if I knew, I wouldn't tell you. Only thing we care about is when a guy is in a territory where we can sign him. Sign players and keep my mouth shut. The less you talk, the less you get in trouble" (Bruns 2015, 149). This don't ask, don't tell mentality allows MLB to sustain a plausible deniability that it hopes does not fray the fabric of giving back to communities and clean-cut "American" nationalism that the game strives to project, but does not exempt it from responsibility in its role of abusing or exploiting international talent, even if that role is indirect. Indeed, Mike Gillerman, executive director of the Santa Clara University Institute of Sports Law and Ethics, views MLB's stance of willful ignorance as problematic, stating, "I think reasonable people would look at it and say . . . This is our labor force. These are our ambassadors. If we want baseball 100 years from now to be held in esteem, let's do something" (Bruns 2015, 150). Though MLB does not wield the political power to change US policy vis-à-vis Cuba, it can certainly apply pressure from its position as an extremely lucrative corporation. After former president Barack Obama visited Cuba in December 2014, a visit that included attendance at a baseball game, MLB stated that it would closely monitor Obama's decision to renew diplomatic relations with Cuba, knowing that this could mean a new stream of talented men of color to labor in its ballfields. In fact, MLB had worked out an arrangement with the Cuban Federation of Baseball in December 2018 so that players could be signed to MLB from Cuba, thus ending the danger of defecting and using human traffickers. Lamentably, the Trump administration annulled that arrangement in April 2019. It is not enough to simply do nothing. If MLB wishes to instill and follow socially responsible behavior, it should also act, or at a minimum publicly state that it denounces the Cold War–era diplomatic tensions that underpin stories such as that of Yasiel Puig.

Conclusion

Returning to "Foul Play," the episode of *Law & Order* mentioned at the beginning of this chapter, in conversations about the disposition of the case among district attorneys, district attorney Nora Lewin laments that the American dream should mean more than just playing baseball and that no one even pretends that the young Latin American men who dedicate their lives to baseball also need an education. This observation belies the global capitalist system that fuels MLB labor recruitment of Latin Americans, despite the organization's publicly stated commitment to social responsibility and investment in poor communities of color in the US and beyond. Indeed, in public presentation and in practice, MLB has struggled to navigate race and global capitalism. Amid public criticisms that the organization insufficiently attends to recruitment of domestic men of color, with interest in baseball diminishing in communities of color in the US, MLB has highlighted the presence of Latin/o American players, though in a carefully curated way so as to not alienate its predominantly white, middle-class, male fan base. MLB largely defines race publicly through a handful of stellar players, particularly Jackie Robinson and the desegregation of baseball, and Roberto Clemente as the great legend who died at the service of others on a hurricane relief flight to Nicaragua. The public is largely unaware of the complicated systemic and structural aspects of MLB recruitment practices that send young Latin American men the message that dedication to baseball, potentially at the cost of education, is the path out of poverty as they join a ceaseless labor stream that feeds MLB from the minor to the major leagues.

The diminishing recruitment pool and interest in baseball, particularly among urban youth of color since the 1970s, as well as MLB's limited entry into the global labor market, gave way to the current labor structure of MLB. Faced with the need to increase its labor pool in the face of rapid labor changes in urban contexts in the 1970s, and gesturing to racial inclusivity in its player pool, the 1980s ushered in MLB's participation in RBI to address baseball recruitment among men of color in the US, and a robust growth in the *academia* system in the Dominican Republic that would guarantee a constant stream of cheap black and Latin/o American labor throughout the system. As some have argued, this allows MLB to diversify its ranks with a black population that is less politicized, less familiar with how racism operates in the US, and thus easier to control than black Americans. I would add that black Caribbean players embody and perform a more ambiguous blackness that does not threaten US racial hierarchies in the same way as black American players do. Indeed, as Spanish-speaking men of African descent, these players straddle black and immigrant identities, and so MLB personnel, media workers, and fans understand them primarily within immigrant labor narratives.

Indeed, the labor recruitment practices and narratives analyzed here illustrate that MLB's Latin/o American players serve as a means of negotiation of racial hierarchies and Chávez's Latino threat narrative. From the structural inequalities embedded in the commodification of young black Caribbean bodies in the Dominican Republic and Venezuela, to the literal trafficking of Yasiel Puig's Afro-Cuban body as an act of economic and political defiance of Cuba's socialist government, global capitalism has framed the movement and reception of male bodies of color within the Americas. Within this labor flow, there is always a preoccupation about what will happen if and when these bodies no longer perform baseball labor. In this way, this discussion of MLB's Latin American labor recruitment, one that only partially evinces its purported commitment to corporate social responsibility, reveals that despite the level of wealth involved, gendered global migration flows continue to subordinate Latin American men and consume their bodies via systemic inequality.

CHAPTER 5

"The Blizzard of Oz," "A-Fraud," "Manny Being Manny," and "Deadbeat Dad"

MLB and the Limits of Latino Character

We win the World Series and still 80% of Chicago are Cub fans.
Is it because we're poor and on the South Side?

—Former Chicago White Sox manager Ozzie Guillén,
on winning the 2005 World Series

When I leave Chicago, they're going to miss me because a lot
of people aren't going to make a lot of money.

—Ozzie Guillén

Mi primer idioma fue el español. Is that good enough?

—Former Chicago Cubs manager Lou Piniella,
when asked by the media if he spoke any
Spanish to relate to the Latino players

THE ABOVE QUOTES from Guillén and Piniella capture some of the tensions surrounding race, class, and Latinidad in the US. Guillén maps class directly onto space and perceptions of the South and North Sides as he asks why the fact that even winning a World Series does not raise the profile of the White Sox, whose park is on 35th and Shields, in the heart of the city's working-class South Side. When Guillén uttered these words in a press conference, the frustration in his voice was palpable, as one would think that winning the top honor in MLB would earn the team more respect and fans. Guillén further pushes back in recognizing that he himself has become a commodity in stating that media workers use him for their own economic gain. Guillén seems well aware that issues of class and race weigh more heavily on fan and media perceptions than do skill and talent. In fact, throughout his time in Chicago as both a player and manager, but especially as a manager, Guillén came to embody a fiery, passionate, salt of the earth and working-class Latinidad, as noted in frequent media coverage, both vilified and celebrated for these qualities by Latina/os and non-Latina/os alike.

Conversely, Piniella's Latinidad is actually called into question. As he is a lighter-skinned, US-born Latino with no audible Spanish accent, some members of the media and fans seem to not even know that he is Latino. Many fans and announcers assume that he is Italian American and claim that his last name sounds Italian One wonders to what extent this assumption of whiteness is also associated with the location of the Cubs' ballpark, Wrigley Field on Clark and Addison Streets, on the upwardly mobile North Side. Though media often present Piniella as quick-tempered and passionate in ways similar to Guillén, the issues of language and whiteness are significant as he is afforded certain privileges, and as a result his Latino identity flies under the radar. In fact, misreadings of him led to questions as to whether he would be able to adequately manage a significant part of his team, Latin/o American players with whom he shares some cultural terrain.[1] As a result, he must evoke the "racialized marker" of the Spanish language (Picker and Sun 2012) in defense of his identity and his credentials. Indeed, language and accent, used to Other and often discredit Guillén, legitimate Piniella with regard to his relationship with Latin/o American players.

For roughly four years (2007–2010) in Chicago, Latin/o Americans managed both of the city's MLB teams: Ozzie (Osvaldo) Guillén, born in Venezuela, managed the White Sox, and "Sweet" Lou Piniella, of Spanish/Cuban descent and born in Tampa, Florida, managed the Cubs. While Piniella had already established himself as an elite manager in the game and had a reputation for winning, Guillén started his first managerial job with his former team; he had played shortstop for the White Sox from 1985 to 1997. Both men inherited a passionate fan base in the city of Chicago, eager for a World Series win as neither team had won a World Series since the early twentieth century, the Cubs in 1908 and the White Sox in 1917. Both men also entered very raced and classed contexts around the city's two teams and their geographic locations. While the Cubs inhabit a North Side neighborhood associated with

---

1. I use the phrase "some cultural terrain" because it is important to understand that the heterogeneous Latin/o American player population in MLB, many born in the Caribbean or Latin America, share some aspects of culture, such as language and cultural knowledge, but hierarchies and tensions also exist between US-born and (im)migrant Latina/os in the US (Jimenez 2009), a context that undoubtedly impacts player/manager relations.

young, upper-class, primarily white professionals and the gay community, the White Sox live in a South Side neighborhood, experiencing ethnic and racial succession and backlash from a white, working-class population associated with the poorer, "salt of the earth" reputation of the South Side in general as compared to the North Side. These two managers, and constructions of them in Chicago during their careers, embody broader tensions in terms of Latina/o social positionality, Latino masculinities, and issues of race, class, and gender as mapped onto socially constructed geographies. The election of Barack Obama to the US presidency in 2008 ushered in a political and media-constructed supposed "post-racial" US society that maintains that race no longer constitutes a significant barrier to equality, power, and privilege as it once did (Wise 2010). MLB's Latin/o American players' bodies and receptions from fans and media prove the extent to which the "post-racial" moment is a myth.

For the June 30, 2008, Crosstown Series, an interleague series where the Chicago White Sox and Cubs play each other, Chevy featured a commercial where Ozzie Guillén and Lou Piniella rap about their teams in order to fuel a crosstown rivalry, featuring the tag line, "I'm a South Side Guy / I'm a North Side Guy." Both the choice of the rap format and the geographically driven south/north "beef" between Guillén and Piniella reveal much about how fans and marketers understand Guillén, Piniella, and the teams and parts of the city they represent. The commercial opens with Guillén rapping about being a "South Side guy" and Piniella countering with his role as a "North Side guy." While brighter images background the Piniella footage as he raps in front of Wrigley Field, including a street sign for Clark Street, where the ballpark is located, Guillén raps at night, and "35th and Shields," the intersection where US Cellular (now Guaranteed Rate) Field is located, is written in graffiti. Indeed, Guillén raps, "At 35th and Shields, we ballin' after dark." The greatest taunt comes as the two men walk toward each other in downtown Chicago, more "neutral" territory, as Piniella quips, "At least I ain't stuck in no South Side Cell." While these references to "after dark" and "South Side Cell" are probably meant as puns since the Cubs play more day games and the White Sox play more night games, these representations cast the two managers in significant ways as Latino men. While Piniella appears surrounded by light, only teased by Guillén for his paunch, Guillén's darker body and accented voice appear at night; the word *hell* is bleeped from his rap, "So you can go to hell"; and Piniella criminalizes him and the White Sox via the image of the "South Side Cell." Given the overall higher poverty and crime rates in South Side neighborhoods, as well as the high incarceration rates for Latinos, Native Americans, and African Americans (Noguera et al. 2012; Ríos 2011), this goes beyond harmless barbing to sell Chevys and signals power differentials embedded in representations of men of color and masculinities that merit further study.

The above characterizations of Guillén and Piniella, as well as those of Latin/o American MLB players more broadly, illustrate a perpetual characterization of Latino men in the US media and beyond tied to passion, aggression, crime, and greed in the pursuit of money. Latina/o media studies scholars locate past and present representations of Latino men with the history of colonization and conflict with Latin America, particularly Mexico.[2] These constructions of Guillén and Piniella as too aggressively Latino (Guillén) or not Latino enough (Piniella) reveal the tensions over authenticity and aggression often associated with men of color in the media and echoed by fan receptions of these men.

Thus, the cases of Guillén and Piniella illustrate the nuanced and complicated nature of defining and embodying Latinidades. Guillén and Piniella inhabit opposite poles of a spectrum of representations and constructions of Latino masculinities through Major League Baseball. Parting from the tensions around Guillén and Piniella, this chapter seeks to unpack the range of constructions present in the public personae and careers of a cohort of players as sites of Latinidades onto which fans and media workers map tensions, anxieties, and exotifications of Latin/o Americans as a result of social and political climates around issues of immigration, economic development, masculinities, and language.

Such representations carry real-world outcomes for Latino men in the US in terms of educational outcomes, incarceration rates, and access to the labor market. Despite their economic success and hard work, media and fan receptions of MLB's Latin/o American players illustrate that institutional racism contours the lives of even the wealthiest elite class, particularly men of color,

---

2. Despite their sustained relative invisibility in media overall (Negrón-Muntaner 2014), scholars have long studied the relationship between media representations embedded in historical and political discourses and Latina/os access to power and privilege. In a long-range study titled "The Latino Media Gap," researchers found that if anything, Latina/o representations in and control of media have decreased since the 1940s, despite their sustained population growth (Negrón-Muntaner 2014). Ethnic studies, cultural studies, and media studies scholars have documented images of Latina/os in the media as functions of national identity, social control, and public policy of the time. Bender (2003) traces the history of representations of Latina/os as a social problem from early Hollywood to the present moment, arguing that such representations built on stereotypes "ensure their legal detriment" (1). Bender cites the 1940s and 1950s as the most significant period for the media criminalization of Mexicans and Puerto Ricans, particularly men, via the Sleepy Lagoon and Zoot Suit Riots in Los Angeles in the 1940s and a New York City murder in 1959 by Puerto Rican gang members including Salvador "Capeman" Agrón (5). The type of urban violence associated with Latina/os described by Bender persists today via representations of gang members and dangerous immigrants in multiple media forums.

and call for sustained social policy reform. This chapter, along with the previous chapters framed within the Latino threat narrative, completes the analysis of race, class, gender, and the consumption of Latin/o American MLB players. It raises questions of the viability of meritocracy and the American dream for Latinos and other men of color as, even when they acquire economic status, these men suffer institutional racism. Media and fan consumption perpetuates these conditions despite some pride these players might inspire in their Latina/o fans.

As such, the exploration and analysis of incidents in the careers of four Latin/o American players/managers will reveal the tensions and long-standing racist and classist tensions embedded in media representations of these men's careers. The analysis begins with Ozzie Guillén during his time as manager of the Chicago White Sox and Miami Marlins. Always outspoken during his playing career, Guillén emerged as an even more outspoken and polemic manager, often taking on issues related to Latin/o American players in MLB as he led the White Sox to their World Series win in 2005, before eventually moving on to manage the Miami Marlins, where he made controversial comments regarding Fidel Castro, igniting the fury of the team's Cuban (American) fans. A study of Alex Rodríguez, one of the most alternately celebrated and vilified Latin/o American players in recent MLB history, follows the Guillén case. From marital conflict and a high-profile dating life to his connection with performance-enhancing drugs, Rodríguez provides a fertile case for media and fan scrutiny, particularly in the wake of his February 2015 apology letter to fans and MLB. Another former polemic player, Manny Ramírez, follows Rodríguez. Like Rodríguez, Ramírez has been connected to the use of performance-enhancing drugs, but unlike Rodríguez, who is normally cast as savvy, in pursuit of fame, money, and the upper echelons of baseball performance, Manny Ramírez is more often portrayed in almost childlike terms, seemingly unable to control his aggressive and passionate instincts, as evidenced by "The Oh Manny Song," a spoof of his career with the Boston Red Sox. Finally, Robinson Canó received much media attention related to a child custody dispute, pending in the Dominican Republic, with the mother of his son around the time of his move from the New York Yankees to the Seattle Mariners. As with Ramírez, media characterizations of Canó often focus on a natural talent but a stubborn lack of focus and unwillingness to work hard as a player. Taken together, these four player case studies underscore the extent to which perceptions of the Latino threat narrative come together in characterizations of Latino men as at best unworthy of full access to US American citizenship and civic participation and at worst a threat that must be curtailed.

"The Blizzard of Oz": (Ir)Rationalizing Ozzie Guillén and Impassioned Latin/o American Masculinities

"We [the Chicago White Sox] are the bitch of Chicago." This is how Ozzie Guillén has described the rivalry between the Chicago White Sox and Cubs vis-à-vis the city's fans. The usage of the term *bitch* here uncovers the multilayered nature of gender construction and contemporary popular usage. While winning in sports usually does establish privilege consistent with a masculine gender role, until recently public perceptions cast the Cubs as "lovable losers" who play in one of the oldest parks in baseball, in an upwardly mobile neighborhood on the North Side. On the other hand, the White Sox play the role of perpetual underdog of the South Side, playing in a relatively newly constructed park, surrounded by marginalized communities. In fact, many described the team's 2005 World Series win as a "fluke," couched in the working-class union discourse of a team of journeymen players, in contrast to the endless stream of highly paid superstars on the Cubs.

Guillén plays with the construct of potency, fully aware that the Cubs have succeeded in establishing hegemony in Chicago via marketing and the construction of space. An examination of key moments of his career as manager of the Chicago White Sox and the Miami Marlins—including an on-field hit-by-pitch controversy; a scandal involving sex dolls in the White Sox clubhouse; the White Sox World Series Parade; and Guillén's comment, made during his time managing the Marlins, that he respected Fidel Castro—captures the ways that media and fans use Guillén to negotiate and understand Latino masculinities and Latinidad both through and beyond the *bandido* figure. Of particular interest here is how masculinities, race, and class intersect in constructions and receptions of Guillén.

On June 14, 2006, Texas Rangers pitcher Vicente Padilla hit Chicago White Sox catcher A. J. Pierzynski with pitches in his first two at-bats. As manager, Guillén interpreted both hits as deliberate, and thus he ordered rookie relief pitcher Sean Tracey to hit Rangers hitter Hank Blalock in retaliation, as is common practice in Major League Baseball. Tracey did not succeed in the planned hit, and later apologized for not following his manager's instructions. Later, Guillén warned Padilla that he would retaliate if he hit another White Sox player in their next series. On June 16, 2006, in an article titled, "Judgment Call: Time to Worry about Ozzie?," *Chicago Sun Times* sports columnist Jay Mariotti took Guillén, to whom he refers as "the Blizzard of Oz," to task for his decision to retaliate and order a young pitcher to make the hit. Mariotti further argued that Guillén humiliated Tracey when he scolded him later for not having hit Blalock. Shortly thereafter, Tracey was sent back to the minor leagues. Mariotti (2006) asks, has Ozzie Guillén "officially lost his mind?" He draws a parallel between Ozzie Guillén and a mafia boss when he reprimands him for making Tracey his "goon-on-demand," referencing images of instability and criminality often used to describe mafia culture in the mainstream US media. This prompted the following response from Guillén: "He called me a gang member, a mafia guy [on April 23, 2005]. When you say mafia man here, that's not easy to say. Now he's sitting on national TV talking about me. I make him famous and make him more money" (Mariotti 2006).

Guillén answered Mariotti's accusations by evoking his own masculine image, calling Mariotti a "fucking fag" and not "man enough" to talk to him directly about the situation. When Guillén was forced to apologize for inflammatory anti-gay remarks, he justified his comments in stating that his use of the word *fag* had nothing to do with homosexuality and that he had nothing against gay men. In Venezuela, his country of origin, the Spanish translation of the word *maricón* does not necessarily signify homosexuality, but rather cowardice, and describes males who are not "real men." The incident gained much attention in the Chicago press because Guillén had won the World Series as White Sox manager only a year before. As a result, Guillén has become a significant, if problematic, Latino public figure locally and internationally. Indeed, on the South Side of Chicago, Guillén has come to embody the working-class "salt of the earth" persona associated with the South Side. For Latina/os in particular, he means a great deal, not only as one of a handful of Latin/o American former players who have arrived at the managerial level in Major League Baseball but also as a Venezuelan-born native Spanish speaker of modest upbringing who has learned enough English and acquired enough social capital to literally speak his mind. Such is his significance as a Chicago public figure that after the White Sox won the 2005 World Series, cable channel Comcast Sportsnet produced a bilingual documentary about Guillén from his youth in Venezuela to the present titled *Ozzie Guillén: A Mi Manera* (*Ozzie Guillén: My Way*), a title that connects Guillén's individual masculinity with that of Frank Sinatra's hit song "My Way." This connection belies a consistent emphasis on individualism in US constructions of masculinity, as well as equating ethnic masculinities (Venezuelan and Italian American, respectively), as aggressive.

In addition to Guillén's public position as a well-known, wealthy Latino, the hit-by-pitch incident and Guillén's rivalry with Mariotti must be read within a larger framework as they serve to illustrate the complex points of negotiation that US Latino males undergo in the formation of their identities at the levels of culture, class, and race. Mainstream US cultural production often constructs them as transgressors, outside of legitimate society and beyond redemption. The case of Guillén problematizes such readings as his class position and fame afford him access to a great deal of cultural and economic capital, and according to some, allow him to blur the boundaries of appropriate and inappropriate behavior in what have been described in the press as his all-too-frequent rants.

This dynamic has played out in economic terms. In a pre-game interview after having been ejected from the previous game for arguing with umpire Phil Cuzzi, Guillén simply stated that he did not like Cuzzi and the feeling was mutual. He further quipped that he would set aside $100,000 to pay fines from MLB that season so that he could say whatever he wanted. Given such resources, what are the consequences of Guillén's actions if he can simply buy himself out of trouble, a privilege typically associated with white masculinity? Does this whiten Guillén? Though his access to capital does afford him a level of privilege, higher in fact than most white men, sports figures such as Guillén do little to improve the material conditions of men of color in general. What interests me here, with regard to the Guillén case, is that despite his having significant power in the public sphere, characterizations of him continue to highlight his being ruled by passion as opposed to reason, and his "foreignness" as a Venezuelan, though he has lived much of his adult life in the US and became a US citizen in 2006.

All of this has led to an ambivalent response to Guillén's controversial remarks, where members of the press, particularly Mariotti, claim that MLB must take a firm stand with Guillén and that he must be stopped, while many White Sox fans, including gay men, have come out in his defense. In fact, the gay community responded to this scandal over the use of the inflammatory term by naming a drink after him: The "Effin Ozzie Guillentini," a martini served with fresh fruit and a complimentary copy of the *Chicago Sun Times,* offered by the Kit Kat Supper Club on Chicago's North Side. The gay community also benefitted economically from a Guillén controversy. Interestingly, Guillén fans and detractors defend their positions using the same rhetorical points, namely, lack of education and cultural misunderstanding, particularly attributed to Guillén's (lack of) command of English. Cowley (2006) used this "cultural misunderstanding" to explain Guillén's behavior. This shared rhetoric, though employed to support opposing viewpoints, portrays Latino men as primitive and ruled by illogical emotional responses, and in so doing occludes the assumptions underlying Guillén's statement regarding homosexuality and maleness, namely, that "real men" are not gay.

As noted earlier, in the article that sparked the controversy, Mariotti refers to Guillén as "the Blizzard of Oz," clearly identifying the manager with an erratic weather front that leaves destruction in its path. Furthermore, he openly questions Guillén's mental stability and whether his mental status has compromised his priorities in managing the team. Mariotti again evinces a temper-based irrational persona when he likens Guillén to a mob figure who hires a "goons-on-demand" and notes that he "hates snitches" after word was leaked from the White Sox organization that Guillén "went nuts" after the failed hit-by-pitch incident (Mariotti 2006). All of the images mentioned thus far index nonwhite masculinities; thus, despite his economic status, Guillén does not fare much better than other Latinos cast as passionate lovers and criminals, notoriously outside the heroic white masculine figure whose passion and rebellion are seen as attributes of power.

While one could certainly dispute the use of hit-by-pitches as a retaliatory practice in baseball, Guillén did not act outside the bounds of conventionally accepted baseball norms. Mariotti's construction of the Venezuelan manager and his actions highlights the Latino outlaw or *bandido* figure present in mainstream US culture since the emergence of romanticized westward expansion and Manifest Destiny in the Southwest, embodied by the white "cowboy" and the indigenous "Indian." I deploy the example of the Guillén/Mariotti controversy to foreground the tensions and ambiguities around constructions of masculinities on and from a transnational and economic perspective that tests the boundaries of who may and may not be called a man. Additionally, to what extent does economic capital inform tensions over power associated with masculinities of color?

A 2008 scandal involving the Chicago White Sox made front-page news in Chicago, further complicating media conversations about Guillén's Latin/o American masculinity. During a losing streak, the team used a controversial "slump-buster," a ritual to try to change the team's luck. In this particular case, an unnamed player set up two blow-up sex dolls surrounded by the bats of most of the players and affixed one sign to each doll. One sign read "Go White Sox" while the other read "You've got to push." The dolls were displayed in the visitor's clubhouse in Toronto during a White Sox road trip on Sunday, May 4, 2008. The incident sparked debates about appropriate behavior in the clubhouse as well as feminist issues related to the image of the dolls. *Chicago Sun Times* columnist Carol Slezak (2008) wrote a scathing article blaming Sox leadership, specifically Guillén, for allowing the stunt. Slezak lamented that neither Ozzie nor any of the players were "man enough" to stand up and say, "This is wrong." She goes on to contrast Guillén, whom she is certain "was born without a sensitivity chip," with then New York Yankee manager Joe Girardi and former Boston Red Sox manager Terry Francona, whom she could not imagine allowing such behavior from their teams. Guillén came under criticism from the feminist community but refused to back down, and in fact defended the actions of his players on the grounds of leadership and privacy.

In statements to the press following the incident, Guillén refused to apologize but took responsibility for the controversy. He defended his players' actions on the grounds that they are adults and their clubhouse should be a private space, casting it in homosocial terms:

> Everyone in the clubhouse, 100 percent of the people in the clubhouse, they are 18 years old and that's a private thing. If the players do it in the dugout so everyone in the public can see it, or did it in the lobby . . . we did it in the clubhouse. A lot of worse things happen in the clubhouse. I don't really know why people are making a big deal. If people got their feelings hurt because of that . . . they don't really know much about baseball. (Spak 2008)

While many have criticized Guillén for deploying a "boys will be boys" defense for his players, the issue of interest here is the way that this is read as just another rant from the volatile Ozzie Guillén, another incident attributed to his perceived deficient grasp of US cultural norms. Furthermore, Guillén's claim of privacy in the clubhouse reinforces the idea that, in part, space constitutes appropriate gendered behavior; if no one sees it, it's just men releasing stress. Like his feud with Jay Mariotti, which the media attributed to his lack of education in Venezuela and lack of English proficiency, readings of what was termed "Dollgate" (a reference to Watergate) missed an integral part of the story. Guillén is undeterred in his claim that he will continue to say whatever he wants, pointing out that the press makes money off of him and so should be glad he is so outspoken. He sums up his position and indexes his manhood in stating, "I'm pretty strong. I took all kinds of punches last year, and I'm still up" (Cowley 2008). The fact that Guillén often referenced his value to the Chicago media as "making them a lot of money" during his time as White Sox manager attests to the fact that Latino men are well aware of how the media and culture market profit from characterizations of them as volatile and out of control.

This awareness on the part of Guillén extends to his identity as a Latin/o American and Venezuelan player. Guillén has often used his fame and media attention to call attention to Latina/os and Latin America. When the White Sox won the World Series in 2005, the city of Chicago sponsored a parade through downtown and the South Side neighborhood of Bridgeport, where the Sox play. Guillén sat atop a double-decker bus with a Venezuelan flag draped over his shoulders. In a speech at the end of the rally, Guillén dedicated his team's trophy to the Venezuelan people. During the off-season, he took the World Series trophy to Venezuela so that his countrymen could share in the White Sox accomplishment. Despite the fact that some South Siders felt that he should not dedicate the victory to Venezuela, Guillén consistently presents himself as Venezuelan first and foremost. For this reason, he has become an even more important public figure in Venezuela than in the US, appearing on then Venezuelan president Hugo Chávez's show *Aló Presidente*.

By the time Guillén parted ways with the White Sox organization after an eight-year acrimonious relationship with general manager Ken Williams, he had gained a reputation among baseball organizations and fans alike as a volatile Venezuelan who could fire up players but also divide organizations due to his irrationality and outspoken nature. In fact, when Guillén accepted a position managing the Miami Marlins, *Sports Illustrated* coverage of the move focused on the team's big spending on talent and a new ballpark through metaphors of mental illness. A March 5, 2012, cover story featured Guillén and shortstop José Reyes, with the title, "Marlinsanity?: Betting Big That Binge Spending, a Psychedelic Park and Mad New Talent Will Create Baseball Mania in Miami" (Reiter 2012; figure 7). The article indexes images of mental instability through the use of the words "insanity" and "madness" to explain changes made by the Marlins organization particularly to cater to Miami's large Latina/o population, many of whom are from the Caribbean, where baseball enjoys a high level of popularity. According to Census Bureau data for 2013, Miami–Dade County's Latina/o population was 65.6 percent. Guillén would only briefly stay with the Marlins organization. He was fired on October 23, 2012, after one season with the team amid a series of controversies.

All of these measures to improve infrastructure and talent were meant to awaken baseball interest in arguably the most Latina/o city in the US, where such interest had not materialized since the formation of the organization as the Florida Marlins in 1993. The *Sports Illustrated* article evinces Latinidad and aggressive masculinity in its description of the locations of the ticketing office and ballpark as well as the hiring of Guillén:

> To make good on one of the biggest gambles in baseball history, the Miami (né Florida) Marlins have established their ticket sales headquarters above a small medical center on a corner lot in Little Havana, abutting a fenced-in yard of squawking chickens. Catty-corner to the two-story building, as if it had recently come to rest after an interstellar mission, is soon-to-open Marlins Park, a sleek Kubrickian vision of white stucco, metal and glass that cost $515 million, seats 37,442, and has a retractable roof that closes in 13 minutes. (Reiter 2012, 36)

FIGURE 7. *Sports Illustrated*, "Marlinsanity," on the Miami Marlins' hiring of Ozzie Guillén, 2012

The article describes Guillén's entrance to the Marlins organization and to their physical facility as follows:

> Then an accented voice boomed from the doorway of the room: "Hey, for f—— $10 million, I'd f—— fly from the moon!" It was Ozzie Guillén, who after eight brash, generally winning and invariably profane seasons as the White Sox manager, replaced the re-retiring McKeon last September. Guillén, who received a four-year, $10 million contract, wasn't brought in merely to be a manager. He is expected, with his honest energy and loose-cannon quotability, to give the franchise a dose of personality and help invigorate the Marlins' fan base. (Reiter 2012, 37)

These two quotes illustrate the ways that aggressive Latino masculinities fuse with the Latinidad of Miami and the marketing of baseball to a fan base of Latina/os who would supposedly identify with Guillén's Marlins playing in a ballpark described in garish terms in Little Havana, among the ubiquitous chickens associated with Caribbean diet, sport, and masculinity. Marlin's leadership also courted non-Latina/os whose interest presumably would awaken amid Guillén's performance of mascuLatinidad, feeding into long-held perceptions of Latino men in entertainment.[3]

Such masculine performances would get him in trouble early in his Marlins career. In an interview with *Time* magazine published on April 9, 2012, Guillén stated, "I respect Fidel Castro. You know why? A lot of people have wanted to kill Fidel Castro for the last 60 years but that [expletive] is still here" (Gregory 2012). These remarks sparked a firestorm among Miami's staunch anti-Castro Cuban population that would contribute to Guillén's separation from the Marlins. The Marlins suspended him for five games as a result of his remarks. As soon as the story broke, the Cuban and Latina/o communities of Miami as well as the Marlins' front office reacted. Local politicians including Miami-Dade mayor Carlos Gimenez and Joe Martinez, head of Miami-Dade Board of County Commissioners, implored the Marlins to address Guillén's remarks, asking for his resignation. Cuban exile group Vigila Mambisa planned a boycott (J. L. Ortiz 2012). Indeed, those boycotting the Marlins protested outside Marlins Park carrying signs bearing Guillén's name in a circle with a line through it, with the caption "NO APOLOGIES FIRE HIM NOW."

---

3. I use the term *mascuLatinidad* here in accordance with Domino Rudolph (2012), who developed the construct as a way of unpacking the tensions of performances of masculinities and Latinidades. MascuLatinidad questions the extent to which performances of Latino masculinities that index aggression, passion, and capital acquisition both advance and limit Latino identities in the public sphere.

In response, the Marlins issued the following press release: "There is nothing to respect about Fidel Castro. He is a brutal dictator who has caused unthinkable pain for more than 50 years. We live in a community filled with victims of this dictatorship, and the people in Cuba continue to suffer today" (J. L. Ortiz 2012). Guillén similarly retracted his comments, evoking Latinidad in his apology to the Cuban community: "I feel sad because I know I hurt a lot of people. I'm Latino. I live in Miami. I have a lot of Cuban friends and players. They know who I am. They know how I feel" (J. L. Ortiz 2012). Guillén subsequently gave a press conference at Marlins Park to repair his standing in Miami's Latina/o community.

Ozzie Guillén would also evoke Latinidad in his press conference at the Marlins' ballpark just a few days after the incident. At the press conference posted to YouTube by DailyWorldwideNews in 2012, Guillén spoke in Spanish and English to address the community he had unintentionally hurt with his remarks, beginning the conference in Spanish and switching to English during the question-and-answer period when requested to do so by a reporter. Guillén's apology and remarks focused on his regret at having hurt the Latina/o community and how a miscommunication and misunderstanding with the *Time* reporter resulted in his remarks.[4] Guillén frequently cited miscommunication and his linguistic limitations in English when reporters asked him to clarify his comments, insisting that his intention was to say that he wonders how it is possible that someone who has done so much damage could still be in power. He stated this clarification in Spanish as follows: "¿Cómo era posible que una persona que ha hecho tanto daño en el mundo esté en el poder?" (How was it possible that a person who has done so much damage in the world still be in power?) (DailyWorldwideNews 2012).

In addition to his explanation based on language, Guillén expressed his regret and sorrow as a Latin/o American and as a representative of the Latina/o community: "I don't represent just myself. I represent Latin America. I represent the ball club, and I represent the organization" (DailyWorldwideNews 2012). Acknowledging his error in judgment, Guillén stated, "He herido a una comunidad, a toda Latinoamérica" (I have hurt a community, all of Latin America) (DailyWorldwideNews 2012). He most strongly connected himself and his apology to a group identity:

A toda la familia cubana, nuevamente, mi perdón, mi cariño, y espero que cuando salga de aquí, entienda mejor y sepa un poco quién es esta persona

---

4. For a more thorough analysis and discussion of language politics in the US and MLB, see chapter 3.

y de verdad qué es lo que siento por ellos y por el régimen castrista y por el régimen de Venezuela, y el de Nicaragua, y el de Ecuador, y el del Perú, y lo que Ud. quiera.

(Again, to the entire Cuban family I beg your pardon and give you my affection, and I hope that when you leave here you understand a bit better and know a bit more who I am and what I truly feel for you and for the Castro regime and the regimes of Venezuela, Nicaragua, Ecuador, and Peru and wherever else.) (DailyWorldwideNews 2012)

Through the description of the "Cuban family," as well as the mention of several Latin American countries, Guillén deploys Latinidad in an attempt perhaps to defuse the charged political nature of the mention of Castro. He implored the audience to accept the sincerity of his apology because this was only the second time in his managerial career that he is apologizing; the first was when he questioned Alex Rodríguez's Dominican nationality when Rodríguez played for the Dominican World Baseball Classic team.

During the question-and-answer period, Guillén continued to negotiate his two languages, as well as a reporter asking him if this was another example of his craziness and erratic behavior, to which Guillén responded, "No soy loco" (I'm not crazy), instead explaining his remarks as a lapse of respect and communication. This is consistent with the tone of "the Blizzard of Oz" that has become ubiquitous in media representations of Ozzie Guillén. He insisted that he will work to mend his relationship with the aggrieved Latin/o American community via a Spanish saying, "Las palabras, se las lleva el viento, las acciones se quedan," roughly equivalent to the English "Actions speak louder than words" (DailyWorldwideNews 2012).

The YouTube posting of Guillén's press conference generated a lengthy comment stream debating Cuban nationalism, "American" nationalism, freedom of speech, masculinity, and the role of the media. Quotes from two commentators particularly capture the tensions around media and Latin/o American masculinities at the heart of this study. Raul Gomez stated:

I guess there are a lot of Cubans in the US, especially in Florida, who don't like the idea of freedom of speech, like the MLB and the privatized, biased media. The media wants to make a big deal about [that] so the people don't even dare to speak their minds. That is why they made Ozzie apologize (poor fool). It is anti-American to not let someone speak their mind. Freedom? In the US? LOL . . . don't make me laugh. Who should really be apologizing? (DailyWorldwideNews 2012)

Gomez's comments reflect the knowledge that media outlets construct the news content that we all consume and are complicit in market-driven production of stories to awaken interest and generate revenue regardless of the possible consequences. He further implicates MLB as part of the problem as their response to the incident shows more of a concern for image and profit than for human dignity and freedom.

With respect to masculinity and machismo, a masculine behavior and performance specifically attributed to Latino men, Kemiztri commented, "AT THIS POINT AMERICANS ARE VERY DOCILE; LOOK AT AMERICAN MEN THEIR BECOMING MORE FENEMIZED??? LOOK THEY SAY HOW MACHISMO IS BAD AND YET THEY DONT REALIZE MACHISMO IS WHAT MADE THE USA . . . ITS AMAZING HOW MEN ARE DUMB DOWN. . . ." (DailyWorldwideNews 2012).[5] This comment represents a disturbing justification of historical violence against people of color by way of a gendered construct associated with a racialized group, Latina/os. This commenter advocates for white masculine violence as a point of nation building as well as maintenance of the nation in the present moment in the face of threat to an undefined "American" machismo that presumably grants unchecked power to white men over all others.

In this way, Ozzie Guillén's managerial career illustrates the sociopolitical tensions around Latina/os in the US, especially Latin/o American masculinities, which are understood by fans and media through optics of aggression, passion, irrationality, and criminalization of accepted behaviors among MLB's white elite managers. While Guillén does indeed provoke debate via his performance of self as he engages questions of politics, masculinity, and power within MLB, media outlets both provide a forum for and embellish incidents of "the Blizzard of Oz" or "Ozzie being Ozzie" that circulate in media features and fan comments on Ozzie's behavior.[6] As such, Guillén, media workers, and fans all collude in the perpetuation of the masculine "Latino threat" dating back to the early days of Hollywood and the *bandido* figure, which has evolved into the dictator/urban criminal, and I would argue the outspoken, wealthy, retired athlete that is Ozzie Guillén. The fact that Guillén understands the dominant perceptions of his actions and the market value of them as fodder for media workers to make money and online commentators to process

---

5. All YouTube comments are reproduced as they appear on the site. Corrections or clarifications will be made when the meaning or context is unclear.

6. The "Blizzard of Oz" metaphor stems from reporter Jay Mariotti's depiction of Guillén during his managerial career in Chicago. "Ozzie being Ozzie" is an offshoot of the "Manny being Manny" description ascribed to Dominican outfielder Manny Ramírez.

Latin/o American social, political, and gender issues pushes us to critically engage class and Latin/o American masculinities in baseball because, to some extent, Ozzie Guillén's economic capital allows him a level of power in the public sphere afforded to few men of any ethnic or racial group. While there are consequences, such as with the Cuban/Latina/o community in Miami, constructions and receptions of Guillén buttress a socioracial hierarchy that benefits him as an individual, while the larger Latin/o American male community continues to suffer the material consequences of the stereotypes ascribed to him. This analysis of Guillén's managerial career maps a range of representations, tensions, and fan reactions that I will further develop through analysis of key moments in the careers of Alex Rodríguez, Manny Ramírez, and Robinson Canó.

"A-Fraud": Embodying Bad Behavior

Though Ozzie Guillén has garnered a great deal of attention and criticism in his managerial career, Alex Rodríguez embodies many of the controversies that tarnish MLB as an institution of "America's game" and a source of national pride. Rodríguez's association with ongoing steroid use among MLB's elite players and his bloated contracts with the Texas Rangers and then the New York Yankees have provided for endless debate among media outlets and fans as passionate baseball followers lament the turn in baseball to a game of capital gain, far removed from the national pastime of yore depicted in movies such as *Field of Dreams* and *The Sandlot,* which cast baseball as a panacea of class and racial harmony. Rodríguez has become the face of the steroid scandal. A 2015 article on the arrest of a steroid supplier in Florida featured a picture of Rodríguez because one of his trainers had allegedly purchased steroids for him from the supplier. Rodríguez's biographer, Selena Roberts (2009), argues that an obsession with notoriety and bodily perfection, as well as a competitive nature, have marked his career such that, in reference to his feelings of competition toward Derek Jeter, Yankee teammates nicknamed him A-Fraud (7).

Questions of character and masculinities tied to class and ethno-racial identities and linked to Latin/o American MLB players mark Rodríguez's publicly crafted persona in ways both similar to and diverging from the case of Ozzie Guillén mentioned above. In both cases, media workers highlight having been born or resided partly in Latin America, or a majority Latina/o–populated area, as in the case of Alex Rodríguez, as explanations for or strongly contributing factors to their actions. However, Selena Roberts's framing of Rodríguez's need for attention focuses on his estranged relationship with his father as a catalyst for his obsession with attention and pursuit of bodily perfection. Though this relationship undoubtedly has shaped Alex Rodríguez's character and sense of self, the burden of representation of Latin/o American men via the cultural construct of machismo, which sometimes includes familial abandonment, must be taken into account so as to not excessively pathologize Latino character. Aware of this himself, Rodríguez initially crafted a public persona rooted in his dedication to family and baseball, though over time he would not shy away from the public spotlight in his dalliances, including very public relationships with Madonna and Jennifer López. As such, along with the other players discussed in this chapter, Alex Rodríguez presents a challenge for fans and cultural critics in understanding and processing Latin/o American masculinities without reducing them to a set of character flaws related to the Latino threat narrative proposed by Leo Chávez fueled by economic, historical, and political contexts that cast Latin/o American men as, in part, irrational, excessively passionate, violent, and hostile to "American" values of hard work and integrity.

Characterizations of Rodríguez often underscore his arrogance and excess in bodily care and presentation through rigorous exercise as well as his taste for expensive clothing and accessories. The back cover of Robert's biography reveals a sharply dressed Rodríguez lighting presumably a Cuban cigar. Rodríguez's arrogance surfaces not only in media coverage of his behaviors as a ballplayer but just as often in the tabloids as a bad-boy celebrity, particularly during his very public relationship with Madonna. The negotiating tactics of agent Scott Boras throughout his career have also contributed to portrayals of Rodríguez as an alternately lost young man still seeking approval in the wake of his father's absence in his life and a cunning superstar who has allowed a high level of privilege to strain his moral character. However, by far the most controversial aspect of Rodríguez's career and media coverage has been his link to steroid use.

Rodríguez's name has surfaced in connection with steroid use in various moment of his career. Most media workers and MLB insiders agree that steroid use has existed for a long time in the sport, but that for many years the organization did not dedicate significant attention and resources to addressing it. The MLB Players' Association has advocated for players, and according to some, enabled the media-termed "steroid era." One unnamed player asserts that the players' union fought hard to stop steroid testing, dismissing the dangers of steroids, and advised players to buy steroids outside the US to avoid detection (Roberts 2009, 136). The key moment for MLB came in 2002, when

Ken Caminiti confessed to steroid use in *Sports Illustrated*.[7] In 2003, the US Congress forced MLB to initiate a testing policy. The Mitchell Report of 2007 publicly documented the investigation into steroids and MLB. Though initial testing attempted to keep players anonymous, names emerged in the course of the investigation and Alex Rodríguez was among those linked to steroids (Roberts 2009, 143). Media coverage of Rodríguez revealed that he obtained MLB-banned substances from trainers in both the US and Dominican Republic, stating that his Dominican cousin had provided him with unnamed medicines that he knew "were not Tic Tacs." Though the problem extends much further, on US soil, this strategy links steroids to a permissive "foreign" Latin American country that provides illegal substances to MLB players fueled by economic greed, a "Latino threat" to America's pastime.

After serving the longest suspension in MLB history for use of performance-enhancing drugs (PEDs), the entire 2014 season, Alex Rodríguez issued a handwritten letter of apology to fans in February 2015. This was a complicated moment for the Yankees as, at that time, they still owed Rodríguez $61 million over the next three years as well as a $6 million home run bonus if he hit six more home runs and tied Willie Mays for fourth place on the all-time list. Though the Yankees had offered him the use of Yankee Stadium for a public press conference in order to confront the situation before the start of the 2015 regular baseball season, Rodríguez stated in his letter, "It was gracious of the Yankees to offer me the use of Yankee Stadium for this apology but I decided the next time I am in Yankee Stadium, I should be in pinstripes doing my job" (King 2015). The letter has been published by media outlets in its handwritten form amid criticisms that it is an insincere attempt at apology; further, Joe Scarborough, host of MSNBC's *Morning Joe,* speculated that the penmanship appears to be that of a woman. Rodríguez himself acknowledges that most will probably not believe and accept his apology, given his history of not telling the truth, taking ownership for his actions in stating, "That's on me" (King 2015). In addition to putting forth a discursively humble apology, Rodríguez self-infantilizes and self-deprecates as he explains his connection to the PED Biogenesis scandal, claiming he thought the pills he was given were placebos: "Only a dope like me would do that stuff and have the two worst statistical seasons of my career" (King 2015).[8]

---

7. In a May 2002 *Sports Illustrated* cover story titled "Steroids in Baseball: Confessions of an MVP," Ken Caminiti told of his own use of steroids, including during his 1996 MPV season, and alleged that about half of MLB's players were using as well (Lamovsy, Rosetti, and DeMarco 2007, 300).

8. Rodríguez's name was linked to the Biogenesis antiaging clinic in South Florida, which supplied human growth hormone, among other medications, to MLB players (Solomon 2013).

On February 17, 2015, the *New York Post* published the letter in an article titled "A-Rod Issues Handwritten Apology Letter to Fans." This article generated a lively comment stream among fans sounding off as to whether to accept Rodríguez's apology, especially within the history of the New York Yankee organization as one of the elite institutions of MLB. With very few exceptions, a consensus emerged within the comment stream that his apology letter is hollow in and of itself, and if he truly wants to repair his relationship with fans and recover his dignity as a ballplayer, he must back up his words with some sort of redeeming action. The themes that emerged centered on issues of masculinities, power, and capital, with many fans angered at the financial gains he has and will continue to receive despite having cheated.

Two representative comments frame the apology and its lack of legitimacy as a restorative act within larger issues of MLB steroid use and manhood. One fan identified as theenforcer posted this response to a prior post asking why David Ortiz has not been publicly implicated in the PED scandal as has A-Rod:

> Still, the only three players names vetted from the list of 100+ players who tested positive were Ortiz, Manny [another part of the comment references Ramírez's baggy uniform] and Rodriquez. The Red Sox team was given a pass by ex- senator Mitchell who conducted the PED investigation for MLB because he was on the RED SOX PAYROLL! Lou Merloni in an interview with the Boston Globe stated that the red sox organization conducted a one and a half hour briefing on PED usage for their players at one time—the article was never reprinted and Lou was immediately hired by the red sox-owned NESN as a sports-reporter! Although Arod has brought a lot of the negative attention on himself, the sportswriting fraternity, starved for original and creative subject matter, chooses the easy-way-out, and piles on Arod to attract a reading audience! (King 2015)

This comment casts the steroid users as cowards, hiding their bulked-up bodies behind a uniform in the case of Manny Ramírez, an issue indexed in discussions of MLB's uniform fit and presentation code, with sportscasters sometimes implying that Ramírez uses an urban aesthetic associated with a baggy shirt as a means to pad his hit-by-pitch statistics as he leans in during at-bats, and thus is not performing honorably in his job. The comment further indicts media workers around baseball as irresponsible transmitters of information, interested only in sensationalism as a means to attract readers. Though other posters refute the veracity of some of the above claims about the Red Sox organization, this rendering of the PED scandal and its focus on three Dominican players underscores the ways in which fans and media workers co-construct images of laziness, cowardice, and market-driven newsfeed in their understandings of Latin/o American players like Rodríguez, Ramírez, and Ortiz. It is important to note that though other posts did reference non-Latino players such as Mark McGuire and Andy Petite as part of the steroid era of MLB, the burden and type of representation associated with Latin/o American players has tended more toward issues of laziness and lack of character, as such men are often perceived as so desperate to escape poverty that they are willing to break the rules. This desperation intersects with the special hunger identified by Samuel Regalado (2008), where Latin/o American players try to excel on the field motivated by harsh economic conditions in their own countries and belief in the meritocracy of the American dream, as well as the Latino threat narrative in that it functions as an impelling force for the massive migration decried by many anti-immigration and nativist groups, without sufficiently attending to the global economic power differentials that structure Latin/o American lives.

A second comment posted by ruthian directly references manhood and "being a man" as well as reparations to the community as ways of legitimating an otherwise empty and rhetorical apology:

> Arod can pay-it-forward by donating his home run bonuses (if he hits and if the Yankees pay) to an inner city charity for disadvantaged kids. Since his "record" is a sham to begin with, why not give every red cent of his bonuses to a worthy cause? An apology letter means nothing—he deceived every kid that believed in him. Does he have the balls now to really be a man and give something back to community? Until then, he's a circus show with no credibility to anyone that loves the true nature of the game, or what's left of it—not to mention that he, Bonds, Clemens, Ortiz?, Sosa, McGuire, and every other cheat should not even be mentioned in the same sentence with the old time record holders (Maris, Aaron, etc)—or they should have an asterisk placed next to their names with an explanation of cheating the fan base and MLB record holders in their illegitimate pursuit of records. Yeah you can argue that everyone cheats a little but the old-timers didn't have PEDs to pump up their home runs (and head size) especially when they were aging. (King 2015)

This second comment casts Rodríguez's career and apology letter squarely in terms of capital and manhood. The idea that Rodríguez should "pay it forward" indexes a restorative justice model where giving to children in need could in some way pardon the greed that presumably drove him to use performance-enhancing substances in the first place. By then asking, "Does he have the balls now to really be a man and give something back to [the] community?" this fan links financial capital to productive masculinity, and is particularly preoccupied with Rodríguez having betrayed the kids that believed in him. The premise that an elite athlete can or should buy his way out of disgrace after cheating belies the tenuous position of sports stars, especially men of color who are recruited to push their bodies to their physical limits as a source of entertainment for a massive audience of spectators, and to represent an ethos of hard work and physical strength as a testament to strength of character. As Todd Boyd (1997) has argued in his work on black NBA players, this system highlights the ways in which historical race and class tensions are mapped onto bodies of color, where individual athletes may exploit the very same capitalist system that has denied them full access for so long. The fact that this fan implores us not to mention the current record-holding players accused of PED violations with old-time record holders such as Maris and Aaron, and that there should be an asterisk next to their names, reiterates a strong work ethic associated with an imagined pure baseball past, before the availability of help via pharmacology, and before the extreme greed driven by inflated players' salaries.

The asterisk on Rodríguez's career frames "The Education of Alex Rodríguez" in *ESPN Magazine*, by J. R. Moehringer, published on February 18, 2015. Moehringer chronicles the time of Rodríguez's suspension within a wider context of his life and development as a man, explaining that the two things that Rodríguez most wanted out of life, and did not receive, were the presence of his father and a college education: "No father, no college. Those are his two gaping wounds" (Moehringer 2015). The idea of the education of Alex Rodríguez structures the article and serves as a way of understanding constructions of Rodríguez by himself and others. Moehringer details the psychological barriers that Rodríguez has confronted since his suspension and his search for redemption in therapy, journaling, and education, taking a course in marketing at the University of Miami. Moehringer captures Alex Rodríguez's career and fall from grace through the tensions wrought on his body and persona:

> Rodriguez was born with an embarrassment of physical riches—power, vision, energy, size, speed—and seemed designed specifically for immortality, as if assembled in some celestial workshop by baseball angels and the artists at Marvel Comics. He then had the annoyingly immense good fortune to come of age at the exact moment baseball contracts were primed to explode. Months after he was old enough to rent a car he signed a contract worth $252 million. Seven years later: another deal worth $275 million. Add

to that windfall another $500 million worth of handsome, and people were just waiting. Fans will root for a megarich athlete who's also ridiculously handsome (body by Rodin, skin like melted butterscotch, eyes of weaponized hazelness), but the minute he stumbles, just ask Tom Brady, they'll stand in line to kick him in his spongy balls. (Moehringer 2015)

This characterization of Rodríguez draws on images of male beauty and power, casting his body as if it were a work of art, or the iconic pop culture image of a superhero, but above all else as a symbol of capital. The emphasis on the wealth generated by his body stands in direct proportion to the fan hatred born of his misuse of that body and its beauty.

Rodríguez's body, admired and vilified for the reasons mentioned above, stands in for a host of tensions related to social positions of Latin/o Americans in MLB. While it is certainly true that Rodríguez has violated MLB PED policies and has spent his career in pursuit of corporeal perfection and excess, media workers have also highlighted the lack that has contributed to such pursuits, a lack sometimes understood in terms of Latin/o American masculinities rooted in aggression and the inability or unwillingness to father their children. In fact, Moehringer argues that lack has led to the creation of A-Rod, an excessive alter ego to the "virginal" and "bicultural" Dominican boy, not fully comfortable in English or in Spanish (Moehringer 2015). This characterization of infantilization versus excess merits further study as these two constructions of Latin/o American players share some common ground, as shall be seen in the case of Manny Ramírez, another Latin/o American player understood as having struggled with migration from the Dominican Republic and never having grown up due to the absence of a father, but construed as less calculating and more childlike than Alex Rodríguez.

"Manny Being Manny": Between Latino Threat and Infantilization

Like Ozzie Guillén and Alex Rodríguez, Manny Ramírez has emerged as one of the most polemic players in recent MLB history. Like Rodríguez, his place in the game and his public persona engage the core issues surrounding Latin/o American players as well as players at large. He has been implicated in MLB's steroid era as well as a controversy over spousal abuse, and he is often constructed as a self-centered and lazy player, interested more in his own salary and success than that of his team, despite several coaches attesting to Ramírez's strong work ethic, coming to the park early before games and working tirelessly to correct flaws in his hitting. Having played the majority of his career for the Boston Red Sox, Ramírez was instrumental in the 2004 and 2007 Red Sox World Series victories after an eighty-six-year championship drought. As with Ozzie Guillén, media and fan constructions of Manny Ramírez often index passion, visceral reactions, and lack of self-control, termed "Manny being Manny."[9] Also, as with Alex Rodríguez, media discourses often position Ramírez as selfish and egocentric. In contrast to Guillén and Rodríguez, Ramírez often emerges in media discourse as childlike in his pursuit of baseball greatness, a hitting savant oblivious to his surroundings, particularly when at bat. In this way, the Ramírez case contributes to and pushes beyond the Latino threat narrative proposed by Chávez, providing for further nuance in our understandings of Latin/o American players and Latino masculinities.

Questions of Ramírez's development as a man and his integration into MLB fame as a transnational player born in the Dominican Republic frame Rhodes and Boburg's authorized biography, *Becoming Manny: Inside the Life of Baseball's Most Enigmatic Slugger*, a project the authors describe as challenging due to Ramírez's erratic nature and unwillingness to fully commit to the project. *Becoming Manny* provides a greater context for understanding media and fan-generated representations as it includes research on Ramírez's early life and career as well as interviews with family members and key figures in his life. Indeed, instead of simply demonstrating ways that media workers and fans demonize Latin/o American players, it is important to understand these depictions within the behaviors of these men as wealthy men of color, negotiating transnational masculinities and social systems and the pressure to produce as players, contexts that sometimes lead to destructive behaviors.

According to Rhodes, the impetus for writing Ramírez's story grew out of her own interest in mentoring, having met Ramírez's mentor, Carlos "Macaco" Ferreira. She felt it was important to understand how the presence and absence of men in key moments of Ramírez's life shaped his growth and formation in adulthood. As such, *Becoming Manny* contextualizes Ramírez's life within paradigms of transnationalism (Ramírez having been born in the Dominican Republic and arriving in the US at twelve years of age) and anthropological research on gender and family construction in Latin America, citing scholars in these fields. For example, to understand Ramírez's behavior, the authors cite a study from *Family Planning Perspectives*, which emphasizes the primacy of male children in Latin/o American families such that they are treated as "little

---

9. Mickey White, a scout for the Cleveland Indians, coined the phrase "Manny being Manny" to describe Ramírez's seemingly oblivious behavior in contrast to his extreme concentration on hitting (Rhodes and Boburg 2011, 290).

kings" (Rhodes and Boburg 2011, 19).[10] While this research does lend a wider context to Ramírez's life—mentioning the primacy of male children in Latin American families and women's desire to give birth to them despite health risks and economic constraints, as well as the role of male children within the family structure—it also indexes similar problematic images of Latin/o American masculinities as driven by passion, aggression, and violence, dangerous images as they can be deployed to marginalize and justify the criminalization of Latino men.

Incidents in Ramírez's career range from the aggression of pushing the Red Sox sixty-three-year-old traveling secretary Jack McCormick, to ducking in and out of the Green Monster while taking his defensive position in left field, to running onto the field waving a small flag after becoming a naturalized US citizen on May 10, 2004 (Rhodes and Boburg 2011, 233). Toward the end of Ramírez's time with the Red Sox, media and fan coverage began to emphasize both the violence associated with the incident with Jack McCormick and what allegedly amounted to a work stoppage as Ramírez began to miss games due to injuries. The theory went that his agent, Scott Boras, orchestrated this in order to force the Red Sox to release Ramírez from the last year of his contract to pursue a more lucrative deal elsewhere.

As with other Latin/o American players, narratives of Ramírez in his biography and via media outlets emphasize the rags-to-riches struggles of a young man who grew up amid poverty, violence, and a lack of adequate formal education but who, due to talent and some level of hard work, overcame these circumstances to rise to elite MLB stardom and emerge as a hero in both the US and his native Dominican Republic. Biographers Rhodes and Boburg point out that violent acts such as pushing the traveling secretary over a game ticket dispute are inexcusable, and as such *Becoming Manny* provides an explanation of his behavior couched in special talent, power imbalance, and psychology.[11] According to Rhodes and Boburg (2011):

> During formative teenage and early adult years, an unnatural alignment of youth and power led him into someone who is slightly more oblivious to the people and events around him and less schooled in manners, obligations, and constraints than the rest of us. Psychologists have referred to this

---

10. In addition to the *Family Planning Perspectives* study already mentioned, Rhodes and Boburg also cite Peggy Levitt's (2001) work on Dominican transnational practices to lend a greater context to Ramírez's life and behavior. In this way, *Becoming Manny* differs significantly from the other biographies of this study.

11. It is important to note that author Jean Rhodes holds a PhD in psychology and teaches at the University of Massachusetts at Amherst.

as *acquired situational narcissism,* a sort of clinical self-absorption that can sometimes afflict the rich and famous. (287–88)

Though this explanation, which Rhodes and Boburg acknowledge only partially explains Ramírez's behavior, draws much-needed attention to the power differentials that surround fame and behaviors of the famous, it does little to undercut the power differentials inherent in the Latino threat narrative that informs readings of Latin/o American players like Ramírez by media workers and fans. As we shall see via analysis of and fan reactions to "The Oh Manny Song," a satirical spoof of Ramírez's career originally posted to YouTube in 2008, understandings of Ramírez index lack of control, aggression, and moral lapses just as they lionize his ability to produce as a powerful hitter, underscoring the complexities of Ramírez and other Latin/o American MLB players as elite athletes and as representative of the national and local pride ascribed to MLB. While for some, winning earns players respect in the face of bad behavior, for others the hyperbolic pursuit of capital inherent in MLB careers renders the league and its players as undeserving of respect.

Fan reactions to Ramírez's erratic and enigmatic persona vary widely. While for some, he represents an ultimate hitting genius, for others he represents Latino pride and success as a public figure, and for yet others he is simply another spoiled athlete allowed to behave in destructive ways without sufficient consequences. A song criticizing Ramírez for his behavior indexes images of Manny as a threat but also as a buffoon, a common image associated with Latina/os in media discourse from the early days of Hollywood to the present. "Oh Manny," written by Jeff Mans and performed by Jonesy, circulated in the media and among Red Sox fans and was posted to YouTube on August 4, 2008, with a second version posted on September 18, 2009, after he was traded to the Los Angeles Dodgers. "Oh Manny," based on Barry Manilow's hit "Oh Mandy," inventories the many reasons why the Red Sox were justified in trading Ramírez and portrays him as a toxic presence in the Boston organization.

The "Oh Manny" song's satirical rendering of Ramírez's career celebrates the day that the Boston Red Sox are finally rid of Manny Ramírez, despite numerous coaches and managers attesting to the great amount of work that Ramírez dedicates to improving his hitting and the prolific career he forged there, contributing to two World Series wins. The song portrays Ramírez as above all lazy and lacking in character: "Your work ethic's crappy." The song's opening lines cast him in terms of bad character and low class: "You're a major pain in the ass. You're overpaid with zero class." As the song progresses, the message is that Boston is better off without Manny, and that Los Angeles will soon realize that he is not worth what it takes to manage his character as a player. This is accomplished via portraying Manny as a coward, "Run fast as you can. Off to LA's where you'll go," and a direct reference to the supposed work stoppage mentioned earlier via reference to a knee injury, "Well you claim that your knee is still achin'. Toward the end of the song, Manny Ramírez is summarily dismissed from Red Sox Nation via the proclamation, "No more crap from you will we be takin'."

The images that accompany the "Oh Manny Song" on YouTube evince a similar discourse of laziness and lack in character, captured primarily in performance and representation of Ramírez's body. Aside from the BostonSportz.com logo that opens the video, footage of Ramírez on the field and in the dugout comprises the vast majority of the video's content: For example, hugging teammates and smiling broadly, sporting a large reddish-blond afro (MRSLANEY7 2008). The most direct visual and auditory correlation comes early in the song as an image of Ramírez's posterior accompanies the lyrics, "You're a major pain in the ass." Other similar images casting Ramírez as buffoon include him from his lower back down to his feet, and kneeling on the field to clean under his fingernail, a shot from behind as he climbs the left field wall to high-five a fan, and picking his nose in the dugout. Similarly, his facial expressions throughout the video depict a playful nature, as opposed to the intensity usually associated with elite professional athletes. For example, in one image, he dons a childlike smile as he touches his pine tar–covered batting helmet.

Since Ramírez played left field for the Red Sox, the mythical Green Monster that houses seating and a manual scoreboard in Fenway Park also features prominently in the video as Ramírez was often known to enter the Green Monster during pitching changes and other game delays. The video opens with images of him hugging the Green Monster mascot and sitting inside and talking on his cell phone as he waves to fans, some of which have become iconic moments of "Manny being Manny." After footage of him in a Los Angeles Dodgers uniform standing alongside Tommy Lasorda, the video concludes, symbolically marking the end of Manny's career in Boston with an image of him emerging from the Green Monster holding a handwritten sign stating, "The new episode in Manny being Manny."

The selection of these images, along with one of Ramírez selling a grill on eBay, construct him in particular ways that highlight laziness and a lack of professionalism, and diminish his contributions and abilities as an athlete and one of MLB's best hitters of his generation (RedSoxNationVideos 2009). Such constructions of his body and place in Red Sox history underscore fan ambivalence, where any perceived breach of loyalty results in expulsion from Red

Sox Nation. In the case of Manny Ramírez, these images and subsequent fan comments on the video must be understood within the framework of Latino masculinities with the Latino threat narrative as well as the long history of representations of Latino masculinities in media. The laziness associated with Ramírez in these representations echoes the drunken buffoon images in early Hollywood.

The substantial comment stream following "The Oh Manny Song" posted on August 8, 2008, ranged from hatred to support of Ramírez and his impact on the Red Sox during his time with the team, especially the two World Series Championships of 2004 and 2007. Fans justified their opinions of Ramírez primarily in this perceived productivity or lack thereof. Indeed, a prevailing sentiment emerged that despite any personality issues or violations of MLB policies, Ramírez's numbers should speak for themselves, as many fans quoted his career statistics or specific playoff appearances, particularly his ability to produce under the pressure of playoffs. Those who did criticize him and found him to be toxic for the Red Sox organization cited his having pushed traveling secretary Jack McCormick (unacceptable because McCormick is an "old man") and teammate Kevin Youkilis. Some fans decried such behavior but did not feel that should overshadow Ramírez's accomplishments over a long career. Though a split emerged among fans, the tone of comments overall emphasized a discourse of meritocracy where Manny is basically "goofy," often referencing "Manny being Manny" as a defense for a flawed human being described as a "beast" on the field and "one of the best hitters in the game." Indeed, comments in defense of Ramírez intersect images of masculine power related to batting and home run production, and a playful orientation toward life.

The second post, of September 18, 2009, differs from the first in two significant ways: The small number of comments, and language—half of the comments are in Spanish or Spanglish. These comments index similar aspects of Ramírez's career in terms of home run production and capital, but those in Spanish more closely reference questions of manhood, strength, and character. While the comments in Spanish and Spanglish overwhelmingly support Ramírez as one of the greatest players of his generation, one negative comment indicts his character. Rolando jeter posted, "Que estupido video como todos los fanaticos de boston porque? no lo ponen fumando marihuanaa al hijo de perro ese que deshonra para este deporte, produce nahuseas la mierda esa" (What a stupid video just like all Boston fans. Why don't they show him smoking marihuana, that son of a bitch, what a dishonor for this sport, this shit produces nausea) (MRSLANEY7 2008). Though comments on both postings reference Ramírez's cowardice by way of homophobic insults, this sole comment specifically lambasts Ramírez as dishonoring baseball. One comment on this second post also indexes the racialized marker of Ramírez's dreadlocked hair as "ugly," intersecting it with a description of him as a "fag" in an attempt to vilify him. With few exceptions, comments on both video postings bolster an ideal of meritocracy associated with US ideology where merit and capital gain are used alternately to support or criticize Manny Ramírez as a player and as a man.

All of the constructions and understandings of Manny Ramírez mentioned engage tensions over capital and Latino masculinities that shape wider understandings of Latin/o American men in the US. In pursuit of his own American dream, Ramírez has violated MLB policy and showed questionable judgment in dealing with others and in negotiating the power differentials of MLB and the teams he has played for. By embodying the rags-to-riches story, akin to Regalado's special hunger narrative, Ramírez has awoken admiration from those who understand his behavior from a sometimes problematic deficit model of lack of male mentoring and consistency growing up in poverty in the Dominican Republic and then in Washington Heights in New York City. For others, his stature as an elite MLB player demands that he be held to a high standard of character, despite whatever socioeconomic, gendered, or global power differentials inform his formation as a man. Though debates over character partially frame perceptions of Manny Ramírez, the case of Robinson Canó and his departure from the New York Yankees more acutely highlight tensions around morality.

"Deadbeat Dad" and Yankee Betrayal: Robinson Canó and the Limits of Latino Character

On December 12, 2013, Robinson Canó finalized a move to the Seattle Mariners after spending his entire major league career thus far with the New York Yankees. The deal, at ten years and $240 million, is among the most lucrative in MLB history (Associated Press 2013). Canó's move and media constructions of his narrative as a player reveal the competing discourses of sainted baseball man of the people whose talents lifted him from squalor in the Dominican Republic and the lazy, overpaid, privileged sports star of color lacking in moral character so often part of the Latino baseball story.

On December 14, 2013, on the heels of the Canó signing, *Seattle Times* staff writer Larry Stone wrote a profile of Canó spanning his career from his recruitment in the Dominican town of San Pedro de Macorís, an iconic baseball town that has produced superstars like Sammy Sosa, to the recent signing and what Mariners fans were getting in Canó. Stone emphasizes his charity work at a New Jersey children's hospital but also underscores baseball insiders' perceptions of him as naturally talented but lazy. The article constructs him via similar imagery as other Dominican players, such as Manny Ramírez (Domino Rudolph 2012), who seem to have innate natural talents that allow them to perform at a high level, which is sometimes misconstrued as laziness as these men take on an industry-wide perception of them as lackadaisical and unmotivated despite the actual work they might do to hone their bodies and their craft. According to former coach Bill Masse, "Put it this way: He wanted to show up at 6:55 and play at 7. He wanted to perform. It took a lot of hard work to teach him how to practice correctly. I always said that once he learned how to work and learned how to get into his routine, he'd be a superstar. Sure enough . . ." (Stone 2013). Masse then stated of a more mature Canó, "He got the rap that he didn't run balls out, was lazy at times, he's a dog or whatever. Nothing could be further from the truth. Things came so easy for him it looked like he didn't try. It's just that his actions were so fluid. He was getting to balls no one else would have been within five feet of" (Stone 2013). Both descriptions of Canó render him a passionate, instinct-driven player who does not fit into the working-class bootstraps work ethic associated with baseball, where supposed hard work will net a young man fame and fortune in Major League Baseball.

The article goes on to profile Canó's life growing up between the Dominican Republic and New Jersey. In fact, the family's relocation back to the Dominican Republic was a result of not only the tensions between black Americans and Dominicans in the neighborhood but also José Canó's desire to provide his son with the best chance of pursuing a career in baseball—a prospect that was much more likely in the Dominican Republic than New Jersey due to scouting practices that favor communities of color in the Caribbean as opposed to communities of color in the US (Rhodes and Boburg 2011). José Canó juxtaposed baseball and education in his proposition to his son to return to San Pedro de Macorís: "Do you want to play baseball every day in the Dominican or go to school up here?" (Stone 2013). Press coverage casts Canó's story as one of rags to riches via the attainment of the American dream so often associated with Latin/o American players, mentioning that in addition to his fame and fortune, Canó is now a US citizen, perhaps moving him closer to becoming a national hero despite being a man of color, born in another country, whose first language is Spanish.

Despite these more positive narratives of hard work and US citizenship, another side of the Canó story has also emerged as a result of his move to the Mariners. On the heels of the move, on December 12, 2013, the *Daily News* published an article on Canó with the following headline: "Robinson Cano a Deadbeat Dad? Judge in Dominican Republic Orders Increase in Child Support for Son" (Red 2013). The story profiles Canó's protracted child support dispute with his son's mother, which had already been in court for several months. Though Canó certainly should support his son and share his wealth with his child, the timing and the characterization of the story, which was also featured on MSNBC and ESPN the same week, connects this personal matter with Canó's professional decision to change teams, deployed as a means to discredit and villainize him as a traitor to Yankees Nation. This strategy is often used to Other Latin/o American players as it calls into question their conduct and characters as men. Markovitz (2011) terms such incidents "racial spectacles," where a spectacle is created in the media to distract people from the material and racialized conditions of modern capitalism so as to minimize social protest against such conditions and to buttress a nationalist ideology (4–5). Quotes from the lawyer for Canó's son's mother, Jackelin Castro, emphasize abandonment and capital: "Sadly, we cannot force a judge to tell Robinson to love his son more. We want to secure the boy's future and have something saved for him" (Red 2013). Later in the article, she goes on to make the case for an increase in child support as follows: "We're talking about someone who made $15 million last season. Robinson, the son, he doesn't have a secure income as of now. That's a shame" (Red 2013).

Again, the issue in question here is not Canó's obligations as a father, as he does have a responsibility to his son, but rather the timing of the story and the emphasis on images of the "deadbeat dad" and the greed of capitalism so often associated with men of color sports stars. Indeed, readers' comments posted after the article demonstrate a similar viewpoint. Comments on the *Daily News* article engage in a heated debate over Canó's duties and character as a father and as a Dominican man. This debate centers primarily on gendered constructions of Jackelin Castro as an insufficiently attractive woman for a man of Canó's status and a gold digger. Readers cast Canó as a wealthy man whose sexual and economic potency need to be checked either by wearing a condom or by forcing him to share his wealth with his son. Economic and legal issues in the debate further cement the binary of the US as a civilized and wealthy country while the Dominican Republic is uncivilized and poor, as many readers felt that in the US Canó would be held more accountable to pay adequate child support based on his salary. Some argued that $600 to $1,200 monthly is more than sufficient to live comfortably in the Dominican Republic, the perception being that the Dominican legal system is unlikely to require Canó to pay a larger portion of his salary. The point here is that the Canó child support debate that emerged in the wake of discontent over his baseball loyalty—a fact not lost on a handful of readers who commented—eschews issues of the burden of representation and media construction in favor of the sensationalizing of a personal matter and utilizing it to fuel fans' discontent and reiterate problematic gendered constructions of Latin/o American men as absentee fathers as a result of their unrelenting pursuit of capital.

Media narratives casting Robinson Canó as a traitor to the Yankee organization and MLB after these organizations provided him with a means to escape poverty, focusing on his contentious paternity case in the Dominican Republic only after his decision to move to Seattle, highlight how media and popular culture serve as crucial sites of debate over the Latin/a/o American presence in the US. Given the pseudo-nationalism associated with sports consumption and fandom, MLB's Latin/o American players provide a crucial set of examples to unpack the place and constructions of Latina/os in the US in terms of race and class due to the significant numbers of players and the varied media and fan reactions to these players.

Conclusion

Constructions and representations of all of the men analyzed here—from the Guillén/Piniella dichotomy to Guillén's managerial career, Alex Rodriguez and Manny Ramírez's performance-enhanced bodies as contested sites of integrity and MLB policy, and Robinson Canó's loyalty and moral character as a father—indicate a sense of lack, be that cultural/linguistic competence in US norms and social practices or adequate male role models to support their development as men of integrity and character. Such understandings of Latin/o American men stem from perceptions of Latin American culture as deficient, compared with the US, and also align with broader understandings of men of color from a deficiency model long criticized by sociologists and anthropologists (Noguera et al. 2011). The cases presented here demonstrate the ways that narratives of lack and deficiency serve both to foster color-blind narratives circulating in post-Obama media discourses and to occlude racist local and hemispheric structures, in deference to individual character. As such, readings of Ozzie Guillén, Alex Rodríguez, Manny Ramírez, and Robinson Canó impel policy shifts that engage racialization and difference instead of embracing a color-blind rhetoric that emphasizes meritocracy, ignoring the reality of an uneven playing field.

CONCLUSION

"Yo quiero jugar como David Ortiz"

Final Thoughts on Race and the Viability of MLB's
Latin/o American Dream in the US Context

AFTER WINNING the World Series in 2018, the Boston Red Sox did not immediately announce their customary White House visit, despite such visits being customary since the 1960s. Similar to the Chicago Cubs' 2016 World Series win, political tensions and Latinidad foregrounded the White House visit. Controversies surrounding anti-immigrant politics and race during the Trump administration have seen a decline in such visits, most notably the cancellation of the Philadelphia Eagles' visit due to low attendance from players. In the case of the Red Sox, attention focused on Puerto Rican manager Alex Cora's critique of Trump administration and its handling of the relief efforts in Puerto Rico following Hurricane Maria. Cora believes that Trump politicized the controversy over the official death count and dehumanized Puerto Ricans, being unwilling to accept the level of devastation suffered on the island and unwilling to take responsibility for relief aid as president of the United States. The team eventually did agree to a visit, which team president Sam Kennedy stressed was optional, though the visit was postponed to May 2019 due to the December 2018 government shutdown. Cora initially said that he would go and use the visit as a platform to represent his people: "I'm going to use my platform the right way. I'm not going to embarrass anybody. Actually, I'm going to represent 4 million people from back home the right way when we go there" (Boren 2018). Later, he decided not to be a part of the May 9 visit. Cora's decision not to visit the White House and use his platform the "right way" to protest Trump's stance on Puerto Rico as a way to represent the island reminds us of the duality of Latin/o American masculinities that must walk a thin line between pride and advocacy on the one hand and respectability on the other.

Media coverage and reactions to performance-enhancing drug (PED) use in MLB, in addition to player retirements, provide a space to interrogate some of the tensions around this duality and Latinidad in the US, embedded in a post-racial notion of nationalism. David "Big Papi" Ortiz has emerged, not only as one of the greatest hitters of his generation but as a role model and aspirational example for Latin/o Americans, especially Dominican (American) males living in harsh economic conditions. Conversely, the circulation of scandals and controversies surrounding Dominican players has cast a pall on perceptions of Dominican character and ethics. In recent years, press reports that Ortiz was among a group of players who tested positive for PEDs in 2003, and the 2018 suspension of Robinson Canó for violation of MLB's PED policy, remind us of the tensions around conduct, masculinity, and Latinidad that continue to circulate via media, fans, and MLB personnel. Ortiz's 2016 retirement complicated perceptions of him as both celebratory and accusatory of cheating. Though his name was included in the Mitchell Report of roughly one hundred players who tested positive for PEDs in 2003, Ortiz maintains that he never used steroids and fears putting such chemicals into his body. In 2003 MLB tested for steroids for the first time to gain an understanding of how widespread steroid use was in baseball at that time. The results were to be kept confidential, but a leaked list revealed some of the names of those who tested positive. The results were later seized by agents investigating the use of PEDs by professional athletes as part of the Mitchell Report and have resulted in protracted litigation between the federal government and the players' union.

I highlight media coverage and reactions to the retirement and PED allegations of Ortiz and the PED suspension of Canó to deepen the present analysis of race, class, masculinity, and MLB as a means to move conversations on gendered national identity, immigration, and Latinidad forward. Ortiz's continued status as a role model, and perceptions of Canó as increasingly problematic, read within both players' associations with PEDs, highlight the complexities and limits of the post-racial era in the US from 2007 to 2016, marked by the election and presidency of the first black American president of the United States, Barack H. Obama, and leading to the election of Donald J. Trump, resulting in an even more hostile racial climate. Obama's election ushered in a post-racial moment defined by "the belief that skin color or other physical markers of racial or ethnic identity are irrelevant" (Molina-Guzmán

2018, 3). Whereas the lauded, famous black body of David Ortiz, like that of Barack Obama, sends the message that race doesn't matter, the vilified famous black body of Robinson Canó reminds us that race still very much matters in the daily lives of men of color. Arguably, the fact that Ortiz has been associated with PEDs but never formally accused or suspended provides enough plausible deniability to shield him from the scorn visited on Canó. Also, the individual success of Ortiz, and his presentation of self, one that does not often foreground his blackness, underscore the conventional wisdom that racism and discrimination are individual, as opposed to structural and systemic, issues, since Ortiz has enjoyed a successful career and largely unblemished reputation.

Ultimately, this conclusion argues that the MLB case study illustrates the ways in which, regardless of class status, the racialization of men of color buttresses a nativist political agenda. As famous or "spectacular bodies," MLB's Latin/o American players make public a host of structural inequalities that continue to contour the life experiences of ordinary Latin/o American men in the US as an exploited and vulnerable labor force and threat to "American" national identity (Canó), but also reassure US Americans that racism depends on the individual in the post-racial US (Ortiz). The conclusion also puts forth final observations about Latinidad in baseball and examines the extent to which Latin/o American players' success and reception symbolically contest nativism and institutional racism and function as tools of Latina/o pride and strength. Finally, I indicate Brazilians, and the recent media attention to São Paolo native Yan Gomes, as an area for future studies on MLB and Latinidad.

"Yo quiero jugar como David Ortiz": David Ortiz as Post-Racial Role Model

Two autobiographies, *Big Papi: My Story of Big Dreams and Big Hits* (2007), coauthored with Tony Massarotti, and *Papi, My Story* (2017), coauthored with Michael Holley, tell David Ortiz's story from his viewpoint, a story that upholds the baseball-as-American-dream narrative espoused by MLB, a narrative that lauds meritocracy and follows the post-racial script of the US as a place where race no longer matters when it comes to achieving success. This is also consistent with constructions of race in the Dominican Republic that erase blackness as part of Dominican heritage and focus more on social class as a mechanism of systemic inequality. As Ortiz is an Afro-Dominican who is racially marked as black in the US, it is striking that he mentions race but asserts that blackness has not been a significant barrier, or even a factor in his trajectory to MLB, evincing a color-blind US perspective or a silenced blackness that often circulates in the Dominican context. In crafting his official persona, Ortiz relies heavily on discourses of uplift, hard work, and familial love in the face of hardship as foundational to his narrative. He casts his baseball career within the context of hard work and struggle to persist at the major league level, contrasting his struggles with the Minnesota Twins with his success finding a home with the Boston Red Sox. In addition to his three World Series Wins with the Red Sox, Ortiz highlights becoming a US citizen and supporting the city of Boston in the aftermath of the Boston Marathon bombing in 2013. When asked to speak on behalf of his team at Fenway Park, a week after the bombing, Ortiz reclaimed Boston pride: "This is our fucking city. And no one is going to dictate our freedom. Stay strong" (Ortiz and Holley 2017, 191). Ortiz weaves together his pride in being an American citizen and the commitment to Boston's recovery after the bombing with the Red Sox's visit to the White House in April 2014, after winning the World Series in 2013. Ortiz presented President Obama with a number 44 jersey as Obama spoke, honoring the team. For Ortiz, this was a critical moment as he recalled Obama's speech a year earlier, speaking to the strength of the city of Boston in the wake of the bombing, and the show of pride and commitment from its sports teams via their parade in support of Boston's healing (Ortiz and Holley 2017, 211–12). The symbolic gesture of the jersey presentation and the selfie he took with Obama, as well as Ortiz's narrative framing of their meeting within the two men's mission to uplift the city of Boston in a time of crisis—a crisis rooted in many US Americans' greatest fear, terrorism—further cements Ortiz, along with Obama, as evidence of the supposed irrelevance of race and the hyper-relevance of merit, hard work, and ethics in the post-racial US. This has been the dominant narrative surrounding Ortiz's retirement.

Among the myriad social media well wishes and articles celebrating Ortiz's prolific career, *Sports Illustrated* and the *Boston Globe* issued commemorative issues on Ortiz's retirement. Both publications feature photojournalistic representations of David Ortiz from his youth in the Dominican Republic as a prospect to the three World Series Championships with the Boston Red Sox leading up to his retirement in 2016. Both publications craft a narrative of Ortiz's life and career within discourses of hard work, compassion, and his "big personality," casting him as a fun-loving man who has proven himself to be dependable, honorable, and a team leader. Both publications also emphasize his support for the city of Boston after the Boston Marathon bombing in 2013. Featuring articles by well-known sports writers, as well as teammate Pedro Martínez and Red Sox owner John Henry, *Sports Illustrated* and the

Boston Globe institutionalize Ortiz as a baseball hero, making the case for his entry into the Hall of Fame despite the cloud of PED use that continues to haunt his career narrative.

Despite any unresolved suspicions of PED use, in 2017 the Boston Red Sox offered Ortiz a lifetime contract as an advisor/ambassador for the organization. Among Ortiz's main responsibilities will be serving as a mentor for current players, helping recruit free agents, making special appearances for the organization, and working in a business development capacity for Fenway Sports Management and its partners. Red Sox principal owner John Henry explains in a statement: "His skill and success on the diamond are rivaled only by his spirit, compassion, and big heart. I cannot think of a better representative for our organization. I'm happy we can now say officially what we have long known, David is family. For over a decade and a half, we have gotten to know what kind of man David is both on and off the field" (Joyce 2017). In the team press release, Ortiz states, "I'm happy to be able to help the Red Sox organization I love in any way I can. Whether that's offering advice to a young player, helping convince a free agent that there's no better city to play in than Boston, or representing the club in the community and with its partners, it's great to be part of the Red Sox organization. It feels like I never left" (Joyce 2017). Mixed fan reactions offer a somewhat more complicated Ortiz narrative as some allude to steroid use and stealing signs while others honor his legacy. Fan skepticism notwithstanding, this announcement's narrative aligns with the persona steeped in family, honor, and compassion that Ortiz's camp has crafted for him. Though Ortiz never served a suspension for PED use once MLB instituted an official policy beginning in 2005, some media workers and fans assert that he is as guilty as players listed on the Mitchell Report who have served suspensions. Players such as Alex Rodríguez, Manny Ramírez, and Sammy Sosa, whose names were also on the 2003 list, and who have served suspensions, have not fared as well in retirement and will likely not enter the Baseball Hall of Fame. Indeed, the exceptionalism of Ortiz contrasts with the story of Robinson Canó's PED suspension, one steeped in the negative perceptions of Dominicans as corrupt and eager to cut corners in their pursuit of MLB success, also seen in the narratives of Rodríguez, Ramírez, and Sosa.

The "Dominican Way": Robinson Canó and the Corruption of Dominican Character

The May 2018 suspension of Robinson Canó sparked a strong reaction in his native Dominican Republic. His suspension came not long after Starling

Marte's suspension, followed by Wellington Castillo shortly after. All three Dominicans received suspensions as a result of violating MLB's performance-enhancing drug policy. Though in recent years such suspensions have become fairly common, three in close proximity affected Dominican fans strongly. As one of MLB's elite current players, Canó's suspension caused the greatest stir. Canó had tested positive for furosemide, a diuretic sometimes used as a masking agent, before the 2018 season. Canó retracted his appeal when MLB was able to make the case that the drug was used as a masking agent (Soldevilla 2018). Media and fan reactions to the Canó suspension further illustrate the systemic tensions around nationalism, labor, race, masculinity, and baseball at the core of this study. Ranging from disbelief to rage at the shame Canó's suspension brings to Dominican baseball, these reactions serve as a reminder of MLB's ongoing struggle with PEDs and the systemic inequality that leads so many players from Latin America to use them.

The Facebook page "La Vida Baseball" captures the meanings and tensions surrounding the suspensions of Marte, Canó, and Castillo, but especially Canó. In "Dominicans Shaken by PED Suspensions," Soldevilla (2018) notes the significance when the news of Canó's suspension broke: "Comments on social media showed how big the news was in the Dominican Republic. Minutes after the rumor spread thanks to a tweet by Dominican sports journalist Franklin Mirabal on his account, @elreydelaradio, Canó was the most trending topic in the Dominican." This indicates that much more than Canó missing eighty games is at stake for Dominicans here. Canó, and his behavior as a representative of the Dominican Republic, became a referendum on corruption and Dominican character via fan and media workers' reactions. The burden of representation emerged as some noted that history treats superstar players like Canó more harshly than players of average talent: "Bartolo Colón is praised now for his longevity and his easygoing ways while others like [Manny] Ramírez [considered one of the greatest hitters of his generation] have been exiled even from conversations about the all-time greats" (Soldevilla 2018). This burden of representation gives way to a more nuanced debate about Dominican character and ethic surrounding Dominican baseball via the varied responses to Mirabal's tweet.

The Canó debate ranges from defenders of Canó who cite his good works and blame corrupt influences for the violation, while others see this as one more example of how baseball intersects with Dominican corruption more broadly. Some advocate for him based on his charitable work in his hometown of San Pedro de Macorís, and his role as captain of the 2013 Dominican World Baseball Classic team, which he led to victory, with many noting that individual players often get caught up in a corrupt system of PEDs allowed to flourish in the Dominican Republic, controlled by handlers, trainers, and scouts who do not necessarily have players' best interests at heart. Detractors blame what they call the "Dominican Way," a term that refers to the idea that on the island, both the government and individuals take "shortcuts" instead of working to attain their goals (Soldevilla 2018). Informal and official responses to the news underscore the gravity of PEDs in Dominican baseball and the need for systemic change that is likely not forthcoming as concerned Dominicans call on the government to enact stringent laws regulating these substances, while MLB's Dominican office did not immediately comment due to the delicacy of the situation. The initial silence from MLB's Dominican office and the government's historic unease with strictly regulating the presence, activities, and influences of MLB in the Dominican Republic allow stories like Canó's to continue to impugn Dominican character and feed conventional wisdom about Latin/o Americans from a transnational perspective based on superficial and stereotypical representations, and individual blame, disconnected from global systemic inequality, a topic to which I shall now turn as the Ortiz and Canó cases push us to consider the intersections between elite Latin/o American baseball masculinities and systemic racism and structural inequality.

Final Considerations on MLB and Latinidad

Throughout this book, I have sought to broaden and problematize understandings of Latino masculinities from an intersectional perspective, as a means of engaging wider conversations about the Latino threat narrative and immigration, increasingly relevant topics in the current political climate of the US. Of particular interest to the current study is the intersection of class in this narrative. Little has been written about the ways that wealth contours Latina/os' experiences of systemic inequality. Conventional wisdom would indicate that wealth moves structural barriers and systemic inequality, similar to the popular adage in Latin America that "money whitens" as a metaphor for the intersection between wealth and white privilege. I would argue instead that, similar to the politics of respectability argument that some have marshaled as an antidote to discrimination to racism against black Americas, wealth has not significantly moved barriers impeding inclusion of Latin/o Americans to full access to social privilege. The argument that "respectability" in dress and behavior would bring greater social acceptance to black Americans has proven to be unfounded (Entman and Rojecki 2000; Omi and Winant 1994; Ray 2018). Similarly, while some of MLB's Latin/o American players have indeed gained access to economic wealth, both the structure of MLB as an industry and many of the narratives circulating around individual players and Latin/o Americans in general, via media worker and fan production, continue to perpetuate and uphold the Latino threat narrative, in particular as it relates to Latin/o American men.

The trajectory of the argument put forth in *Baseball as Mediated Latinidad: Race, Masculinity, Nationalism, and Performances of Identity* demonstrates that MLB continues to uphold larger neoliberal corporate practices in labor recruitment and compensation, as well as socially and politically rooted anxieties about Latin/o American men as perpetual immigrants who threaten to fray the fabric of US nationalism. Evidence of this exists from the historical roots and representations of Latin/o American players, be it in the differences in opportunities for and perceptions of players based on skin color and name, to present concerns about language and national identities embodied by players. Through exploring a group of case studies that locate contemporary players within the historical contexts of Latin/o Americans in MLB, as well as current social and political climates and debates, I have sought to show that individual players' narratives reveal the intricacies of structural inequality and racism in the US and Latin America as these men embody and straddle transnational identities, loyalties, and socio- and geopolitical contexts. Media production, circulation, and social media interactions have become the main platforms through which to debate issues of nationalism, loyalty, race, and immigration. Since the proliferation of social media platforms such as Facebook, YouTube, Instagram, Twitter, Snapchat, and others, as well as blogs and comment streams on newsfeeds, media production about MLB has become a vital site of negotiation and debate where fans and media workers around the world can debate who may sing the US national anthem at the All-Star Game; how much Spanish, if any, we should hear in MLB dugouts and ballparks; the implications of Sammy Sosa whitening his skin; the ethics of racialized recruitment of MLB players in the Spanish Caribbean; or the importance of personal character among MLB's superstars as role models whose spectacular bodies come to represent Latin/o American male identity for many fans. At the root of all of these cases is whiteness and the ways that the US and Latin American nations construct, understand, and deploy whiteness as a social construct to limit access for some while granting it to others.

Beginning with the ongoing case of Sammy Sosa's skin bleaching, media workers and fans sustain a debate around whiteness, access, black pride, and the fraught history of African enslavement and Spanish colonization in the Caribbean. Indeed, as of this writing, pictures of a whitened Sosa circulate on the internet via memes, jokes, and blogs and webpages dedicated to black pride. These uses belie the continued pain that circulates in countries that have not yet reckoned with the historical traumas of enslavement and colonization that sustain white supremacy to the present. In fact, the case of Puerto Rico, which many argue remains a US colony in supposedly postcolonial times, highlights this relationship between white supremacy and trauma, as many MLB fans mark the body of US Puerto Rican salsa singer Marc Anthony as nonwhite and un-American and thus unable to perform "God Bless America" at the 2013 All-Star Game. Vividly aware of this dynamic, mainland and island-based Puerto Ricans mobilized around Team Puerto Rico's success in the 2017 World Baseball Classic as an act of nationalism, particularly in the final game between Puerto Rico and the US, as a metaphor for the struggle many Puerto Ricans feel between the two nations. Though Puerto Rico lost, amid an era of economic austerity and control via PROMESA legislation, the team's outstanding performance in the tournament united Puerto Ricans around national pride in baseball, if only temporarily. The devastation of Hurricane Maria roughly six months later, and the US government's inadequate response, reminds us of the daily struggles of colonialism embedded in grossly unequal power differentials. MLB, and many individual players, especially Puerto Rican players and managers, used their economic and social capital to collect relief funds, hosting charitable events at ballparks and elsewhere, as well as via social media. The traumas and pride rooted in Dominican and Puerto Rican blackness and national identity in these cases function similarly in transnational and US contexts via Spanish language use, labor recruitment, and media worker and fan constructions of players through conventional wisdom of Latino masculinities as at best problematic and at worst destructive to US nationalism and economies.

English language use has long been associated with US nationalism, and not speaking English, or speaking languages in addition to English, calls into question the loyalty of US citizens and residents as part of the national mythology. Spanish especially, given the conflictive relationship with Mexico over the shared border with the US, has been racialized and coded as "un-American" and associated with undocumented immigration. Well aware of this dynamic, and eager to retain its position as "America's pastime" and root itself in white US nationalism, MLB has always had a tense relationship with the Spanish language, from de facto to de jure policies and practices that silence or minimize Spanish use among MLB's significant Spanish-speaking labor force. Only in 2016 did MLB officially institute a policy mandating translators for Spanish-speaking players, though Japanese players often have escort interpreters when they arrive in the US, highlighting a racialized inconsistency in MLB policy. As we saw with the backlash against the 2013 Spanish language broadcast of the World Baseball Classic game between Puerto Rico and the Dominican Republic on ESPN, MLB has cause to treat the Spanish language with caution, lest it alienate significant parts of its fan base. It has only been through the advocacy work of former and current players and managers such as Ozzie Guillén and Carlos Beltrán that MLB finally institutionalized interpretation services for its teams. Policy notwithstanding, de facto language policing still exists for Spanish-speaking players. During the 2018 season, Chicago White Sox president Ken Williams assured fans and media workers that Cuban infielder Yoan Moncada does speak English despite his working with the team translator for media interviews. Williams has also implored Moncada to speak English more so that he can connect to fans. Williams's stance illustrates the extent to which the Spanish language continues to be perceived as distancing and unwelcome in mainstream US institutional and social settings. Thus, the racialized marking of Spanish joins the labor recruitment practices and concerns around character and Latino masculinities tied to MLB players as evidence that wealth does not move systemic racism and parallels the experiences of undocumented Latin/o American laborers.

Labor and Latin/o American masculinities coalesce in the body of Yasiel Puig and his defection and journey from Cuba to the US. MLB has for years both housed and trained young men in the Dominican Republic and Venezuela in what essentially amount to labor camps while also turning a blind eye to the harrowing journeys of Cuban players like Yasiel Puig who sometimes risk their lives to come to play for MLB in the US. Puig embodies the risks and rewards associated with MLB labor recruitment, as well as concerns over Latin/o masculinities via his well-documented and life-threatening voyage to the US, and his life of excess since his arrival, including several speeding infractions and a guest appearance on the television series *Angie Tribeca*. Puig's strong black body, like those of other players such as Ozzie Guillén, Manny Ramírez, Alex Rodríguez, and Robinson Canó, has been read by some media workers and fans within the "black brute" imagery associated with men of color. Infractions by all of these men, be they speeding, performance-enhancing substance use, or child support cases, circulate through this lens in media and fan-generated content. A post wishing Manny Ramírez a happy birthday on the Facebook page "La Vida Baseball" inspired mixed comments. Though many were supportive, several fans admonished his PED use and perceived disloyalty to the purity of baseball, with some referencing his lazy defensive play. In contrast to lionized retired player David Ortiz, some media workers and fans connect the power and disciplining of male bodies of color, so prized in Ortiz, to transgression and character flaws that they perceive to be part and parcel of Latin/o American masculinities in the bodies of Guillén, Ramírez, Rodríguez, Canó, and Puig.

In the summer of 2018, media coverage celebrated the appearance of Yan Gomes, the first Brazilian to play in an MLB All-Star Game in 2018. Gomes, born in São Paolo, in addition to MLB executives, lauds this historic moment as a signal that more Brazilian players will likely enter MLB in the future, particularly via burgeoning recruitment efforts in São Paolo. This attention to Brazil evidences MLB's globalized search for new sources of cheap labor outside the US to fill its minor and major league systems, and centers Latin America and Latinidad in that search. Yan Gomes serves as a safe initial representation of Brazilians in MLB as his light skin marks him as white in the US, much like early white Cuban players during MLB's segregation era. As Brazil is the Latin American country with the largest black population, Brazilians will likely follow in the footsteps of Dominicans in their racialized integration into MLB if recruitment there increases. It is also unlikely that mainstream white US MLB fans will embrace Portuguese any more than they have Spanish, if they are even aware of the linguistic differences. Finally, Brazilians provide a fertile space for future studies of Latinidad in baseball and beyond in terms of their social and linguistic incorporation into the current MLB player structure. One thing is clear: MLB exemplifies how institutional racism and the Latino threat narrative continue to function within the ideological context of the post-racial US, and shows that individual wealth and fame of the "spectacular bodies" of MLB stars sustain inequality and post-racial narratives, while some individual players, like David Ortiz, provide Latin/o American fans moments of pride and pleasure, rooted in mediated baseball Latinidad.

BIBLIOGRAPHY

Alderson, S. (2009, September 23). Alderson report. Retrieved from https://archive.org/stream/608594-alderson-report/608594-alderson-report_djvu.txt.

Alim, H. S., J. R. Rickford, and A. F. Ball (Eds.). (2016). *Raciolinguistics: How language shapes our ideas about race*. New York, NY: Oxford University Press.

Alou, F., and P. Kerasotis. (2018). *Alou: My baseball journey*. Lincoln, NB: University of Nebraska Press.

Amazon. (n.d.-a). *Ballplayer: Pelotero* [Customer reviews]. Retrieved from https://www.amazon.com/gp/video/detail/B008FRI4JE/ref=pd_cbs_318_7#customer-review-section.

Amazon. (n.d.-b). *Rumbo a las grandes ligas / Road to the big leagues* [Customer reviews]. Retrieved from https://www.amazon.com/Road-Big-Leagues-Vladimir-Guerrero/dp/B0036GoTGo/ref=sr_1_1?s=amazon-devices&ie=UTF8&qid=1535462874&sr=8–1&keywords=rumbo+a+las+grandes+ligas#customerReviews.

Amazon. (n.d.-c). *Sugar* [Customer reviews]. Retrieved from https://www.amazon.com/Sugar-Algenis-Perez-Soto/dp/B002MBEHLS/ref=sr_1_1?ie=UTF8&qid=1535463186&sr=8–1&keywords=sugar+baseball+movie#customerReviews.

Anderson, S. (2018, April 27). 27% of Major League Baseball players are foreign-born. *Forbes*. Retrieved from https://www.forbes.com/sites/stuartanderson/2018/04/27/27-of-major-league-baseball-players-are-foreign-born/amp/.

Andrews, D., and S. J. Jackson. (2001). *Sports stars: The cultural politics of sporting celebrity*. New York, NY: Routledge.

Anzaldúa, G. (1987). *Borderlands / La frontera: The new mestiza*. San Francisco, CA: aunt lute books.

Aparicio, F. R. (1998). Whose Spanish, whose language, whose power?: Testifying to differential bilingualism. *Indiana Journal of Hispanic Literatures, 12*, 5–25.

Aparicio, F. R., and S. Chávez-Silverman (Eds.). (1997). *Tropicalizations: Transcultural representations of Latinidad.* Hanover, NH: University Press of New England.

ASAP sports. (2017). National Baseball Hall of Fame Induction Ceremony Ivan Rodríguez Speech. Retrieved from http://www.asapsports.com/show_interview.php?id=132649.

Associated Press. (2013, December 12). Robinson Cano and Mariners finalize huge contract. *USA Today.* Retrieved from http://www.usatoday.com/story/sports/mlb/2013/12/12/robinson-cano -and-mariners-finalize-huge-contract/4000471.

Austerlitz, P. (1997). *Merengue: Dominican music and Dominican identity.* Philadelphia, PA: Temple University Press.

Axisa, M. (2017, March 23). Watch: Puerto Rico holds WBC parade even after championship game loss to USA. Retrieved from http://www.cbssports.com/mlb/news/watch-puerto-rico -holds-wbc-parade-even-after-championship-game-loss-to-usa/.

Babiak, K., and R. Wolfe. (2013). Perspectives on social responsibility in sport. In J. L. Paramio-Salcines, K. Babiak, and G. Walters (Eds.), *The Routledge handbook of sport and corporate social responsibility* (pp. 17–34). New York, NY: Routledge.

Báez, J. (2009). *Latinas talk back: The Latina body, citizenship, and popular culture* (Unpublished dissertation). University of Illinois at Urbana–Champaign.

Báez, J. (2014). Latina/o audiences as citizens: Bridging culture, media and politics. In A. Dávila and Y. M. Rivero (Eds.), *Contemporary Latina/o media: Production, circulation, politics* (pp. 267–84). New York, NY: New York University Press.

"Baseball been berry, berry good to me!"—the famous SNL catchphrase of Garrett Morris as Chico Escuela. (2018, December 9). Retrieved from http://www.thisdayinquotes.com/2009/ 12/baseball-been-berry-berry-good-to-me.html.

Beltrán, M. (2002). The Latina Hollywood body as site of social struggle: Media constructions of stardom and Jennifer Lopez's cross-over butt. *Quarterly Review of Film and Video, 10*(1), 71–86.

Beltrán, M. (2009). *Latino stars in U. S. eyes: The making and meanings of film and TV stardom.* Urbana, IL: University of Illinois Press.

Bender, S. (2003). *Greasers and gringos: Latinos, law, and the American imagination.* New York, NY: New York University Press.

Bever, L. (2014, April 7). After David Ortíz selfie, White House draws red line. *The Washington Post.* Retrieved from https://www.washingtonpost.com/news/morning-mix/wp/2014/04/07/ after-david-ortiz-selfie-white-house-draws-red-line/?utm_term=.co4ac1fc308f.

Bhabha, H. (1990). The third space. In J. Rutherford (Ed.), *Identity, culture, community difference* (pp. 207–21). London, UK: Lawrence and Wishart.

Bhabha, H. K. (1994). *The location of culture.* New York, NY: Routledge.

Birrell, S., and M. G. McDonald, (Eds.). 2000. *Reading sport: Critical essays on power and representation.* Boston, MA: Northeastern University Press.

Bjarkman, P. C. (2016). *Cuba's baseball defectors: The inside story.* Lanham, MD: Rowman & Littlefield.

Bleacher Report. (2017). Puerto Rico is having all the fun and the World Baseball Classic. Retrieved from https://www.facebook.com/bleacherreport/?hc_ref=SEARCH Bleacher Report Facebook.

Boden, A., and R. Fleck (Directors). (2008). *Sugar.* United States: Sony Pictures Classics.

Bonilla-Silva, E. (2014). *Racism without racists: Color-blind racism and the performance of racial inequality in America*. Lanham, MD: Rowman & Littlefield.

Boorstin, D. J. (1992). *The image: A guide to pseudo-events in America*. New York, NY: Random House.

Boren, C. (2018, December 4). Red Sox to visit the White House, with Alex Cora promising to use platform "the right way." *The Washington Post*. Retrieved from https://www. washingtonpost.com/sports/2018/12/04/red-sox-visit-white-house-with-alex-cora -promising-use-platform-right-way/?noredirect=on&utm_term=.3a885c93c797.

Boston Globe. (2016). *Big Papi: The legend and legacy of David Ortiz*. Chicago, IL: Triumph Books.

Boyd, T. (1997). *Out of bounds: Sports, media, and the politics of identity*. Bloomington, IN: Indiana University Press.

Bretón, M., and J. L. Villegas. (1999). *Away games: The life and times of a Latin ball player*. New York, NY: Simon & Schuster.

Brito Ureña, L. M. (1987). *El merengue y la realidad existencial del hombre dominicano*. Santo Domingo, DR: Editorial Universidad Autónoma de Santo Domingo.

Bruns, R. (2015). *Finding baseball's next Clemente: Combating scandal in Latino recruiting*. Santa Barbara, CA: Praeger.

Buckland, J., and B. Reiter. (2018, July 2–5). Where are they now: Sammy Sosa. *Sports Illustrated*, 42–52.

Burgos, A. (2007). *Playing America's game: Baseball, Latinos, and the color line*. Berkeley, CA: University of California Press.

Burgos, A., and F. Guridy. (2010). Becoming suspect usual places: Latinos, baseball and belonging in El Barrio del Bronx. In G. Pérez, F. Guridy, and A. Burgos (Eds.), *Beyond el barrio: Everyday life in Latin/o America* (pp. 81–99). New York, NY: New York University Press.

Burke, T. (2013a, March 10). "Is it me or has ESPN been taken over by wetbacks?" Viewers react to tonight's WBC ESPN Deportes simulcast. *Deadspin*. Retrieved from http://deadspin.com/ is-it-me-or-has-espn-been-taken-over-by-wetbacks-vie-5989829.

Burke, T. (2013b, July 15). People were angry about ESPN's bilingual interviews of Cuban players. *Deadspin*. Retrieved from http://deadspin.com/people-were-angry-about-espns-bilingual -interviews-of-794474276.

Burns, K. (Director). (2010). *Baseball: The tenth inning*. United States: PBS.

Camper, C. (Ed). (1994). *Miscegenation blues: Voices of mixed race women*. Toronto, CA: Sister Vision Press.

Candelario, G. E. B. (2001). "Black behind the ears"—and up front too? Dominicans in the black mosaic. *The Public Historian, 23*(4), 55–72.

Candelario, G. E. B. (2007). *Black behind the ears: Dominican racial identity from museums to beauty shops*. Durham, NC: Duke University Press.

Castillo, J. (2014, April 25). Carlos Beltran speaks out against lack of interpreters for Spanish-speaking major leaguers. Retrieved from http://www.nj.com/yankees/index.ssf/2014/04/ carlos_beltran_speaks_out_against_lack_of_spanish_interpreters_for_players.html.

Castrovince, A. (2017, March 20). Best of both worlds?: Maddon's clever idea. Retrieved from http://m.mlb.com/news/article/219964122/joe-maddon-talks-world-series-v-classic-idea/ ?topicid=209143850.

Cepeda, M. E. (2010). *Musical imagination: U.S.-Colombian identity and the Latin music boom.* New York, NY: New York University Press.

Chávez, L. (2013). *The Latino threat: Constructing immigrants, citizens and the nation.* Stanford, CA: Stanford University Press.

Chicago Cubs. (2014, May 25). *Cubs sign Manny Ramirez to be player-coach at Triple-A Iowa* [Press release]. Retrieved from http://chicago.cubs.mlb.com/news/article.jsp?c_id=chc &content_id=76751562&partnerId=as_mlb_20140525_24y=pr_mlb&ymd=20140525.

Christian, M. (2000). *Multiracial identity: An international perspective.* London, UK: Macmillan.

Collazo, M. (2017, March 20). Make no mistake, this year's REAL March Madness is the World Baseball Classic. *Latino Rebels.* Retrieved from http://www.latinorebels.com/2017/03/20/ make-no-mistake-this-years-real-march-madness-is-the-world-baseball-classic/.

Connell, R. W. (1987). *Gender and power: Society, the person and sexual politics.* Stanford, CA: Stanford University Press.

Connell, R. W. (2005). *Masculinities.* Berkeley, CA: University of California Press.

Couldry, N. (2001). *The place of media power: Pilgrims and witnesses of the media age.* London, UK: Routledge.

Cowley, J. (2006, June 22). Guillén Ozzie Guillen Apologizes For Slur Used Toward Jay Mariotti. *Sports Business Daily.* Retrieved from https://www.sportsbusinessdaily.com/Daily/ Issues/2006/06/22/Franchises/Ozzie-Guillen-Apologizes-For-Slur-Used-Toward-Jay -Mariotti.aspx.

Cowley, J. (2008, May 6). Never a doll moment: "Private thing" Ozzie says he won't apologize for team's clubhouse antics. *Chicago Sun Times.* Retrieved from https://infoweb.newsbank. com/apps/news/openurl?ctx_ver=z39.88-2004&rft_id=info%3Asid/infoweb.newsbank. com&svc_dat=AWNB&req_dat=0E66AEBBA17CB700&rft_val_format=info%3Aofi/ fmt%3Akev%3Amtx%3Actx&rft_dat=document_id%3Anews%252F120803A59F7D66Co.

Crenshaw, K, N. Gotanda, G. Peller, and K. Thomas (Eds.). (1995). *Critical race theory: The writings that formed the movement.* New York, NY: New Press.

DailyWorldwideNews. (2012, April 10). *Ozzie Guillen Fidel Castro press conference* [Video file]. Retrieved from https://www.youtube.com/all_comments?v=RXSN7vodSJU.

Daniel, G. R. (2012). *Machado de Assis: Identity and the Brazilian novelist.* University Park, PA: Pennsylvania State University Press.

Daniel, G. R., L. Kina, W. Ming Dariotis, and C. Fojas. (2014). Emerging paradigms in critical mixed race studies. *Journal of Critical Mixed Race Studies, 1*(1), 6–65.

De Genova, N., and A. Y. Ramos-Zayas. (2003). *Latino crossings: Mexicans, Puerto Ricans and the politics of race and citizenship.* New York, NY: Routledge.

Debord, G. (1967). *Society of the spectacle.* Detroit, MI: Black and Red.

Degler, C. N. (1986). *Neither black nor white.* Madison, MI: University of Wisconsin Press.

DelawareToday. (2010, August 6). Q&A: Ken Burns. Retrieved from http://www.delawaretoday. com/Delaware-Today/September-2010/Q-ampA-Ken-Burns/.

DiAngelo, R. (2018). *White fragility: Why it's so hard for white people to talk about racism.* Boston, MA: Beacon.

Domino Rudolph, J. (2012). *Embodying Latino masculinities, producing masculatinidad.* New York, NY: Palgrave Macmillan.

Domino Rudolph, J. (2018). My family had to learn English when they came, so why is everything in Spanish for them? In S. McClure, and C. Harris (Eds.), *Getting real about race* (85–99). Los Angeles, CA: Sage.

Duany, J. (1994). *Quisqueya on the Hudson: The transnational identity of Dominicans in Washington Heights*. New York, NY: CUNY Dominican Studies Institute.

Duany, J. (2002). *The Puerto Rican nation on the move: Identities on the island and in the United States*. Durham, NC: University of North Carolina Press.

Duk | Big League Stew—Thu, Jan 19, 2012 2:09 PM EST Yahoo Sports. Retrieved from https://sports.yahoo.com/blogs/mlb-grand-league-stew/photo-sammy-sosa-skin-still-very-white-190931256.html.

Dyer, R. (1979). *Stars*. London, UK: BFI.

Dyer, R. (1986). *Heavenly bodies: Film stars and society*. New York, NY: St. Martin's Press.

Entman, R. M., and A. Rojecki. (2000). *The black image in the white mind: Media and race in America*. Chicago, IL: University of Chicago Press.

Escobar, A. M., and K. Potowski. (2015). *El español de los Estados Unidos*. Cambridge, UK: Cambridge University Press.

Feagin, J. (2013). *The white racial frame: Centuries of racial framing and counter-framing*. New York, NY: Routledge.

Finkel, R., J. Paley, and T. Martin (Directors). (2011). *Ballplayer: Pelotero*. USA: Cuacua Productions.

Flores, W., and R. Benmayor. (1997). *Latino cultural citizenship*. Boston, MA: Beacon Press.

FoundationINTERVIEWS. (2012, July 30). *Garret Morris on SNL's Chico Escuela and the news for the hard of hearing* [Video file]. Retrieved from https://www.youtube.com/watch?v=SoGtPwDJywo.

Fregoso, R. L. (1993). *The bronze screen: Chicana and Chicano film culture*. Minneapolis, MN: University of Minnesota Press.

Freyre, G. (1956). *The masters and the slaves: A study in the development of Brazilian civilization* (S. Putnam, Trans.). New York, NY: Alfred A. Knopf. (Original work published 1933)

Gamboa, G. (2013, July 18). Marc Anthony addresses All-Star Game racial controversy. *Long Island Newsday*. Retrieved from http://www.newsday.com/entertainment/music/marc-anthony-addresses-all-star-game-racial-controversy-1.5716688.

García Canclini, N. (1995). *Hybrid cultures: Strategies for entering and leaving modernity* (C. Chippiari and S. López, Trans.). Minneapolis, MN: University of Minnesota Press. (Original work published 1989)

Gigley, C. (2006). Bienvenidos: Foreign-born players must develop more than their baseball skills in the minor leagues. Their will to escape the life they led back home often helps them persevere. *Vine Line, 21*(6), 38–39.

Gil, R. (2009, November 14). *Raymond Pozo version Sammy Sosa* [Video file]. Retrieved from http://www.youtube.com/watch?v=zrhjRu4Jlqc.

Gledhill, C. (1991). *Stardom: Industry of desire*. New York, NY: Routledge.

Gonzales, R. (2015). *Lives in limbo: Undocumented and coming of age in America*. Berkeley, CA: University of California Press.

Gonzalez, J. (2007, May 11). Hey Ken Burns, why shun Latinos? *Daily News*. Retrieved from http://www.nydailynews.com/entertainment/tv-movies/hey-ken-burns-shun-latinos-article-1.252103.

Goodman, J. (Director). (2008). *Road to the Big Leagues / Rumbo a las grandes ligas*. USA: ELEMENT Productions.

Gordon, L. (1997). *Her Majesty's other children*. Lanham, MD: Rowman and Littlefield.

Gregory, S. (2012). Big fish: Outrageous Ozzie Guillen makes the Marlins the talk of baseball. *Time*. Retrieved from http://content.time.com/time/magazine/article/0,9171,2110450,00. html.

Guillen calls A-Rod hypocrite in SI for WBC decision. (2006, February 17). *ESPN*. Retrieved from http://www.espn.com/mlb/news/story?id=2332682.

Gutmann, M. (2006). *The meanings of macho: Being a man in Mexico City*. Berkeley, CA: University of California Press.

Hall, S. (1990). Cultural identity and diaspora. In J. Rutherford (Ed.), *Identity, culture, community difference* (pp. 222–37). London, UK: Lawrence and Wishart.

Hill, J. (2007). Mock Spanish: A site for the endexical reproduction of racism in American English. In J. Healey and E. O'Brien (Eds.), *Race, ethnicity and gender* (pp. 270–85). Los Angeles, CA: Pine Forge Press.

Holmes, J. (2016, April 11). Carlos Correa wants to change baseball's unspoken code of conduct. *Esquire*. Retrieved from https://www.esquire.com/sports/interviews/a43777/carlos-correa -interview/.

Howard, D. (2001). *Coloring the nation: Race and ethnicity in the Dominican Republic*. Boulder, CO: Lynne Rienner.

Hurtado, A., and M. Sinha. (2016). *Beyond machismo: Intersectional Latino masculinities*. Austin, TX: University of Texas Press.

Iber, J., S. O. Regalado, J. M. Alamillo, and A. De León. (2011). *Latinos in U. S. sport: A history of cultural identity, and acceptance*. Champaign, IL: Human Kinetics.

Ifekwunigwe, J. O. (1999). *Scattered belongings: Cultural paradoxes of "race," nation and gender*. New York, NY: Routledge.

IMDb. (n.d.-a). *Ballplayer: Pelotero*. Retrieved from https://www.imdb.com/title/tt1885335/ ?ref_=fn_al_tt_1.

IMDb. (n.d.-b). *Rumbo a las grandes ligas / Road to the Big Leagues*. Retrieved from https://www. imdb.com/title/tt1372294/?ref_=fn_al_tt_1.

IMDb. (n.d.-c). *Sugar*. Retrieved from https://www.imdb.com/title/tt0990413/?ref_=fn_al_tt_1.

Jamail, M. H. (2008). *Venezuelan bust baseball boom: Andrés Reiner and scouting on the new frontier*. Lincoln, NB: University of Nebraska Press.

Jimenez, T. (2009). *Replenished ethnicity: Mexican Americans, immigration and identity*. Berkeley, CA: University of California Press.

Johnson, M. S. (2015, July 10). Béisbol (#1528). *Latino USA*. Retrieved from https://www.latinousa .org/2015/07/10/1528-beisbol/.

Joyce, G. (2017, September 14). David Ortiz signs "forever" deal with Red Sox. *New York Post* Retrieved from https://nypost.com/2017/09/14/david-ortiz-signs-forever-deal-with-red-sox/.

Kallio, T. J. (2007). Taboos in corporate social responsibility discourse. *Journal of Business Ethics, 74*(2), 165–75.

Katz, J. (2014, April 14). Escape from Cuba: Yasiel Puig's untold journey to the Dodgers. *Los Angeles Magazine*. Retrieved from http://www.lamag.com/longform/escape-from-cuba -yasiel-puigs-untold-journey-to-the-dodgers/.

Kelley, R. (1998). *Yo' mama's dysfunktional!: Fighting the culture wars in urban America*. Boston, MA: Beacon.

Kihl, L. A., and S. Tainsky. (2013). Delivery of large-scale CSR efforts through corporate community investment: Lessons from Major League Baseball's Reviving Baseball in Inner Cities Program. In J. L. Paramio-Salcines, K. Babiak, and G. Walters (Eds.), *The Routledge handbook of sport and corporate social responsibility* (pp. 185–97). New York, NY: Routledge.

Kimmel, M., J. Hearn, and R. W. Connell. (2005). *Handbook of studies on men and masculinities.* Thousand Oaks, CA: Sage.

King, G. A. III. (2015, February 17). A-Rod issues handwritten apology letter to fans. *New York Post.* Retrieved from http://nypost.com/2015/02/17/a-rod-issues-apology-letter-to-fans/.

Klein, A. (1991). *Sugarball: The American game, the Dominican dream.* New Haven, CT: Yale University Press.

Klein, A. (2006). *Growing the game: The globalization of Major League Baseball.* New Haven, CT: Yale University Press.

Klein, A. (2009). The transnational view of sport and social development: The case of Dominican baseball. *Sport in Society, 12*(9), 1118–31.

Klein, A. (2014). *Dominican baseball: New pride, old prejudice.* Philadelphia, PA: Temple University Press.

Kramer, D. (2017, September 13). MLB celebrates Hispanic Heritage Month: League expands 2016 initiative Ponle Acento with special events, TV spots. Retrieved from http://m.mlb.com/news/article/254036892/mlb-honors-hispanic-heritage-through-september/.

Kruth, C. (2017, March 20). World Baseball Classic sets attendance record. Retrieved from http://m.mlb.com/news/world-baseball-classic-sets-attendance-record-c220103566.

La Vida Baseball. (n.d.). About. Retrieved from https://www.lavidabaseball.com/about-la-vida-baseball/.

Lamovsky, J., M. Rosetti, and C. DeMarco. (2007). *The worst of sports: Chumps, cheats and chokers from the games we love.* New York, NY: Ballantine Books.

LatinWorks. (2017, May 18). *MLB's "Ponle Acento" case study. Putting the accent on béisbol* [Video file]. Retrieved from https://www.youtube.com/watch?v=9TSCcOaBmzc.

Levermore, R. (2013). Viewing CSR through sport from a critical perspective: Failing to address gross corporate misconduct. In J. L. Paramio-Salcines, K. Babiak, and G. Walters (Eds.), *The Routledge handbook of sport and corporate social responsibility* (pp. 52–61). New York, NY: Routledge.

Levinson, P. (2012). *New new media.* New York, NY: Pearson.

Levitt, P. (2001). *The transnational villagers.* Berkeley, CA: University of California Press.

Limón, J. (1999). *American encounters: Greater Mexico, the United States and the erotics of culture.* Boston, MA: Beacon.

Lippi-Green, R. (2011). *English with an accent: Language, ideology and discrimination in the United States.* New York, NY: Routledge.

Lopez, A. M. (1991). Are all Latinos from Manhattan?: Hollywood ethnography and cultural colonialism. In L. D. Friedman (Ed.), *Unspeakable images: Ethnicity and the American cinema* (pp. 404–24). Urbana, IL: University of Illinois Press.

Maguire, J. (1999). *Global sport: Identities, societies, civilizations.* Cambridge, MA: Polity.

Mahanti, M., and A. Moreno. (2001). Same difference: Towards a more unified discourse of "mixed race" theory. In D. Parker and W. Song (Eds.), *Rethinking mixed race* (pp. 71–75). London, UK: Pluto Press.

Major League Baseball Players Association. (2010, September 9). *USAID teams up with Major League Baseball Players Trust and MLB to benefit Medicines for Humanity in the Dominican Republic* [Press release]. Retrieved from http://mlb.mlb.com/pa/releases/releases.jsp?content=090910.

Maly, M., and H. Dalmage. (2015). *Vanishing Eden: White construction of memory, meaning, and identity in a racially changing city.* Philadelphia, PA: Temple University Press.

Maraniss, D. (2016, September 7). Roberto Clemente fue un fiero crítico tanto del béisbol como de la sociedad estadounidense. *ESPN Deportes.* Retrieved from http://espndeportes.espn.com/beisbol/nota/_/id/2782063/roberto-clemente-fue-un-fiero-critico-tanto-del-beisbol-como-de-la-sociedad-estadounidense.

Marcano Guevara, A., and D. P. Fidler. (2002). *Stealing lives: The globalization of baseball and the tragic story of Alexis Quiroz.* Indianapolis, IN: University of Indiana Press.

Mariotti, J. (2006, June 16). Judgment call: Time to worry about Ozzie. *Chicago Sun Times.* Retrieved from https://infoweb-newsbank-com.peach.conncoll.edu/apps/news/document-view?p=AWNB&t=pubname%3ACSTB%21Chicago%2BSun-Times%2B%2528IL%2529/year%3A2006%212006/mody%3A0616%21June%2B16&action=browse&format=text&docref=news/1125B1F5976931D0.

Markovitz, J. (2011). *Racial spectacles: Explorations in media, race, and justice.* New York, NY: Routledge.

Marks, M. (2015, September 18). Bonehead quote of the week: Donald Trump wants you to stop speaking Spanish. *San Antonio Current.* Retrieved from http://www.sacurrent.com/Blogs/archives/2015/09/18/bonehead-quote-of-the-week-donald-trump-wants-you-to-stop-speaking-spanish.

Marshall, P. D. (1997). *Celebrity and power: Fame in contemporary culture.* Minneapolis, MN: University of Minnesota Press.

Marx, G. (2003, June 29). Cubs odyssey was bad trip, he claims. *Chicago Tribune.* Retrieved from https://www.chicagotribune.com/news/ct-xpm-2003-06-29-0306290354-story.html.

Mastrodonato, J. (2014, April 14). David Ortiz approved of Saturday Night Live skit impersonating him. *MassLive.* Retrieved from http://www.masslive.com/redsox/index.ssf/2014/04/saturday_night_live_skit_pokes.html.

Mayes, A. J. (2014). *The mulatto republic: Class, race and Dominican national identity.* Gainesville, FL: The University Press of Florida.

McDonough, C. (2015, November 23). David Ortiz responds to "Saturday Night Live" skit with hilarious tweet. *NESN.* Retrieved from https://nesn.com/2015/11/david-ortiz-responds-to-saturday-night-live-skit-with-hilarious-tweet-photo/.

McWilliams, A., and Siegel, D. (2001). Corporate social responsibility: A theory of the firm perspective. *Academy of Management Review, 26*(1), 117–27.

Mercer, K. (1990). Black art and the burden of representation. *Third Text, 4*(10), 61–78.

Miller, M. (2004). *Rise and fall of the cosmic race: The cult of mestizaje in Latin America.* Austin, TX: University of Texas Press.

MLB. (n.d.-a). About: Major League Baseball and the Dominican Republic. Retrieved from http://mlb.mlb.com/dr/about.jsp.

MLB. (n.d.-b). Academies. Retrieved from http://mlb.mlb.com/dr/academies.jsp.

MLB. (n.d.-c). Breaking Barriers. Retrieved from http://web.mlbcommunity.org/programs/breaking_barriers.jsp?content=inside.

MLB. (n.d.-d). RBI. Retrieved from http://mlb.mlb.com/mlb/official_info/mlb_official_story_headline.jsp?story_page=rbi.

MLB. (n.d.-e). Social responsibility. Retrieved from http://mlb.mlb.com/dr/social_responsibility.jsp.

MLB. (2017). About the 2017 World Baseball Classic. Retrieved from https://www.worldbaseballclassic.com/info/about.

Moehringer, J. R. (2015, March 7). The education of Alex Rodríguez: Six months, four cities, two coasts, one Batman suit—we chronicle the fallen slugger's winding road back to pinstripes. *ESPN*. Retrieved from http://espn.go.com/espn/feature/story/_/id/12321274/alex-rodriguez-return-new-york-yankees.

Molina-Guzmán, I. (2010). *Dangerous curves: Latina bodies in the media*. New York, NY: New York University Press.

Molina-Guzmán, I. (2018). *Latinas & Latinos on TV: Colorblind comedy in the post-racial network era*. Tucson, AZ: University of Arizona Press.

Molina Guzmán, I., and A. Valdivia. (2004). Brain, brow and booty: Latina iconicity in U. S. popular culture. *The Communication Review, 7*, 205–21.

Moya-Pons, F. (1995). *The Dominican Republic: A national history*. New York, NY: Hispaniola Books.

Mr. Inoa. (2009, November 13). *La crema de Sammy Sosa* [Video file]. Retrieved from http://www.youtube.com/watch?v=wooX9uFI7wM.

MRSLANEY7. (2008, August 4). *The oh Manny song* [Video file]. Retrieved from https://www.youtube.com/watch?v=SCd8LV9ewEE.

Natividad, A. (2017, April 14). How an ad agency got Major League Baseball to put Spanish accents on its jerseys: LatinWorks' well-deserved accent on America's pastime. *Adweek*. Retrieved from http://www.adweek.com/creativity/how-an-ad-agency-got-major-league-baseball-to-put-spanish-accents-on-its-jerseys/.

Negrón-Muntaner, F. (2014). The gang's not all here: The state of Latinos in contemporary US media. In A. Dávila and Y. Rivero (Eds.), *Contemporary Latina/o Media: Production, circulation, politics* (pp. 103–24). New York, NY: New York University Press.

Newcomb, A. (2014, April 1). Why "Big Papi" got paid to take selfie with President Obama. *ABC News*. Retrieved from http://abcnews.go.com/US/david-ortizs-selfie-president-obama-promoted-samsung-twitter/story?id=23148152.

Noguera, P., A. Hurtado, and E. Fergus (Eds.). (2011). *Invisible no more: Understanding the disenfranchisement of Latino men and boys*. New York, NY: Routledge.

Oboler, S., and A. Dzidzienyo (Eds.). (2005). *Neither enemies nor friends: Latinos, blacks, Afro-Latinos*. New York, NY: Palgrave Macmillan.

O'Callaghan, T. (2009, November 10). What could have made Sammy Sosa's skin lighter? *Time*. Retrieved from http://healthland.time.com/2009/11/10/what-could-have-made-sammy-sosas-skin-lighter/.

Omi, M., and H. Winant. (1994). *Racial formation in the United States: From the 1960s to the 1990s*. New York, NY: Routledge.

Orozco, J. (2008a). Caribbean cruise: Having derived its name from the Italian word for "little Venice" because of its villages built on water, Venezuela is a rising player in the game of baseball. *Vine Line, 23*(2), 32–33.

Orozco, J. (2008b). Caribbean cruise: Having derived its name from the Italian word for "little Venice" because of its villages built on water, Venezuela is a rising player in the game of baseball. *Vine Line, 23*(3), 34–35.

Ortiz, D., with T. Massarotti. (2007). *Big Papi: My story of big dreams and big hits*. New York, NY: St. Martin's Griffin.

Ortiz, D. with M Holley. (2007). *Papi: my story.* Boston, MA: Houghton Mifflin Harcourt.

Ortiz, F. (1947). *Cuban counterpoint: Tobacco and sugar* (H. de Onis, Trans.). New York, NY: Alfred A. Knopf. (Original work published 1940)

Ortiz, J. L. (2005, August 6). Alou offended by radio host / KNBR suspends Krueger after comments. *SF Gate.* Retrieved from http://www.sfgate.com/bayarea/article/Alou-offended-by -radio-host-KNBR-suspends-2618251.php.

Ortiz, J. L. (2012, April 10). Ozzie Guillén on the hot seat over Fidel Castro remarks. *USA Today.* Retrieved from http://usatoday30.usatoday.com/sports/baseball/nl/marlins/story/2012-04 -09/ozzie-guillen-castro-controversy/54136806/1.

Pacini Hernandez, D. (1995). *Bachata: A social history of a Dominican popular music.* Philadelphia, PA: Temple University Press.

Padilla, D. (2017, March 23). Puerto Rico: U. S. players misinterpreted planned celebration. *ESPN.* Retrieved from http://www.espn.com/mlb/story/_/id/18981934/puerto-rico-team-says-us -team-misinterpreted-planned-world-baseball-classic-celebration.

Páez-Pumar, L. (2017, March 22). Puerto Rico is running out of blond hair dye because of World Baseball Classic. *Remezcla.* Retrieved from http://remezcla.com/sports/puerto-rico-blond -dye/.

Passan, J. (2012, July 2). Searching for truth in a land where it's fleeting. *Yahoo Sports.* Retrieved from https://sports.yahoo.com/news/story-of-miguel-sano-chronicles-ugly--sleazy-side-of -baseball-s-dominican-talent-pipeline.html.

Perea, J. (1998). *Immigration and citizenship in the twenty-first century.* Lanham, MD: Rowman and Littlefield.

Pérez Cabral, P. (2007). *La comunidad mulata: El caso socio-político de la República Dominicana.* Santo Domingo, DR: Cielonaranja.

Perez-Firmat, G. (1994). *Life on the hyphen: The Cuban American way.* Austin, TX: University of Texas Press.

Pérez-Torres, R. (2006). *Mestizaje: Critical uses of race in Chicano culture.* Minneapolis, MN: University of Minnesota Press.

Picker, M., and C. Sun (Directors). (2012). *Latinos beyond reel: Challenging a media stereotype.* United States: Media Education Foundation.

Ramírez, H., and E. Flores. (2013). Latino masculinities in the post-9/11 era. In M. S. Kimmel and M. A. Messner (Eds.), *Men's lives* (pp. 32–40). Boston, MA: Pearson.

Ramírez, R. (1993). *Díme capitán: Reflexies sobre la masculinidad.* Rio Piedras, PR: Ediciones Huracán.

Ramirez-Berg, C. (2002). *Latino images in film: Stereotypes, subversion, resistance.* Austin, TX: University of Texas Press.

Ray, R. (2018). If only he hadn't worn the hoodie . . . : Race, selective perception, and stereotype maintenance. In S. M. McClure and C. A. Harris (Eds.), *Getting real about race* (pp. 72–84). Los Angeles, CA: Sage.

Red, C. (2013, December 12). Robinson Cano a deadbeat dad? Judge in Dominican Republic orders increase in child support for son. *New York Daily News.* Retrieved from http://www. nydailynews.com/news/national/240-million-dead-beat-cano-striking-dad-article-1.1546458.

RedSoxNationVideos. (2009, September 18). *Oh Manny song* [Video file]. Retrieved from https:// www.youtube.com/watch?v=7cJifRrlvoI.

Regalado, S. (2008). *Viva baseball: Latin major leaguers and their special hunger.* Urbana, IL: University of Illinois Press.

Reiter, B. (2012, March 5). Marlinsanity?: Betting big that binge spending, a psychedelic park and mad new talent will create baseball mania in Miami. *Sports Illustrated, 36–40.*

Rhoden, W. (2010, August 3). Guillén clarifies comments on Spanish-speaking players. *New York Times.* Retrieved from https://www.nytimes.com/2010/08/04/sports/baseball/04rhoden.html.

Rhodes, J., and S. Boburg. (2011). *Becoming Manny: Inside the life of baseball's most enigmatic slugger.* New York, NY: Scribner.

Ríos, V. (2011). *Punished: Policing the lives of black and Latino boys.* New York, NY: New York University Press.

Rivera, M. (2017a, April 17). For Betances, repping the Yankees is an American dream. *ESPN.* Retrieved from http://www.espn.com/mlb/story/_/id/19316029/yankees-star-dellin -betances-growing-dominican-repping-hometown-team.

Rivera, M. (2017b, May 6). Dellin Betances: "Mi sangre siempre ha sido dominicana y Yankee." *ESPN Deportes.* Retrieved from http://espndeportes.espn.com/beisbol/beisbolexperience/ nota/_/id/3122317/dellin-betances-mi-sangre-siempre-ha-sido-dominicana-y-yankee.

Robberson, T. (2013, July 5). Marc Anthony controversy underscores a racist, ignorant tide in America. *Dallas Morning News.* Retrieved from http://dallasmorningviewsblog.dallasnews. com/2013/07/marc-anthony-controversy-underscores-a-racist-ignorant-tide-in-america. html/.

Roberts, S. (2009). *A-ROD: The many lives of Alex Rodríguez.* New York, NY: Harper.

Robinson, J. (1995). *I never had it made: An autobiography.* New York, NY: Ecco. (Original work published 1972)

Rodríguez, C. E. (1997). *Latin looks: Images of Latinas and Latinos in the U. S. media.* Denver, CO: Westview Press.

Rodríguez, R. (2004). *Hunger of memory: The education of Richard Rodriguez.* New York, NY: Bantam. (Original work published 1982)

Rojas, E. (2009, November 10). Sosa: Cream has bleached skin. *ESPN.* Retrieved from http:// espn.go.com/mlb/news/story?id=4642952.

Root, M. P. P. (Ed). (1992). *Racially mixed people of America.* Thousand Oaks, CA: Sage.

Rosaldo, R. (1995). Foreword. In N. Garcia Canclini, *Hybrid cultures: Strategies for entering and leaving modernity* (C. Chippiari and S. López, Trans.; pp. xi–xvii). Minneapolis, MN: University of Minnesota Press.

Rosaldo, R. (1997). Cultural citizenship inequality, and multiculturalism. In W. Flores and R. Benmayor (Eds.), *Latino cultural citizenship* (pp. 27–38). Boston, MA: Beacon Press.

Rose, T. (2008). *The hip hop wars: What we talk about when we talk about hip hop-and why it matters.* New York, NY: Basic Books.

Rosen, J. (2012). The people formerly known as the audience. In M. Mandiberg (Ed.), *The social media reader.* New York, NY: New York University Press.

Roth, W. D. (2012). *Race migrations: Latinos and the cultural transformation of race.* Stanford, CA: Stanford University Press.

Rúa, M. (2005). Latinidades. In S. Oboler and D. González (Eds.), *The Oxford encyclopedia of Latinos and Latinas in the United States* (Vol. 2, pp. 505–7). New York, NY: Oxford University Press.

Ruck, R. (1998). *The tropic of baseball: Baseball in the Dominican Republic*. Lincoln, NE: University of Nebraska Press.

Ruck, R. (2011). *Raceball: How the major leagues colonized the black and Latino game*. Boston, MA: Beacon.

Sagás, E. (2000). *Race and politics in the Dominican Republic*. Gainesville, FL: University Press of Florida.

Samuel, E. (2016, October 17). Adrian Gonzalez refused to stay at Trump hotel when Dodgers played in Chicago. *New York Daily News*. Retrieved from http://www.nydailynews.com/sports/baseball/dodgers-adrian-gonzalez-refused-stay-chicago-trump-hotel-article-1.2834189.

Sanchez, J. (2016a, January 14). Beltran's vision realized with translator program. Retrieved from http://m.mlb.com/news/article/161857500/carlos-beltran-gets-spanish-translator-program/.

Sanchez, J. (2016b, September 7). MLB celebrates Hispanic Heritage Month: #PonleAcento campaign recognizes rich influence on game. Retrieved from http://m.mlb.com/news/article/200004914/mlb-celebrates-hispanic-heritage-month/.

Sandoval, C. (2000). *Methodology of the oppressed*. Minneapolis, MN: University of Minnesota Press.

Santiago, S. (2001). *The space in-between: Essays on Latin American culture* (T. Burns, A. Gazzola, and G. Williams, Trans.). Durham, NC: Duke University Press.

Schlegel, J. (2010, August 4). Baseball strives to provide for Latino players: Education, translation services part of ongoing programs. Retrieved from http://mlb.mlb.com/news/print.jsp?ymd=20100804&content_id=13018392&c_id=mlb&fext=.jsp.

Sedgwick, E. K. (2015). *Between men: English literature and male homosocial desire* (30th anniversary ed.). New York, NY: Columbia University Press.

Shaw, R. (2010, August 3). Ozzie Guillen speaks truth on baseball's racial double standard. *Beyond Chron: The Voice of the Best*. Retrieved from http://www.beyondchron.org/ozzie-guillen-speaks-truth-on-baseballs-racial-double-standard/.

Shingler, M. (2012). *Star studies: A critical guide*. New York, NY: Palgrave Macmillan.

Shohat, E., and R. Stam. (1994). *Unthinking Eurocentrism: Multiculturalism and the media*. New York, NY: Routledge.

Simmons, K. E. (2009). *Reconstructing racial identity and the African past in the Dominican Republic*. Gainesville, FL: University Press of Florida.

Singer, T. (1998, March). Not-so-remote-control. *Sport, 36*.

Slezak, C. (2008, May 6). White Sox doll blow up- Sexist "shrine" shows lack of leadership by Sox' bosses, team members who weren't man enough to stop infantile display. *Chicago Sun Times*. Retrieved from https://infoweb-newsbank-com.peach.conncoll.edu/apps/news/document-view?p=AWNB&t=pubname%3ACSTB%21Chicago%2BSun-Times%2B%2528IL%2529/year%3A2008%212008/mody%3A0506%21May%2B06&action=browse&format=text&docref=news/120803A535806D28.

SNL transcripts: Eric Idle: 12/09/78: Weekend Update with Jane Curtin & Bill Murray. (2018, October 8). *SNL Transcripts Tonight*. Retrieved from http://snltranscripts.jt.org/78/78hupdate.phtml.

Soldevilla, A. (2018, May 31). Dominicans shaken by PED suspensions: Say it ain't so! *La Vida Baseball*. Retrieved from https://www.lavidabaseball.com/ped-suspension-robinson-cano/.

Solomon, M. (2013, August 2). The Biogenesis PEDs scandal explained. *The Guardian*. http://www.theguardian.com/sport/2013/aug/02/biogenesis-peds-scandal-explained.

Sosa, S., with M. Bretón. (2000). *Sosa: An autobiography.* New York, NY: Warner Books.

Spak, K. (2008, May 6). White Sox doll blow up- Manager defends team using inflatable dolls in clubhouse as "slump busters," but Sox officials admit it was tasteless. *Chicago Sun Times.* Retrieved from https://infoweb-newsbank-com.peach.conncoll.edu/apps/news/document -view?p=AWNB&t=pubname%3ACSTB%21Chicago%2BSun-Times%2B%2528IL%2529/ year%3A2008%212008/mody%3A0506%21May%2B06&action=browse&format=text&docref =news/120803A533C255F0.

Sports Illustrated. (2016). Big Papi special retirement tribute.

Stampler, L. (2014, April 1). Obama takes selfie with "Big Papi" David Ortíz. *Time.* Retrieved from http://time.com/45616/obama-red-sox-selfie/.

Stone, L. (2013, December 14). Robinson Cano's journey to stardom was years in the making. *Seattle Times.* Retrieved from http://seattletimes.nwsource.com/html/larrystone/2022464158 _stone15xml.html.

Sue, C. (2014). Negotiating identity among Mexico's cosmic race. In R. C. King-O'Riain, S. Small, M. Mahtani, M. Song, and P. Spickard (Eds.), *Global mixed race* (pp. 91–118). New York, NY: New York University Press.

Sullivan, P. (2016, November 10). Jake Arrieta's political tweet gets Theo Epstein's attention at GM meetings. *Chicago Tribune.* Retrieved from http://www.chicagotribune.com/sports/ columnists/ct-arrieta-epstein-sullivan-gm-meetings-spt-1110-20161109-column.html#.

Sullivan, P. (2017, January 16). President Obama welcomes Cubs to the White House: "It took you long enough." *Chicago Tribune.* Retrieved from http://www.chicagotribune.com/sports/ baseball/cubs/ct-cubs-white-house-visit-20170116-column.html.

Synnott, A. (1987). Shame and glory: A sociology of hair. *British Journal of Sociology, 38*(3), 381–413.

Thomas, P. (1967). *Down these mean streets.* New York, NY: Vintage.

Torres, M. (2017, July 12). Lost in translation: MLB requires Spanish translators, Royals don't exactly follow rule. *The Kansas City Star.* Retrieved from http://www.kansascity.com/sports/ mlb/kansas-city-royals/article160937659.html.

Torres-Saillant, S. (1998). The tribulations of blackness: Stages in Dominican racial identity. *Latin American Perspectives, 25*(3), 126–46.

US Census Bureau. (n.d.). US Census quick facts. Retrieved from https://www.census.gov/ quickfacts/fact/table/US/RHI125218.

USAID. (n.d.). Major League Baseball—Dominican Development Alliance. Retrieved from https://partnerships.usaid.gov/partnership/major-league-baseball-dominican-development -alliance.

Utting, P. (2004). *Corporate social responsibility and business regulation* (Washington DC UNRISD Research and Policy Brief 1). Geneva, Switzerland: United Nations Research Institute for Social Development.

Valdivia, A. (2010). *Latinos and the media.* Cambridge, MA: Polity.

Vargas, D., N. R. Mirabal, and L. La Fountain-Stokes. (2017). *Keywords for Latina/o studies.* New York, NY: New York University Press.

Vasconcelos, J. (1925). *La raza cósmica: Misión de la raza iberoamericana: notas de viajes a la América del Sur.* Madrid, SP: Agencia Mundial de Librería.

Weekend Update: David Ortiz [Video file]. (2014, April 13). *Saturday Night Live.* Retrieved from http://www.nbc.com/saturday-night-live/video/weekend-update-david-ortiz/2772827?snl=1.

Weekend Update: David Ortiz on Yankee Stadium [Video file]. (2016, October 1). *Saturday Night Live*. Retrieved from http://www.nbc.com/saturday-night-live/video/weekend-update-david-ortiz-on-yankee-stadium/3108912?snl=1.

Weir, T., and B. Bachelor. (2004, April 13). Spanish-speaking players get lessons in American life. *USA Today*. Retrieved from http://usatoday30.usatoday.com/sports/baseball/2004-04-13-cover-latinos_x.htm.

Williams, T. (1997). Race-ing and being raced: The critical interrogation of "passing." *Amerasia Journal, 23*(1), 61–65.

Wise, T. (2010). *Colorblind: The rise of post-racial politics and retreat from racial equality*. San Francisco, CA: City Lights.

World Baseball Classic. (2006, February 28). *Walk Like a Sabermetrician*. Retrieved from http://walksaber.blogspot.com/2006/02/world-baseball-classic.html.

Young, A. (2004). *The minds of marginalized black men: Making sense of mobility, opportunity and future life chances*. Princeton, NJ: Princeton University Press.

Young, R. (1995). *Colonial desire: Hybridity in theory, culture and race*. New York, NY: Routledge,

Zack, N. (1993). *Race and mixed race*. Philadelphia, PA: Temple University Press.

INDEX

GLOBAL LATIN/O AMERICAS

Frederick Luis Aldama and Lourdes Torres, Series Editors

This series focuses on the Latino experience in its totality as set within a global dimension. The series showcases the variety and vitality of the presence and significant influence of Latinos in the shaping of the culture, history, politics and policies, and language of the Americas—and beyond. It welcomes scholarship regarding the arts, literature, philosophy, popular culture, history, politics, law, history, and language studies, among others.

9 780814 255841